DRESSAGE
QUESTIONS
ANSWERED

DRESSAGE QUESTIONS ANSWERED

Charles de Kunffy

ARCO PUBLISHING, INC.
NEW YORK

First Arco Edition, Second Printing, 1985

Published by Arco Publishing, Inc.
215 Park Avenue South, New York, N.Y. 10003

Library of Congress Cataloging in Publication Data

De Kunffy, Charles, 1936–
  Dressage questions answered.

  Includes index.
  1. Dressage. I. Title.
SF309.5.D443 1983   798.2′3   83-11784
ISBN 0-668-05869-2

Printed in the United States of America

Contents

Credits

Illustrations

DRESSAGE
QUESTIONS
ANSWERED

Mme. Liselott Linsenhoff, of the Federal Republic of Germany, riding Piaff. The high standards of form, feeling and beauty that won them the Olympic Individual Gold Medal in Munich, 1972. Their many international victories made this team of supreme athletes one of the most successful in the entire history of competitive dressage. Their harmony and serenity as seen on this picture represents the ideal of horse and rider performing as though they were animated by an outside, invisible force. This effortless appearance is eloquently elegant.

Form, Feeling and The Art of Classical Equitation

Classical Equitation or Dressage: A Definition

The number of riders interested in dressage has grown rapidly—and that gives us cause to celebrate! But many are those who express a desire to know how many kinds of dressage are in existence, and rampant are the speculations about having at one's disposal at least two major attitudes toward dressage from which to choose. And that gives us cause to reflect.

Members of the dressage community have begun to notice two different tendencies in dressage, tendencies which seem to conflict with each other. Dressage as an art seems to conflict with dressage as a technique. Taking time to develop a horse seems to conflict with the urge to produce quickly whatever will suffice in a race to meet competition dates and obligations successfully. Elegant competitors with artistic appeal seem to conflict with mechanically obedient, submissive, and boring ones. Slow moving idealists seem to conflict with pragmatic competitive practitioners. And all in the name of dressage.

Who would have guessed, or even hoped, ten years ago that today there would be enough knowledgeable and observant dressage enthusiasts to be concerned with the questions that are tacitly—yet definitely—raised here. Yet, today, many are concerned. For the validity of the answers we give to these questions will largely determine our future course and the keenness of future questioners.

1

For maximum results, there is only one correct way of gymnasticizing a horse and that is through a single correct system of strategies that can be practiced by only one kind of equitation, one kind of seat and aids. The standards of these gymnastics embodied in the dressage tradition were not arrived at arbitrarily. Nor were they dreamed up by sentimental romanticists. Rather, what has survived centuries of testing is the sum total of pragmatic equestrian knowledge. Everything was tried, contested, experimented with. That which worked was retained.

Classical horsemanship — *dressage* — is called "classical" because it is enduring. Only that which survives epochs by remaining meaningful in the human experience becomes a classic, classical. Dressage has survived for centuries because it consistently produced desirable results in the development of the majority of horses. In classical dressage, only that which is correct in terms of the horse's development toward his full potential is considered beautiful. Out of the most effective horsemanship emerged the concept of beauty and artistry in dressage. That which functions properly in gymnastic terms, and is arrived at without compulsion or force, is inherently awesome and beautiful. A horse moving with beautiful paces, effortlessly covering ground and happily complying with his rider's inconspicuous aids, displays his own artistry. In short, effective horsemanship is an art!

The mischief is caused by the eternal pitting of man's pragmatic instincts against his moral inclinations. On the one hand are those who are concerned with things as they are (the sociologists); on the other hand are those whose primary concern is with things as they ought to be (the philosophers). There is, of course, always a *de facto* situation; reality — actuality — exists without any moral consideration. However, there is always the possibility of a *de jure* situation — an ideal situation that reflects a preference for things as they *ought to be* rather than as they *in fact are*.

Ideally, *de facto* riding should be identical to and representational of *de jure* dressage. In fact, everyday riding should aim at approximating the ideal as closely as possible. That is the whole motivational force behind classical horsemanship — to create the gymnastically ideal horse rather than one that maintains the *status quo*. Dressage, indeed, has its own morality and that, not competition, is its motivational force.

Because dressage is a living tradition, it exists only insofar as its practitioners endorse and demonstrate its ideals. If riders cannot or will not practice or emulate dressage ideals, then the art will cease to explain itself in terms of correct results and will ultimately disappear. There will be riding, and that riding may be called "dressage" — but the name will not mean more than a semantic approximation of the great classical tradition. For an art cannot be practiced in name only and be kept alive.

Classical horsemanship is based on a love for the horse; it is not practiced for the glorification of the rider. Love, according to Erich Fromm, foremost among psychiatrist-philosophers, is the active promotion of the well-being of the love-object—in this case, the horse. Ideally, then, the equestrian should dedicate himself to the horse's best interests—an attitude that logically leads to a commitment to develop the horse to his full potential. To do this painlessly, gradually, and naturally is to practice dressage, which then becomes an expression of loving devotion. That which falls short of such an expression is dressage in name only.

To be an equestrian in the classical sense is not just to be a rider. It is a position in life. It is a stance one takes in relation to life. One must make a choice between self-love—the promotion of the well-being of one's own ego—and love for the horse. That is the fundamental attitudinal decision that earned Xenophon the title of Father of Classical Dressage: *he dared to love a horse!*

If riding that aims at the promotion of classical dressage principles fails to be victorious in competition, it is merely a temporary defeat. Eventually, that which is correct will be discovered to be also good, and in the long run it will succeed. After all, in riding, not the fleeting glory of the ribbon but the enduring thrill of a well-trained horse is what yields the true reward. The ways of any art are slow, but those of the equestrian art are slowest. But through its snail's pace comes enduring validity: and that which endures is once again classical and representative of the finest in our tradition.

The English philosopher Jeremy Bentham suggested that the society which produces the greatest good for the greatest number of people is the best society. So it is with classical horsemanship. For only those techniques and methods endured which consistently produced the greatest good for the greatest number of horses. Bentham also defined "good" on the minimum level as the absence of pain and on the maximum level as active happiness. That should suffice to guide us when we seek to know how we should treat and train our horses.

Not only physically induced pain—the pain induced by a rider's hands!—but the mental anguish created by speedy "riding technology" can produce an unhappy horse. The horse that is happy is a giver! If you cannot tell stories about what your horse is doing for you, there is not much in the way of happiness to talk about.

Riders who are not sure of their art need the reassurance of a ribbon. Those secure in their art accept a ribbon occasionally as an honor rather than a proof. Riders who know what is right because they feel it do not need a judge to verify it for them, nor a ribbon to show to posterity. Their reward is in having achieved something that goes on between themselves and the horse, something they feel and therefore know. The improvement of the horse is its own reward. Such secure riders would never exchange the thrill of improving a horse for a ribbon. For such riders are interested in more than the score; they are primarily interested in the game.

The difference between civilized behavior and the barbaric lies in the difference between compassion, which is a combination of empathy and forgiveness, and compulsion. Classical horsemanship is compassionate; classical horsemanship is civilized. Where there is barbaric riding, there is no representation of dressage. Historically, civilization evolves when there is a surplus of the mundane, when everyday needs are not only adequately but well met. Analogously, proper riding is a civilized luxury that evolves only when the hunger for the "bread and butter" successes in terms of the rider's ego has been satisfied. For the luxury of civilized riding is that success is measured in the *horse's* terms, not the rider's. Is the *horse* improved? Is *he* happy?

Haste is the enemy of any art. Michelangelo took his time with his art until the Pope who commissioned it died and left the bills to his successor. An artist can only be told what he must accomplish; he cannot be given a deadline by which he must accomplish it. The street artist who promises a portrait in five minutes reveals a great deal about himself. So does the rider who quickly "makes" a third-level horse. Competition forces the meeting of deadlines and contesting involves the Ego. Both encourage haste, the enemy of quality. Both encourage a forced rather than a natural development. For centuries, multitudes found it important to travel long distances to marvel at Michelangelo's creations. They came away inspired. Today we need equestrians to whom we might make pilgrimages in the hope of gaining inspiration.

It is known that of all the people who have lived during the last million years, half are alive right now. Thus, the sum-total of the present human experience — that being experienced simultaneously by all of us now alive — equals the sum-total of the life experiences of all our predecessors. Speculation on the equestrian implications of these statistics suggests that all current equestrian experience equals the equestrian experience of all the past. It is safer, however, to surrender to the speculation that in the past the quantitative equestrian experience was far greater than it is today when the horse is no longer a utilitarian animal. Horses are no longer the means of transportation and the substitute for muscle they once were. The half of humanity that has gone before us, however, produced a narrow stratum of practitioners with equestrian wisdom known to us as the classical heritage of dressage. It has endured by its *virtue,* not by *compulsion;* therefore, it is *good!* As the half of humanity that is now alive rides simply for the sake of riding rather than for any utilitarian purpose, we should hope to contribute to the wisdom of dressage at least as much as our predecessors did. If we are to live up to the heritage they left us, our simultaneous performance should at least equal their cumulative one!

The dressage boom is on! As in all booms, there will be many losers and a few winners. Those who think there is more than one type of dressage will be losers. For they will lose out on knowing the intoxication of having been a part of an art both as its creator and as one created by it, both as a participant in it and as an inducer of it. For in classical riding, the unit of horse and rider is both maker and made, both subject and object of the art.

Dressage As Art

I am convinced that when done to the highest degree of expertise and inspiration, riding is an art. One cannot expect agreement on this issue, for riding as art sounds terribly exclusive, unavailable, and therefore pretentious to some. Well, all art is, by definition, exclusive, as is all excellence. Thus, one ought merely to build up tolerance, even respect, for that which is better than average and therefore unattainable for the majority.

All art is based on the knowledge of its traditions and history, and a full mastery of its techniques as well as the use of its tools. Riding, as

Photographed by Herr Werner Menzendorf, Federal Republic of Germany

Andrew Rymill, Esq. of England, riding Reminiscent. Elegance, as seen here, cannot be pretended because it is the by-product of the proper attire, appropriate effort and superb concentration.

an art, is not different from the others. Riding, to whatever degree of great mastery, is still just a skill. Art is based on, yet goes beyond, these skills and techniques. The skilled rider, the technician is the sportsman and finds that calling riding an art is either pretentious or offensive.

Many great riders, many outstanding competitors are outstanding craftsman, that is, fantastically capable sportsmen. Fewer are the artists, and so it should be. The craftsmanship of riding, the equestrian sport, is infatuating and often irresistible. Their pursual is what we witness in the show rings and at competitions (including the Olympic Games). The art of riding is sometimes resplendently displayed in the competition arena but, being sufficient unto itself, is more often part of the everyday existence of its masters.

There goes a horse, with his jaw open, twisted in pain; his lips are flapping around bared teeth; his ears alternately layed back or flipping forward attending to business other than the rider; his tail is twisting, then rotating while he counterflexes his body at corners, his steps rapid and choppy. What is it? Neither a display of riding skills (no technology) nor art. In fact, that is not riding, not even traveling passively. There is disharmony caused by ignorance.

But look elsewhere. There is a horse and his rider, melted into one harmonious unit appearing as if they are oblivious to their surroundings. They appear animated by an outside force! Both horse and rider appear to be in a daze or a state of meditation, attuned to something the spectator cannot detect, for they seem melted into a no-beginning, no-end harmony without being obviously aware of each other. They appear attuned but to an outside, third force, an inspiration, that brought them together. The unit has beauty, for its energy and force are greater than human, greater than equine.

There is the art of riding! When it is seen at a show, you can hear spectators comment on the horse doing the program by himself, as if by memory. The foundation of that art is **total harmony.** All skills, techniques, and knowledge of riding are useless unless they can be effectively employed for the creation of total harmony. All else is subsidiary to that. For if you think of the elements of riding, whatever they may be: relaxation or impulsion or balance or responsiveness to the aids or attentiveness or engagement or whatever, each element is desirable for its contributing to the ultimate establishment of harmony. Nothing is recommended in riding that destroys harmony and all is strongly urged that promotes it!

The skills that contribute to and promote harmony are many. They can be taught, more or less, to riders. The art of riding, the sensitivity to and awareness of harmony, even the desire for it, cannot be taught, merely inspired in others. For to some people the most natural state of existence is a quarrel. To others the favored state may be a stupor of some sort, while for another it may be playful frivolity. But there are those who understand and seek harmony and live by its ethics, and they naturally gravitate towards those efforts in riding that lead to total harmony, and thus the art of horsemanship.

Harmony has its physical bases. Those who have "feel," that mysterious and oft-mentioned but never explained concept, are well on their way toward the art of riding. That feel is predominantly an ability to physically seek harmony through the most accommodating position of togetherness. That is why the rider with feel may not sit as properly or elegantly as a competitor in the Olympic Games but may certainly make the horse happy. Often one can see (with delight) talented young riders with improper skills (mushy abdomen, rounded shoulders, awful style) who make delightfully harmonious companions on their horse's backs. The "natural" always keeps his center of gravity together with that of the horse, enjoys the energy that carries that center boldly forward, enjoys getting obedience from the horse by cajoling it and keeping things smooth. That is why their horses appear very rhythmic: for wherever their balance may be, they never lose rhythm. The rider and horse's centers of gravity are merged in harmony!

Riding is a creative art in that it creates and recreates its own artistic subject, the gymnastic horse. But it is also a performing art, and when the human mind animates effortlessly the horse's body during a display in public, that art carries its own moment. The artistic statement is made by harmony obvious even to the beholder, and anything disrupting it shatters the moment. That is why a performance of high quality is breathless and flows as a unit. For if it is well done, a gymnastic test does not appear laced together of different movements but remains one continuous statement consistent in philosophy, feeling, and existence.

No art is mindless. It has been said that the intelligent, the very bright person is a "genius," an artist. No, not necessarily! Intelligence helps, for the skills on which art is based need intelligent application. Its acquisition is also based on intelligence. But beyond that, *sensitivity* and *insight* are the more important determinants of an artistic effort.

There comes a day, and later on sometimes every day, when you feel that you lose sense of your skills. You become unaware of yourself, become oblivious to your aids and whatever your limbs, torso, and musculature are doing. You become absorbed in an effort that seems independent of your senses and so thoroughly effortless that it suggests a feeling of being in a dream where you can ride but for the first time without awareness of the effort. When you no longer feel what you are doing or that you are busy, you have entered the artistic experience. And there you find the motion, the flight, the suspension that always eluded you before now floating underneath you as if in spite of you.

Often instruction spoils the chances for the artistic development of the rider. Instruction, indispensible for the teaching of riding skills, is no longer necessary during the artistic effort. As in painting, once the artist has learned to use the tools of the craft from his master, he no longer finds use for the overseer. Establishing his own art studio, he seeks solitude and immersion in his own thoughts, inspirations, and feelings.

The artistic rider is often disturbed, annoyed, disrupted by instruction. Important things happen during silences. Thus, when a rider is tuned to the chattering of his coach, he is not fully attending to the communications of his horse. Therefore, in artistic riding, silence is of essence, so that when the rider makes a statement of harmony, it is not a verbal one but a total event.

I had to discuss all this, not for those who do not understand what I am writing about, because they may not have had substantiating experiences. I am taking a chance to reach those who felt lonesome with their artistic experiences. For them, let there be reassurance in knowing that in the art of riding resides the true meaning of the effort and that there is some company for them to share.

The Horse As Our Partner Not A Beast of Burden

The horse, by nature, is an animal who should not carry and cannot carry you easily. He is not an animal of burden at all. Examination of the horse's musculature and skeleton reveal that he is not an animal who should have anything on his back at all, if we want to keep him healthy, happy, and moving beautifully. He is much more suited to pulling, since his motive force derives solely from the hindquarters.

Most of the horse's weight happens to be in front of the hindquarters, not on top, so the forehand serves as a crutch to support the weight. Humans, whose legs support all their weight *and* provide locomotion, move easily and gracefully; pushing a heavy wheelbarrow or a hand plow will simulate the horse's problem: pushing a majority of his weight from behind. So the horse's natural tendency is to put his weight on the forehand and push it by a kicking motion against the ground catapulting forward with as much speed as possible; thus, the thoroughbred on the racetrack most approximates the activity for which the horse was really made.

When you hitch a carriage or buggy behind a horse, he is not unhappy, because his weak joints are not taxed by a burden on top of him, and he can thrust his weight forward to pull this light and reasonably mobile item. The source of locomotion is then in the center of the entire moving system, making the horse's task easy. But a horse has no business carrying additional weight on his back. And yet we make him do that. We not only expect him to live happily ever after, but optimistically expect him not to break down. We also expect him to move well, even better than nature would inspire him to move. This is a tremendous task that we assign to ourselves. We must set about it properly, because if we make a mistake anywhere, we damage the musculature and the joints of the horse faster than we can feel sorry. If you look at a horse's haunches, his power source, you see four joints: hip, stifle, hock, and pastern. So that the horse may propel himself forward with the foreign weight of the rider and equipment without damage to these joints, we must develop the animal gymnastically. The idea is analogous to the development of a human gymnast. What does a gymnast do to look so fabulously coordinated and so beautiful in action? A gymnast has developed his joints and musculature properly, so that with minimum effort, strain and calorie output he can perform movements of incredible power with maximum grace. Similarly, the goal of our equine gymnastics (or dressage, if you will) is to develop the kind of gymnast who with minimum effort floats in suspension above the ground with utmost grace and coordination. This is the goal that we propose to pursue.

In order to develop muscular strength and elasticity and supple joints, we have to put the horse through very careful and progressive gymnastic exercises; if they are not careful and progressive, however, they will break down part or all of the horse's locomotor system. You know very well that if you overburden a horse following incomplete training, he will be prone to tie up or, worse, develop azoturia. A horse's muscle tissue can easily break down or be torn. Look, in the human realm, at a laborer. In the course of a day, he will work at least as hard as, if not more than, most athletes do in the course of heavy training. Yet he seldom possesses the full, finely sculpted body of the gymnast, nor will he move with the gymnast's elegance, and will often appear broken down, even emaciated. Because he does not use his body properly, he cannot have that coordinated grace. But a trained gymnast who works out eight hours daily will look beautiful. His musculature will come alive in the right places, and he will coordinate and move with form and brilliance. Both the laborer and the gymnast work the same number of hours and sweat equally heavily, yet one becomes a beautiful human, and the other can become a broken person. You, as the trainer, will determine which of these directions your horse's development will take. This business of going out and saying, "I'm working my horse, and he will be great," is not necessarily so. If you work him the wrong way, you will ruin him. You will make him a prematurely aged, stiff, broken-down unhappy creature full of pain. This is why it is important to understand, when you look at the joints of the hindquarters, that the hock is a smaller joint than the human knee. The human knee carries only 100 to 200 pounds, yet it is a common sight of arthritis, pain, swelling; it is predisposed to injury. The horse's hock carries from 1000 to 1500 pounds! And in the trot and canter, gaits with moments of suspension, the force absorbed is even greater than 1500 pounds; added to it is the kinetic energy of descent and the considerable force exerted by the horse in his propulsive thrust. And if that hock absorbs the impact in the wrong way and is not allowed to carry the burden with an elastic flexion, we are going to make that hock defend itself against the resultant pain and injury. That hock joint will build up all sorts of tissue and cartilage which will be very painful and eventually, of course, thicken the inner tissues just like regular outer tissue. This is why you see so many horses with a "hitching hock." These horses are unlevel, meaning one hind leg moves shorter than the other, an impure movement. The horse is not clinically lame, nor would a competition judge eliminate him. This kind of problem is called "rein lameness," because it is introduced by the rider using his hands rudely or unknowledgeably. If you sustain pressure on the horse's jaw for a long time or pull on the horse's mouth hard, he will have to oppose that pressure, because nature gave him a certain length of neck muscles that needs to be carried in a comfortable stretch in order to be relaxed. If the rider, for any reason, tries to compact it, it hurts the horse, just like a tight shoe hurts one's toes. Thus, the horse will pit his entire, very strong neck musculature against your hand's power and pull on the bit even after he has already made his jaw stiff by opening it in an attempt to release the offending pressure. Since that awful hand comes back with the gaping jaw and insists on further torturing, the horse has no alternative but to pit his strong neck musculature against the pulling arm. For it takes two to pull! The horse stiffens and pulls in an effort to save his hocks from the whiplash that results from the tug of war in front. It is hurting him! So, if you do this pulling contest, he comes down so hard on his joints and kicks the ground with so much defiant force as he fights the torturous pain in his mouth and neck that he eventually breaks down either one or both hocks, depending on one- or two-handed pulling by the rider.

The other extreme results from work on the so-called "light hacking rein." "Look, I dropped the reins," but you can be rude with a dropped rein, because when somebody asks you to come to the middle of the ring or walk from trot, you take the up to now loose rein and give it an inevitably strong yank and rip at the jaw. At that moment the horse becomes alarmed and whiplashes back on the hock, a painful jolt against which nature builds up arthritic tissues. So whether it is a perpetually pulling hand or an occasionally rough, abrupt hand, you must know that every time you do so you are assuring your horse shortened usefulness and an unhappy life. So the message is, then, why not leave his mouth alone? One possible cause of this fault is that we are visually oriented. We always want to see what we are doing. And the only area of the horse that you see is his neck and head. And you're so mesmerized by the beauty, agility and power of that neck that you want to get it involved, dominated, intimidated. This is one reason riders "move into" the horse's head and take up residence there. Heavy handedness also results from the "too much, too soon" method. Before the rider has an independent, relaxed and balanced seat, he is allowed to handle the reins. In a European academy the rider is lunged sometimes up to eighteen months until he has a perfectly independent, balanced seat without any gripping or slipping. Only these riders are allowed to control the horse on their own. He who lacks this secure seat will find himself in a vicious circle of losing balance and being frightened of falling. Seeking support, like grabbing for the rail on a pitching ship, one seeks a handle to grasp. We don't try to regain our balance with our toes or our earlobes; it's always our hands. So what is in your hand when you are losing your balance on horseback? The reins! You grab at them, supporting yourself on the horse's mouth. With each one of these efforts, you are not only making the horse move clumsily and out of balance, in pain and panic, but you are also ruining his joints and musculature, proscribing any progress towards a more brilliant future. It would be best if riders would understand how to start, to invest the time to learn to sit properly in the correct balance and the correct relaxation, so that their hands are independent of their seats, so that they do not use them to steady themselves, so that they can make their legs independent and available for aiding. (It is a sport of slow development, but most rewarding because the time is there: you can pursue it literally into your seventies and eighties. Many riders continue into their ninth decade.) The moment you have independent and strong legs you can address yourself to the control of the horse's hindquarters. From then on, there is riding.

A Brief, Panoramic View Of Dressage Commitments

Dressage is a French word we continue to use, for lack of a sufficient English equivalent, in connection with the improvement of a horse. It is a word denoting more than training: a total improvement of the horse is implied, both mental and physical. It means something qualitatively different from education, for it is a more intimate and less formalized method. Increasing numbers of equestrians are now riding their horses according to classical dressage principles.

Since horses were in the past the most useful of man's partners, the knowledge of horses and their effective training has been an all-important aspect of human existence. Horses were beasts of burden, extensions and enlargements of man's muscle power and energy. They were the fastest means of transportation, both civilian and military, making them as important in the past as are jets in our day.

Dressage has a tradition, even in writing, that is over two thousand years old, since it is based on the writings of the Greek general,

Xenophon. Over the milleniums, as a consequence of the importance of the horse, everything was tried and that which succeeded in improving the horse has been retained. Since neither the physique nor the mentality of either horse or rider has changed throughout the ages, the traditional principles of dressage remain relevant today.

While the utilitarian value of the horse has declined, its value in sports has concurrently increased, as men find themselves reluctant to leave contact with nature and abandon such a fine partner. It calls for a degree of wisdom and humility to accept traditional principles in the art of riding when we are part of a culture in which technological changes so rapid and dazzling encourage us to think that our forefathers were pygmies in most endeavors and that nothing endures. Also, we are reconciling ourselves to the belief that change is synonymous with improvement, for indeed in technology only that which is an improvement warrants change. But when it comes to the art of riding we must remain scrupulously relevant and not allow ourselves to believe that principles applicable to technology are also applicable to riding. No tradition that developed over milleniums can be discarded in two generations.

I am not advocating rigidity, however. We all know that any art form relies heavily on innovation, ingenuity, resourcefulness and creativity. A good dressage rider possesses and uses these attributes. However, he must use them within the general boundaries of the well-formulated classical principles of dressage, those principles that have ensured equestrian success in practice for centuries.

Dressage has three basic, interrelated meanings:

(1) *Dressage, in general, is all horsemanship that is based on love and respect for horses.* It is aimed at the *improvement of the horse's natural abilities to the ultimate degree.* It results in a happy horse that usually lives longer, stays healthier and performs better and for a longer time than one not dressaged. The method of dressage includes only natural means for the development of the horse. It is based on commitment to the education of the horse. Therefore, it is based on mutual understanding, respect and trust between horse and rider. It is based on kindness and reward rather than punishment and it excludes the use of force.

(2) *Dressage, more specifically, refers also to logical, natural, sequential exercising of the horse in order to improve his natural physical and mental abilities.* When we use the concept of dressage

in this way, we often call it gymnasticizing. The systematic gymnasticizing of the horse will result in a development similar to that
occurring in human gymnasts, figure skaters, or ballet dancers.
While their muscles and joints are improving in strength and their
abilities to use this energy with control also improves, they become
supple. A supple body manifests itself as the harmonious, controlled use of an extremely strong and well-developed musculature.
It enables the body to dispense a great deal of energy with comfort.
It makes possible a maximum performance output with a minimum
of energy dispensation. As the correct joints and correct
musculature are being used for the performance of a task, exhaus-
tion is eradicated and stress, both physical and mental, is reduced.

(3) *Dressage, finally, also denotes a special kind of competition.*
Dressage competition is based simply on the showing of a horse in a
flat arena of prescribed size in which the horse is ridden through
logical gymnastic exercises. Dressage competition is based on valuable
daily gymnastic exercises, the only difference being that these gymnastics are performed in a prescribed area and proceed according to a
well-designed, logical program. Depending on the horse's advancement, he can be shown at different levels of gymnastics.

The horses that are shown in dressage have been trained according
to general dressage principles of the classical riding tradition. They
have been logically gymnasticized daily. They have been successfully
shown through dressage competition programs. Thus they
demonstrate dressage in all three senses of the word.

The daily gymnastic dressage exercises of a horse aim at the following goals:

Physically the horse should be strengthened and balanced in order
to increase his impulsion and as a result he should be able to carry
himself and his rider forward with great strength. The ultimate goal is
to so balance the horse that he carries the majority of the composite
weight of himself and his rider as much on the hind legs as possible, in
other words, is collected and "seated." The horse must also improve
his suppleness (ability to bend). The ultimate goal in suppleness is a
horse that bends in his joints in order to do two things well:
movements on very small arcs, and suspension. Suspension refers to
those moments when some or all of the legs of the horse are in the air.
A supple horse suspends so powerfully and easily that he seems to
float and his feet touch the ground only for short instances. Finally,
the horse must move evenly and in good rhythm in all natural paces.

Mentally the horse should become obedient to his rider through trust based on cooperation and consistent communication of guidance. The rider must represent reason, logic and kindness, much as our thinking ought to represent these trustworthy attributes to the rest of our organism, which willingly obeys its dictates. The horse must also improve his attentiveness. Without an increased attention span as well as an improved sensitivity, a horse cannot accommodate the evermore refined communications of the rider's aids, nor can he improve his facility in self-awareness and resultant coordination.

The horse's physical and mental development take place simultaneously, reinforce each other, and are achieved by systematic, logical and consistent gymnastic exercises. The development has to be gradual, and therefore it is usually slow.

The *gymnastic exercises* that are useful for a horse include basically two kinds. These are exercises that (1) longitudinally bend, or flex, the horse and (2) laterally bend the horse.

Longitudinal bending of the horse refers to the horse's flexion throughout his length. This is something we humans never experience in our bipedal posture and locomotion. As the horse creates all his locomotion in his hindquarters, he cannot correctly propel himself forward without proper and total engagement of his body. In order to totally engage, he has to flex his muscles throughout his body, which results in a longitudinal bend. This bending begins at the hind hoofs, runs through the joints of the hindquarters that create the locomotion, communicates the movement through the back muscles to the front, where the impulsion is fed into the navigational, balancing areas of neck and head, and terminates at the horse's mouth.

Longitudinal flexion results in relaxed but well engaged joints and active musculature, which in turn contributes to the creation of great impulsive, yet controlled energy.

It further results in an improved ability of the horse to (1) carry his rider in correct balance, move with correct weight distribution on all four legs both on straight lines and on arcs; (2) shift the center of gravity of the composite weight towards the hindquarters, which are the only source of locomotion, thereby making movements more effortless and liberating the forelegs for higher and more suspended action; and (3) increase the horse's abilities of collection and extension. This means that the horse's ability to lengthen or shorten his strides in all natural paces without altering the rhythm of his hoof beats increases: in other words, the horse will cover greater or shorter distances per unit of time without either rushing or slowing down. Both rushing and sluggishness tire the horse and make the rider's travel uncomfortable.

Balanced movement is the foundation of all correct riding achievements. Only a longitudinally bent horse can move in balance. This is difficult to achieve, considering that most horses "fall" even when free on a pasture for lack of sufficient musculature, strength and know-how in balancing their own bodies correctly. When the foreign weight of the rider is introduced the horse will unavoidably "fall" in order to keep himself upright on his four legs.

By "falling" I do not mean that the horse literally falls down to the ground! I mean that the horse is incapable of maintaining an even distribution of weight on his four legs. All horses have to be dressaged before they can maintain a correct distribution of weight at all paces and figures. However, there are horses so well constructed that they have "natural balance" and move evenly, lightly, and supplely when free of a rider.

The horse's hindquarters are the source of his impulsion; therefore, the rider must seek to control them. The only way to do this is to flex the horse longitudinally. The best exercises for improving longitudinal flexion are transitions. It is important to know that transitions cannot only take place from pace to pace (i.e., trot to walk, etc.) but also within paces by extending or collecting the horse's strides.

The most collected gymnastic exercises are the *collected walk, the piaffe* (trot on the spot) and *the pirouette at the canter.*

Once a horse moves in perfect balance, the rider must encourage supple movements. As the horse is learning to balance and by dressage his musculature is improved, he will also gradually become more supple. A supple horse yields both mentally and physically; mentally to the rider's wishes and physically to the task of effortless locomotion.

A supple horse engages all his joints and muscles in rhythmic coordination that ensures balanced movement with the least exertion. While looking at a supple horse working, one observes a rippling and swaying of the horse's musculature that brings to mind coordinated and seemingly effortless dancing.

Obviously, less supple horses who have had little gymnasticizing will be less able to bend on an arc than thoroughly elastic, well-gymnasticized horses. Riders must be careful not to overbend one part of the horse's body only, for that will invite him to remain straight and stiff in the rest of his body. The horse's neck is naturally more supple than his bulky trunk which includes a relatively unyielding rib-cage and heavy musculature. A horse can remain rigid throughout his trunk and still bend the neck to reach a fly or scratch way back. However, correct lateral bending occurs only when the horse is evenly bent throughout his body, along his spinal cord.

At the beginning of dressage training the major task is to teach a horse to carry his rider in balance on a straight line. The horse is to move evenly and straight without pushing his shoulders or haunches in or out, his hind legs following the forelegs so that the horse's spinal cord remains the center axis from which the hoofprints are equidis-tant. The rider should never become a passive traveler, and even on a running horse should keep the legs intimately in touch with the horse's sides, teaching the horse the concept that he may move only under conditions of aiding.

Most of the time a horse moves on a bent line. Only seldom is there a straight path to move on. In our small riding arenas there are two long walls and two short walls where a horse should move straight. Otherwise, riding is done on some arcs, circles or the combination of those, whether it is jumping or any other gymnastic exercises or showmanship the rider may pursue. Lateral bending can be exercised in two qualitatively different ways.

The simpler lateral exercises are those done on circular lines, while the horse's hindlegs continue to follow in the direction of the forelegs. The path of the horse then proceeds on an arc. Such are all the corners of a riding arena, those being all parts of an incomplete circle. To that we can add the riding of a full circle, which can be of any size, usually large for a stiffer, novice horse and smaller according to the horse's ability to bend as he advances in his suppleness. Then we can ride serpentine lines, which are more difficult than simple circles, for the horse is asked to bend from side to side in quick succession. Finally we can ride figure-eights, which are rather difficult to do well, as the horse will have to sustain bending for a long while on each side, yet is given only one straight step to change the bend from one side to the other side.

In short, from simple to complex arc riding we proceed from a generous arc, through the circle and serpentine to the figure-eight. We also proceed from generous arcs to tighter, smaller ones as the horse's ability to bend onto them in a continuum improves. Note that the horse should be taught lateral flexion at the walk first, then at the trot or, if possible, in canter.

The more difficult or complex lateral exercises are done on multi-tracks. That means that the horse will not follow with his hind legs toward the footprints of the forelegs on the corresponding side. Rather, the horse will leave either three or four tracks behind. These exercises, in general order of difficulty, are as follows:

The *shoulder-in* and *shoulder-out* exercises can be done only at the walk and trot. In the shoulder-in exercises we ask the horse to be bent around our inside leg, stepping with his inside hindleg toward the footprint of the outside foreleg. He will leave three tracks behind as a result and will bend the joints of the inside hindleg generously by striding deep under the center of gravity. While the horse will progress in space towards the direction of his outside shoulder, he will be bent opposite the direction of progression — to the inside. This is the only movement we ask of a horse where we demand bending opposite to the direction of motion.

The shoulder-out is the reverse position of the shoulder-in. It is not necessary to do it, for by changing the hand one can supple equally both sides of the horse with the shoulder-in alone.

The *haunches-in* and *haunches-out* exercises are a little more sophisticated in their demands on the horse's musculature than the previously discussed ones.

In the haunches-in the horse is once more bent evenly around the rider's inside leg. He is moving towards the side on which he is bent with his hindquarters tracking inside of the rail near which the forehand proceeds. The outside hindleg of the horse strides toward the direction of his inside foreleg.

The haunches-in can be done in all three natural paces, the walk, trot and canter. However, I strongly recommend that it never be exercised in the canter. Horses have the natural tendency to canter crooked, with their haunches in, anyway. That is highly undesirable for it allows the horse to avoid bending his joints correctly and move in stressful lack of balance. Indeed, the rider must encourage his horse to canter very straight. Thus the haunches-in at the canter, while horses are eager to offer it, should be an exercise avoided.

The haunches-out, just like the shoulder-out, is an exercise not necessary to practice, as it can be replaced by changing the hand and performing again a haunches-in.

The half-pass is a more sophisticated lateral bending exercise than the previously described ones. It serves to strengthen the horse's uses of his hips, stifles and shoulders, as opposed to the shoulder-in which aims to strengthen the hocks for collection and suspension. At half-pass the horse moves on a diagonal across the arena space, but should never be allowed to proceed ahead of the inside shoulder. The horse is once again bent around the inside leg of the rider, proceeding towards the direction of this bending. Most important are the maintenance of the forward urge, the evenness and clarity of motion. Half passes can be done at the walk, trot and canter and should be done, indeed, at all three paces. The horse moving in half pass will leave four tracks behind on the ground. The joints it strengthens will improve the horse's ability to extend his strides.

Pirouettes are also lateral bending exercises. They can be performed only in the walk and in the canter. While pirouetting at the walk is a relatively simple gymnastic exercise, doing the same in canter is one of the most difficult. Young horses can soon pirouette at the walk but only the most advanced horses will be able to do the same at the canter, usually many years later.

At the pirouette, the horse is asked to turn around his hindquarters, which are to remain active, but on the spot where the movement was started. One can ride quarter, half, three-quarter or full pirouettes, depending on the horse's level of advancement. During these turns around the hindquarters, the horse has to be gently bent around the rider's inside leg towards the direction of the turn.

Generalizations to remember in connection with lateral bending of the horse:

(1) During all lateral bending exercises horses are bent along the entire length of their spinal column towards one side. That side is the hollow or contracted side of the horse. The other side, called the outside, is stretched longer and feels "full."

(2) While lateral bending exercises can never be done with a straight horse, their purpose remains to help straighten a horse. Lateral bending exercises have very high suppling value which ensures the eventual development of the desired straight-moving horse.

(3) There can never be any successful lateral bending without the horse first being bent longitudinally. In other words, lateral bending can occur only when the horse is "ahead of the legs, driven up to the bit," in perfectly relaxed longitudinal bending.

(4) While longitudinal flexion is a prerequisite to lateral flexion, each reinforces the horse's ability to do the other. In other-words, successful lateral bending will consolidate the horse's ability to remain in longitudinal bending, which in turn will make this prerequisite position more often available to do additional lateral exercises.

(5) Always repeat each lateral bending exercise on both hands. Never exercise the horse's hollow or stiff side more than the other. Always "mirror" lateral exercises and do it in close succession. In other words, if you circled to the right, follow that soon with a circle to the left. If you made a half pass to the right, follow that with one done to the left, etc.

(6) Always combine longitudinal and lateral gymnastics. Longitudinal gymnastics being all transitions, always make a transition after each lateral exercise. As an example: circle right in the trot and reaching the opposite rail, depart into canter on the left lead. Or pirouette left at the walk, and depart at the canter on the right lead when the pirouette is completed. The combinations are literally infinite.

(7) Gymnastic riding can be meaningful only when a planned strategy is pursued by the rider. No exercise should be done on the spur of the moment and without due preparation. During riding, quick succession of changes reveal well-planned gymnasticizing. There is no specific value in riding endlessly in the same pace, on the same line, for a long time. The frequency of transitions is in direct proportion with the value of gymnastic development in the horse.

The dressage rider goes through basically three stages of education and achievement.

The *beginner* should ideally have two instructors: a riding coach and a school horse. This rider must learn to harmonize with all the movements of his horse. In order to do so he must acquire a balanced seat. Then he will be able to follow the horse's movements. He will sit correctly. A school horse can offer quiet tolerance and well-balanced, comfortable, pure movements without much need for alteration from the rider. Thus, the rider can relax into a comfortable position. Lazy horses that need strenuous driving will always stiffen the novice rider. Unbalanced, irregular, unpredictably behaving horses will deny relaxation and good feeling to the rider and will encourage anguish and anticipation in him.

This stage or period is terminated, according to the rider's natural talents, as soon as he acquires an independent, balanced seat in which he can follow all of his horse's movements, and therefore, begin to influence with aids.

In the second stage, the rider learns the *craftmanship* and *technique* of riding. He will also *diversify* and *build routine*. In this stage the rider is taught by the coach and continues to learn from his horse. However, he becomes himself also a partial instructor of his horse.

He should ride as many kinds of horses as possible. He should ride in as many modes of riding as possible. Go on trail rides, jump, and do gymnastic flatwork.

The rider now learns the refined language of aids and how to use them effectively and consistently. Now having an independent seat, he can take the liberty to use any part of his body independently according to need, without the urgency to grip or stiffen. Learning the use of aids also depends on natural talent. Some people will be able to coordinate effective aids consistenly rather soon.

In the third stage the rider becomes *accomplished.* Now he only needs a coach to guide him and do as much of that work cooperatively through consultations and discussions as possible. The rider now is the teacher of his horse. The horse emerges as the sole object of instruction for which the rider and his coach pool their knowledge and energies. The coach should make an effort to deny any function as a "crutch" or dictator.

Some riders will exhibit great skill and craftmanship at teaching their own horses. They will improve throughout a lifetime as experience and routine increase their effectiveness. Few will emerge as artists. Through sensitivity, imagination and creative approaches, they may add their new inspirations to the great body of classical riding knowledge. Dressage has absolutely no room for rudeness, intimidation, cajoling or trickery. The horse's abilities are just as varied and unique as those of human individuals. A dressage rider must proceed at the pace his horse offers; he must understand and respect the individuality of his partner.

At this stage life is full of challenges. Competitions serve as educational experiences. Riders bid themselves against their own performances and seek to improve. They are now totally dedicated to their horse's needs, having no more need to concentrate on their own skills.

During this last stage, it is important for riders to be independent, to exercise their own judgment and base it on their feelings of the horse. No coaching that is authoritarian or tyrannical has any place, for that would limit the rider's essential development.

In the following part of this chapter, I will not discuss the activities of the beginning riders, previously described. Nor will I talk about the work of the accomplished artist of horsemanship. Rather, I will discuss the concepts relevant to the middle group. However, those preliminary to it or past it may also be interested.

The horse's obedience is achieved by virtue of "conversation" that is constantly and continuously going on between horse and rider. The conversation is silent and eventually should become refined enough not to be apparent to an observer's eyes. At first, figuratively speaking, there may be some "shouting" going on, or "loud talk," but later, as the horse's mentality is improved and as he becomes more capable of doing the required tasks, the "conversation" takes on the intimacy of a "whisper."

These communications are always two-way. One is not a rider until one feels clearly and distinctly the communications of his horse and can interpret these in order to react to them properly. Horses will communicate through bodily attitudes. Riders will feel these communications also with their body and reply to them bodily. The language of the rider is called *aids* and that speech which communicates to the horse is *aiding.*

The rider's aids must be *clear, concise,* and *consistent. Without these attributes no human could learn a foreign language, nor can the horse learn the language of the aids. As in all language studies, the teaching of the aids must involve frequent repetition and resemble the drilling of a vocabulary.*

The language of its vocabulary is limited by the physical and mental attitudes of both horse and rider. The rider may communicate with his torso, back muscles, legs and hands.

A rider should basically ride with his upper body, which in no part contacts the horse. Only in coordination with the rider's torso and in support of its actions can we meaningfully work with our legs and hands. The rider's body is mistakenly called "seat." A good rider sits on three points all the time and never allows those to leave the saddle while dressaging. These three points are the two seat bones and the crotch. If the crotch is not on the saddle, but elevated off it, the seat bones also elevate up into the buttocks and meaninglessly roll back and forth in the saddle. This annuls any reasonable communication between the rest of the body and the horse.

So the seat, the two seat bones and the crotch, are to be passively, adhesively, and everlastingly placed in the saddle. Against the seat, which is the contact area, the aiding system may be put to work. Only in the jumping seat (which includes posting) will this seat be replaced by another area of contact and suspension against which the aids will work: the knees.

Now let me outline the four instruments of aiding:

(1) The seat, as described above, *is passive and is the communication center.* The rider and horse, through the saddle, remain in steady contact. This is the area that *never* aids but without which there is no possibility of correct aiding elsewhere. This is the point of stability and suspension which allows for the independent mobility of aiding areas elsewhere.

(2) *The legs serve primarily the purpose of creating impulsion.* Impulsion is the most important output we want from the horse. The rider should never use his legs to maintain his balance in the saddle. The rider should stay in the saddle by virtue of his bodily coordination in such a manner that his perpendicularly positioned torso, pulled by the center of gravity, maintains him in the saddle.

Secondarily, the legs are used for the utilization of impulsion into lengthening or higher strides. They regulate extension and collection. They determine paces because their various uses indicate to the horse which pace he is to move on and with how long a stride within that pace. The use of the rider's legs should be distinctly different in halt, walk, trot and canter. This is not a quantitative (amount of pressure) difference, but qualitative.

Legs also bend the horse and even suggest the degree of bending. In short, the legs control the activities of the all-important hindquarters of the horse.

The body of the rider is used as a transformer. The impulsion generated in the horse's hindquarters runs forward in his body through his back. These various weaving movements in the horse's back are those the rider perceives as motion and with which he variously cooperates in order to keep his seat steady in the saddle. Without these motion weaves we would sit on an unmoving surface much like the seat of a car which gives us no feeling in spite of the locomotion of the car. The horse makes us feel his moves through his swinging back, through which the impulsion-created energies travel toward his front, which merely absorbs these energies. The horse's front never creates locomotive energies, it merely absorbs and supports those coming from the hindquarters. The back is the bridge which transports these energies from points of origin in the rear to points of termination in the front.

(3) *The rider's body sits on this bridge of communication and has the task of transforming these energies.* The rider's body absorbs the energies coming from the rear, effects change and passes them through his shoulders, arms and hands towards the horse's mouth.

The body can be used in *two different ways* in these transforming activities: [1] **As weight.** The torso can tilt forward or backward from the perpendicular position. It can also tilt slightly right or left from the same perpendicular position. It can also weight one or the other of the seat bones by rotating lightly one shoulder forward and the other backward from their parallel positions. [2] **As power.** The rider can flex or relax some or all of his back muscles, thereby indicating cooperation or resistance to the horse's offered movement.

These activities of the rider's body are to serve basically three transformation functions: (a) *drive,* (b) *follow and harmonize as an approval,* and *(c) restrain by bracing.* A rider should constantly be doing one of the three with his body. Furthermore, he should do the appropriate one. Most riders unfortunately yield to the horse only by following his movement, with which they seek to harmonize at all cost. These riders are travelers and impotent as meaningful transformers of the dynamic energies to them by the horse. Bracing begins with the legs that are firmly established on the horse's sides into a steady contact. With this contact the horse is encouraged to continue to work under the weight with his hind legs while the rider creates a point of steadiness against which his muscles can be braced. The torso is braced by rendering the rider's backbone unyielding, and using the lower back muscles so as to bring his seat bones arrestingly and heavily down into the saddle. To get the correct feeling, I recommend you plant your feet firmly on the ground while sitting on a kitchen stool and use your body so as to elevate the two back legs of this stool off the ground. As you will notice, you can determine how high you wish to elevate the stool legs. Equally on a horse you can brace lightly or strongly.

(4) *The hands serve the purpose of guidance and inducers to relaxation as well as appropriate terminating points for the horse's energies.* As such, they are primarily *controlling* mechanisms. They absorb the excesses the legs create and the body cannot handle. As such they should be the least important, least used, most lightly and sparingly engaged units of the aiding group.

Correctly used hands should never punish, should be always as light and as inactive as possible, and should be coordinated with the back muscles while the arms remain relaxed.

A young horse may run because he is losing his balance and is falling forward, rolling like an avalanche on his forelegs, picking up more and more impetus as he goes along. The hands should never jerk the horse's mouth. If a horse is running much, the rider should attempt to slow his rhythm with his torso and circle him frequently on large comfortable circles on which he can bend at this relatively stiff period of his development.

The rider's hands must depend on supple use of all joints starting with the shoulders on down to the fingers. No arm muscles should be in use. Basically, the hands should be a mere extension of the activities of the rider's back, always coordinated with it.

Therefore, the hands, like the body, will do three kinds of things: *drive, restrain,* or *yield.*

The most important general concept in aiding is that at all times, all the aiding mechanisms should be in use and in perfect *coordination* with each other. Thus, aiding is perpetual and the aids must be used consistently. Even harmonious relaxation is an aid, for it tells something to the horse.

There are two basic aiding systems according to coordination of the rider's body. They must be used appropriately and with properly effortless interchangeability. Riders must always be able to shift from one system to the other, according to what they mean to communicate to their horse. These two systems are sometimes called *"unilateral and bilateral"* or *"parallel and diagonal"* aids. I will use the latter pair of terms when describing them.

In the *Parallel Aiding System,* the rider must do exactly the same on both of his sides. He must place the right leg on the horse exactly opposite the left one on the other side. He must use his weight and back muscles the same way on both sides of his spinal column. He must engage his hands identically and of course, carry them in identical positions on both sides.

This aiding system should be in effect when we wish the horse to use himself symmetrically in identical ways on both sides of his spinal column. The occasions where that is desirable are fewer than those when diagonal aids are necessary and are limited to the following:

    (1) When the horse is to halt — all the time

        (2) When reining back — all the time

            (3) When trotting — only on a straight path

                (4) When walking — only on a straight path

At all other activities diagonal aids must be used, as the horse uses each of his sides differently.

The *Diagonal Aiding System* should be in effect much more frequently than the parallel one. Even during as simple a riding activity as trotting around an arena, riders should make eight changes from parallel to diagonal aids and back. Each of the four straight walls must be ridden under parallel aids, while all four corners should be rounded by a horse that is bent by diagonal aids.

As opposed to parallel aiding, in diagonal aiding, the rider must do different things on each side of the horse. Legs, back, torso, hands, all act differently on the right than on the left side. Usually action is initiated on one side of the horse, running through the transforming body to terminate on one hand at the opposite side from the initiating leg. We talk about "inside" and "outside" of a horse rather than right or left. The inside is usually but not always that side which is to the center of the arena, the outside being usually the one towards the rail. All the time the horse is bent more or less to his inside. Therefore, if the horse is in counter-canter, he is bent away from the center of the arena and facing towards the rail. In such a case the "inside" of the horse is actually to the outside.

Where there is no rail, as in cross country riding or when stadium jumping through continuous curving lines, the "inside" is always the side towards which the horse is bent. Thus, the horse is always shorter or "hollow" to the inside and longer or "full" to the outside.

The rider's legs can be basically in two different positions on the horse's sides. The so called *"girth position"* is slightly behind the girth, the rider's toes being directly under and flush with the knees. The so called *"canter position"* is further behind the girth position by about two to four inches. It is important to maintain both of these positions with toes well elevated and heels sunk, and continue to ride with flexed calfs. In diagonal aiding, one leg is in the girth position, the other in canter position.

Hands may be in three different positions.

(1) The *indirect hand* serves the purpose of indicating lateral bending to the horse. *In that position, the rein is so held that were it to continue beyond the hand, it would pierce the rider's breast on the opposite side.* In other words, if the inside rein is held as an indirect rein, it would connect the inside corner of the horse's mouth to the outside breast of the rider (if the rein were to continue beyond the rider's fist). The indirect rein is, therefore, near the horse's neck but never crossing over to the other side of his crest. It is mostly passive. It may never be pulled backwards. In all lateral movements, where aids must always be diagonal, the rider's inside hand may be an indirect hand. It is passive and therefore does not act as a rein in opposition to the inside hindleg of the horse, which is to carry more weight in lateral movements than the outside one. It merely indicates the degree of lateral bending to the horse.

(2) The *direct hand* is used to perform half halts and full halts. It is the hand position designed to effectively communicate the restrictive back actions of the rider to the horse's mouth. It is the hand that asks and invites the horse's head to slow down and wait for the hindquarters to catch up. It is the only hand position that invites backward followed by yielding forward in rhythmic intervals. To this hand the horse responds by supply yielding his jaw, poll and neck. The direct hand may go from contact to opening, avoiding any restrictive invitation, in order to create lengthening of the horse's body when extending the strides.

The direct hand connects the horse's mouth towards the rider's waistline on the same side. In diagonal aiding the outside rein is usually direct. In parallel aiding both reins are used as direct reins. It is important that the activities of the direct rein always be coordinated with the rider's back muscles on the same side. The bracing of the muscles in the small of the back should cause the invitation of the direct rein on the horse's mouth, rather than any tension in the arms of the rider.

(3) The *leading rein* is most often used on young, green horses to offer them exaggerated guidance when needed. The direction of the leading rein is from the horse's mouth towards the rider's thigh on the same side. So it is a rein pointing slightly away from the horse's neck and slightly downward, indicating strongly the track on which the horse is to turn. As the horse advances and accepts the rider's legs for bending and guidance, this direct rein will no longer be necessary and will be replaced by an indirect rein.

Now that so much has been said about the aiding system, let me add as a summary that aiding is successful only if the rider offers it through a sequence:

(1) Rider prepares the horse: warning.
(2) Horse responds to preparation by attentiveness.
(3) Rider aids into movement.
(4) Horse executes the movement correctly.
(5) Rider confirms it by yielding.
(6) Horse relaxes and perpetuates the movement.
(7) The rider harmonizes with his relaxed horse in desired movement.

This sequence takes a very short time to perform. Yet all steps of it must be performed by both rider and horse. If one of them omits one of these responses, the entire sequence must be re-initiated by the rider, who repeats preparation.

It is tremendously important to yield to our horses. Nothing should ever freeze when aiding; nothing should ever be locked; nothing should ever be rigid. Riding is dynamic; it is perpetual movement. Therefore it tolerates no rigidity, which is the stopping of motion. Should any part of the rider become stiff or rigid, the horse will have to become rigid. If any part of either horse or rider is stiff, the whole system suffers discord, and correct gymnastic development is at an absolute end.

In conclusion, let me remind you once more that dressage is beneficial for any horse regardless of its use. After all, dressage is simply the natural, harmonious, kindly way of logical gymnasticizing. It was indeed developed to help promote the usefulness of any horse.

There is no horse in this world who will not improve by becoming stronger, more supple, more elastic, more balanced, more harmonious, easier in understanding light aids rather than force. There is no equestrian endeavor that cannot benefit from a horse whose attention span has been increased and who is more trusting of the rider. There is no performance that cannot be improved by a more obedient horse who is not only willing but also capable of using himself correctly. That is all that dressage aims at and that is all any rider may reasonably desire to achieve.

Dressage Training's Simplest Logical Outline

Imagine a huge box of puzzle pieces that you dump on the floor. The pieces will be hard to fit together without knowing the final picture. The picture printed on the lid of the box gives the guideline for fitting the pieces of puzzle together in the most effective and efficient way. In this article, I will give the whole panoramic picture in brief, as the top of the puzzle box shows the final picture. Later we can look at some of the pieces in detail. By then one should know a little better where the pieces belong in the total picture.

The stages in the horse's development are sequential. One cannot work on a sophisticated movement without having previously achieved the "lower" stage preceding it. The horse's daily work as well as his development throughout the years, therefore is sequential and not helter-skelter. The developmental stages in horse gymnastics *(dressage)* grow in sophistication by repetition. Fulfillment (goals satisfactorily met) will come by maturation of gymnastic exercises. Therefore, each exercise (shoulder-in, etc.) has its own history, beginning with rather hesitant, poor quality performance and maturing toward perfection.

Dressage tests, in fact, are measuring instruments by which the horse's general gymnastic development is evaluated. Scoring of the various movements is done so as to reflect the developmental sophistication required on each specific testing level. Each movement in a dressage test is reflective of a training idea which is basically evaluated by it. While the entire gymnastic development of the horse is a harmonious, continuous effort, movements in dressage tests are designed to reveal specific details of that general development.

Therefore, some movement might predominantly test balance (i.e., flying changes on every stride) while others might test engagement (i.e., pirouette at the canter).

Now let us look at the *stages of developmental sophistications and what observable tendencies they create.* The rider must recognize when and how gymnastic development takes place in the horse. So here is an outline of how *every day* of riding might be built in a logical sequence; how these days logically spent will build into years of work based on the same sequence of activities.

(A) **RELAXATION** is the prerequisite of all gymnastic work. The horse should be relaxed in mind (trusting the rider and accepting his aids) and in body (muscles relaxed, joints rotating properly). When a horse is relaxed, he produces the condition we often call (in my mind wrongly) — *being on the bit.* I rather think that relaxation will result in the *horse accepting* (being on) *the aids.* Primarily, this means the acceptance of, or submission to, the *forward driving aids* of the legs. A horse that submits to the aids will react to the rider's driving leg aids by engaging more — in effect shifting more weight towards the haunches and rotating his joints in a larger circle — rather than hurrying! A horse on the aids will maintain a proper rhythm while being worked with the rider's legs to cajole engagement or bending. A horse that jigs, hurries and plunges forward when ridden by the rider's legs, is not relaxed. Thus relaxation is most obviously manifest in the *longitudinal flexion* of a horse which "rounds out" when driven (elevating back, stepping deeper, rotating joints more slowly, lowering haunches) rather than rushing forward. By "bowing" or flexion in length the horse develops new kinetic energy for improved impulsion. As a bowed whip has kinetic spring the longitudinally-flexed horse has "resident energy" that a strung-out, tense horse, above the bit, does not have. A flexed horse vibrates the movement through his entire body rather than just striding with his legs. The muscles relaxed allow resiliency of vibration throughout and those are the beginnings of general suppling (development through relaxation rather than strain and tension).

First, relaxation is comprised of an *omission* (lack) *of tension.* It is a condition that, in its most primitive form, is based on the *absence of* tensions and resistances. However, with time and sophistication, relaxation will become the substance of all the following — and more sophisticated — stages and will be re-named. These new connotations of basic relaxation are the further stages of sophistications of development. In other words, relaxation, as it becomes sophisticated, is the essence of all stages of development.

When the horse is relaxed with the aids, flexed, submitting to driving aids and producing pure and energetic basic paces, we work on the next stage of sophistication, which is balance.

(B) **BALANCE** is most commonly manifest in, and is achieved with the help of lateral bending throughout the horse's spine without rushing, and in transitions from pace to pace with clear demarcation, purity and grace. A balanced transition is easy to recognize because the last step of the original pace is as clear and balanced as will be the first step of the new pace. If the transition involves a muddle of deterioration of the original pace before "falling" to a new one, awkwardly, balance is missing.

(C) **RHYTHM** is the essence of sophisticating the original relaxation of the horse. Only against the musical measures of the horse's hoof-falls can we work towards sophistication. For if rhythm changes, evasion occurs. Any change of rhythm is an evasion; for, by speeding or slowing, the horse can avoid engagement of the haunches as well as all lateral flexion. Often I feel that the so-called "feel" or talent manifest in many riders (independent of the level of their trained skills) is nothing more than a perfect sense of rhythm, combined with a perfect sense of bringing their center of gravity together with that of their horse. Much as the tight-rope walker, who perpetually adjusts his body to keep his center of gravity perfect and prevent falling, so will the talented rider reorganize himself with every step of the horse's action without making his effort obvious to the observer.

Rhythm is best cultivated (and tested for achievement) by riding for lengthening and shortening strides within the same pace. It is composed of transition work in the same pace. Extending and collecting the horse's strides must go on from the beginning of his training to initiate longitudinal elasticity and allow it to grow into true collection and extension in perfect rhythm.

(D) **IMPULSION** is controlled energy manifest; the opposite of rushing. Displaying, rather slow but more suspended action (not fast and choppy), the joints in the haunches rotate with a rounder, more continuously fluid motion. The elastic motion of the joints is facilitated by a supple musculature (rippling under the skin), propelling the horse with accuracy and grace, yet without haste.

(E) **ENGAGEMENT** of the haunches can be recognized in its sophisticated stage by a more cadenced movement displayed by an increasing time of suspension (flight above ground) proportionate to decreasing but supremely accurate touch down periods. The lightness and harmony of a well-engaged horse is manifested in maximum suspension produced by minimum energy (the economy of perfect gymnastics). The haunches will assume (accept) the majority of weight, liberating the forehand. The lightness of the forehand is demonstrated by the alternate rocking of the withers to a point higher than the haunches, never by a pulled-up neck with a tucked-up head; by movement in which the shoulders are completely free; by lifting the knees high (cannon bone perpendicular to the ground). The forehand seems to "hover and hesitate in dance" as the withers "bounce upward" somewhat dandifying in elegance the truly brilliantly-engaged horse.

Remember that the younger horses will need more time on exercises primarily fostering the first three stages. As a green horse might spend much of the lesson relaxing, a fully-trained horse relaxes and submits often as soon as the rider is placed in the saddle, leaving much of the riding time for engagement efforts. While a truly green horse cannot and will not engage, he will go through a "relative engagement" somewhere during the period of running away with the rider and of finally being controlled to a halt for the breathless rider to dismount.

Relaxation is the real name of all stages. For whether it is the rhythm or the engagement or anything else you might work on, it is only a sophistication over relaxation. Engagement is *committed relaxation* as opposed to *omission* of tension as in the first stage. The horse's musculature and joints are supple and elastic *because they are relaxed.* That is why in the "pool of relaxation" balance, rhythm, impulsion and engagement, which are the developmental sophistications of relaxation, must be cultivated.

Any time spent on a tense horse is a waste of time.

The Dialectics of Success
In Schooling The Horse

The rider has to keep in mind that means and ends should be clearly defined and not confused with each other. Several different *means* (methods, actions) may lead successfully to the same *end* (goal). In fact, a combination of means may more successfully lead to the quicker attainment of certain ends. That is why I find it important to remember Hegel's (a German historian who learned from history that man never learns from history) *dialectics*!

This is what he proposes, in brief:

There is always a THESIS, that is an *action,* that immediately provokes an ANTITHESIS or *reaction.* The two contest and as a result a SYNTHESIS or *solution* will occur. But that synthesis is not static, for it immediately appears as a challenge to which a new antithesis develops with which it has to fight for the next possible synthesis. In short, nothing is permanent, rather all is dynamic, and the only reality is an everchanging process where nothing is ever resolved, fixed and therefore attainable. For as soon as a goal has been reached, it is newly challenged by an antithesis that seeks a renewed goal. A simplified version is presented below:

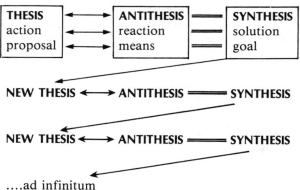

....ad infinitum

What is the importance of this philosophical theory to riders? We are simply reminded that we start with a certain condition in the horse which is our thesis. That could be a *lack of impulsion.* Immediately we must propose our goal or synthesis to be the *establishment of impulsion.* Where we put the question mark in the formula is the antithesis. We must ask what means (methods) should be introduced to fight the thesis and search out the proper antithesis that will predictably come to the desired synthesis, which is improved impulsion. So let us go through the formula with the following simplified chart:

LACK OF IMPULSION ◄——► **WHAT SHOULD I DO?**
A lazy horse, sour to the
aids, moving stiffly and
inattentively...

This is a condition.   **This is where good riding
strategy must be; the means
best suited to our goals
must be found.** In this case:
RELAX the horse to render
him educable. Slow him
further to develop the opportunity to drive. Follow
the slightest impulse offered
after the drive by traveling
passively on that miniscule
energy. Then drive again
and harmonize the gain, until the horse becomes quite
attentive to the aids and offers beyond relaxation a
balanced and rhythmic
movement which is sus-
tained without perpetual
nudging aids.

TO IMPROVE IMPULSION
This is my GOAL

Where do riders go wrong? They can usually identify the problem, which we are calling the thesis. But they then proceed to propose as the antithesis what ought to be the synthesis. In other words, they go wrong by trying to use as means their goals! So they get a different end result because the one they wanted was spent as a means and those means create an unpredictable result! Let us go through the example again the way it will go wrong:

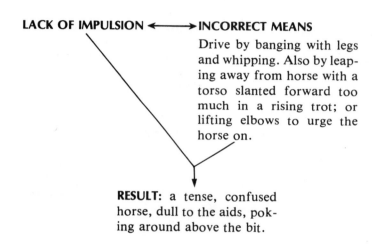

LACK OF IMPULSION ←——→ INCORRECT MEANS

Drive by banging with legs and whipping. Also by leaping away from horse with a torso slanted forward too much in a rising trot; or lifting elbows to urge the horse on.

RESULT: a tense, confused horse, dull to the aids, poking around above the bit.

So remember that a rider who pursues his goals by riding his goals will never achieve them. But a rider who pursues various proper means leading to a goal that is a genuinely new condition, will progress. Remember that when we define our goal as being a horse that moves straight forward with good impulsion, we employ the means of bending, for it is through bending that the horse becomes straight. That is why riders who just ride straight on their green horses will always have green horses, because through straightness you get crookedness but through bending you get straightness. In the same way, through stretching the young horse you will eventually have a collected horse with a tall neck in self-carriage, but by elevating his neck early and artificially, by force, you will have the opposite, a horse on the forehand, rushing "down hill." It is well for us to learn from Hegel's dialectics that those who confuse the means with the ends are the losers!

The Athletic Horse Performs Gymnastically Well

Becoming An Athletic Horse Is Not By Food Alone

The formal education of any animal, including the human, is much influenced, even determined to some degree by the hereditary package the animal is born with on the one hand and his early life experiences on the other. Formal education will have to deal with an animal that is limited by his inborn abilities, aptitudes, talents and potential and one that has also had past experiences, prior to the beginning of his formal education. Consequently, the horse's background warrants some attention.

The hereditary package (the genetic background) of a horse is very important in determining how much education the horse will be able to receive. It will determine how well the horse will perform. The best upbringing, the best education, the best training will not be able to eliminate hereditary shortcomings, whether they are of a physical or mental nature. This is the reason why selecting the right young horse for our educational purposes is paramount to success.

The upbringing of the young horse from his birth to the time his formal education commences will also be of great importance. The best hereditary traits can easily be thwarted, inhibited or ruined by incorrect upbringing. A young horse can easily be physically stunted and

Photographed by S. Gail Miller

Reigen, the eighteen months old Hannoverian colt, son of Rondo is owned by Dr. and Mrs. Jerry Martin of Flagstaff, Arizona. His upbringing, as represented here by romping in the snow, demonstrates the wisdom that an athlete must be hardy and develop through motion and exercise. Liveliness, energy, balance and speed, all there!

mentally ruined much before he is mature enough to receive a formal education or training. Damage in early life can cause irreversible and incorrigible shortcomings.

Like all living organisms, the horse too exists in several contexts as a result of his interrelationship (interaction) with his environment. The horse's "present" as we work with it in training does not exist in a vacuum. It represents two relevant dimensions: (1) *The "present" of the horse is a result of his past — his memories, in particular. By the same token, his "present" is becoming the past of his future; whatever we do to him, he will remember.* (2) *The horse will always naturally interact with his current environment, which, while training, includes us.*

To experience his word sympathetically is, therefore, the first and foremost principle of the upbringing of a horse. We must consciously adopt an attitude of empathy toward the horse. We should try to experience the world (including ourselves) through his senses and as if through his thinking. This attitude presumes not only willingness to comply and eagerness to play at "being a horse" but also a solid academic knowledge of the horse's nature.

To know our goals for the horse and chart our course to fulfill them is the second most important element of a successful training plan. Goals should be formulated in a hierarchical pattern. The cumulative, overall, paramount goal should always be to develop our horse's innate potential to its utmost. If we selected our young candidate properly, then his potential will guarantee that as he develops it, he will fulfill our equestrian ambitions too, as if by coincidence. Lesser goals will have to be designed by the years, months, weeks, daily lessons and even minute to minute. As the scheme is hierarchical, lesser goals must always remain supportive of greater ones. We cannot hope to succeed in a year's program unless we do only such things from minute to minute as will enhance (contribute to) that yearly goal. In this short outline of training suggestions, I will address myself to the task of suggesting major goals to accomplish, of more or less a year's duration.

From birth to six months of age a foal is nourished by his mother, Therefore his life is with his mother. They could be part of a herd of brood mares with foals under them or could be in an area just as a pair. They should, however, in either case, be in a large area where they should be allowed to move about at leisure and at their chosen pace. Food should be plentiful and include natural pasture. When herding to pasture is necessary it should be done at the leisurely walk, ambling along, giving the opportunity to feed all the while.

From six months to two years of age the weaned foal should ideally join a herd of similarly aged youngsters. The horse is a herd animal with well developed social instincts. For his unfolding, the society of other horses is essential. Competition horses shying from others, kicking at others in a warm-up ring, reveal great social inhibitions and resultant impairment. Horses correctly raised in a herd will not usually exhibit such undesirable and abnormal behavior. While sheltered overnight in a more confined and well protected area, the young horses should remain free (untied) and together in their shelter. During the daytime and weather permitting, they should be herded out to pasture for the day's duration and back at evening time. As they grow older both the length of the herding distance and the quality of its challenges can gradually be

Photographed by Mrs. Susan Derr Drake

Atilla, here three years old, Hannoverian stallion out of Argus. Owned by Mrs. Susan Derr Drake of Pomona, California, he is given the best of every opportunity to develop into a great athlete. Working without the burden of a rider, develops the natural paces. Here you can see the fine suspension at the canter, as it is performed by a horse who is strong, deep and wide of chest and is "pegged at the four corners" by straight and powerful legs.

increased. The morning and evening herding times are those of purposeful exercise. Young horses should get an ever increasing "mileage into their feet" and be moved over terrain that will contribute to the development of good hoof and joint conditions.

These twice-a-day exercising periods should present physical and mental challenges by small climbs, slides, ditches, ravines, brooks, ponds, logs, etc., such as the local terrain would naturally offer. Should the area be void of surface challenges by nature, herding paddocks should be constructed that will contain obstacles built to accommodate the desirable exercises.

From two to three years of age formal schooling of the horse begins. The young horse now periodically and eventually for most of the time is segregated from his fellows. He is tamed for human companionship. He will receive a halter to wear, will be groomed, housed in a separate box or paddock, and his hooves will be trimmed and shod. He will become familiar and, if handled properly, friendly with people. He will accept a multitude of equipment.

For now his training begins. At first he will be handled on the halter, then gradually lunged. At first he will be lunged from the center of the circle. His balance is to develop and his familiarity and even love of people result in his obedience to his handler. When the young horse obeys verbal commands given from the center of the circle on which he is lunged, he will be trained to accept two lunge tapes. The second tape is added to the outside of his body, running under his tail, and leading on to the handler who holds it in the center of the ring. Lungeing on two tapes adds to the control of the horse, especially encouraging his later bending onto the arc of the circle. It also prepares the horse for the next step in his training.

While the horse is continually warmed up on the lunge tapes from the center, he will now also be driven from behind. The two tapes will be held and handled as if driving a horse hitched to a buggy. The trainer must follow the horse on foot at an ample distance to prevent being kicked. He should aim to teach the horse to walk without excitement straight in front of him. Any time the horse deviates from the straight line of his progress, the trainer must step behind him, making himself invisible and insisting on the horse's continued trust in him, but without threatening. When the young horse lunges well, both on a single tape controlled from the middle of a circle and from double tapes being driven from behind, he is ready for the next step of his education.

The horse will now be driven in a buggy or cart. There are several good books on how to teach a horse to pull and what proper equipment should be used while doing so. The importance of driving a horse from a buggy, or rather his pulling something, is enormous. As you have gathered by now, during each step of the horse's training attention is paid to both his physical and mental development. By driving a horse, he will be straightened. He will develop his muscles further, while developing strength and stamina. He will acquire rhythm, especially through periods of trotting. He will develop trotting muscles. He will be able to perform transitions which are important gymnastics for muscle and joint development. The horse will supple, particularly through transitions. He will learn to accept the bit and the handling of aids that communicate to him through complex equipment. Mentally, the horse's attention span will grow. He will be called upon to sharpen his focus on small but meaningful communication devices. He will have to submit himself to his driver through trust. More than from the ground, his handler can now communicate to him, put demands on him and intensify meaningful gymnastic exercises.

Needless to say that driving is a great pleasure to the horseman and teaches him good hands and the use of the whip as an aid rather than an instrument of punishment. Being driven should be a joy to the horse too. For pulling a light buggy or cart should be no strain, yet the pleasure of running on straight stretches at a good clip, being liberated from a tedious lunging circle or the tedium of walking on two long tapes, should encourage his impulsion and zest.

From three to four years of age the well-founded horse will move under the saddle with his rider on his back for the most time. He will still be lunged to "warm him up" in order to supple and relax him before each session of riding. He can occasionally still be driven from a buggy. Since much of his time spent in schooling will be under the saddle, now for the first time the three year old becomes a riding horse. The foundation of his career as a sports horse functioning under a rider is now being laid. The horse should move in a generous "frame," free of hindrances and interferences from the rider. The rider should concentrate on harmonizing with his horse. This is no simple task, for the young saddled horse will lose his balance often. He will be uneven and insufficient in his gaits. He will rush. He will "fall through" turns. He will be stiff in his joints, shy in using his muscles, will tire easily, will resist. All these will be expected symptoms of those shortcomings that are due to lack of physical fitness. To help him, the rider must sympathetically follow with his center of gravity to harmonize with that of the shifting center of gravity of the young horse. The rider should plan to ride his horse as much as possible over open country. Freedom, both from the rider's restrictions and from confinement in a small arena, are essential. The horse will best gymnasticize and best find his balance under the foreign weight of his rider by moving over irregular terrain, by climbing, sliding and taking small leaps.

About twice or three times a week the horse should be gymnasticized in an arena. These sessions should include cavaletti work too. Again, there is good literature concerning proper cavaletti work. In the arena more attention to the rider can be asked for and careful attention can be paid to lateral work. The arena work should be mentally more, but physically less demanding than the cross-country work.

This year in the horse's training is critical in affecting his future career as a sports horse. The literature that is concerned with how to train young and green horses is vast and should be consulted. This is the year during which the horse learns all the basic aids. His rider must teach him the meaning of these aids. Therefore, over-demanding is a mistake. The method of conversation should be established but the new language should not be used to discuss "philosophy."

From four to six years of age the horse should be "generalized." His training should be that of a combined event horse's training. He should be dressaged, moved over open country and jumped in an arena. Horses should not jump higher than 4.0 feet before they reach four years of age, for their joints can be over-taxed and permanently damaged. But now the time has come to work the horse harder.

Also, competition may be pursued during these two years. The horse should learn all about competition environment, including the mental state of his rider, for all competiton environments will alter the behavior of both rider and horse.

From age six on the horse has arrived! He will be properly specialized. For greater demands in performance, time spent with the horse will have to be focused on particular tasks. The horse will either be most suitable for dressage or for jumping or for the continuation of combined event performances. One of these competition areas should be selected and pursued by proper training.

The Athlete   *"Atilla"*

Photography by Susan Derr Drake

The great competition athlete is a horse that grew up through motion and exercise, not by food alone. In a species which survived by flight, the "survival of the fittest" will favor those individuals who grew up moving.

The Compatibility of Jumping and Dressage

Jumping has had, for a long time, a wide appeal among American riders. But dressage is rapidly gaining in popularity throughout the country, and as more and more riders are becoming aware of it, the question whether dressage and jumping are compatible will invariably come up whenever dressage is discussed. Jumping enthusiasts are being exposed to a new, competitive appeal of dressage. and it is therefore necessary to answer this question.

Paraphrasing one of Oscar Wilde's many witticisms will remind my readers that questions are often more important than answers. They reveal needs and therefore deserve our full attention. There may be, in my opinion, the following reasons for questioning the compatibility of dressage and jumping:

(1) Some riders do not know what dressage is all about. They may have read some highly technical books on the subject that omitted to mention anything about its applicability to riding in general. They also may have witnessed some "dressage demonstrations" that had no more in common with dressage than the ill-applied use of the term. Such demonstrations may have displayed a confined, curbed, hindered and totally unhappy horse that was forced to do something unnatural, thus producing a feeling of uneasiness if not disgust in any tactful rider.

(2) Then there are equestrians who would like to do both jumping and dressage but wonder if by doing both with the same horse they may not diminish their chances to reach the top. There is much in our culture and our education that shows that success and attaining perfection can only be the result of specialization. Not knowing really what dressage is all about, these thinking riders believe that it is so vastly different from jumping in goals, ideals, methods and principles as to endanger their horses' chances for success.

(3) Related to the above reasons is the total absence, in this country, of horses that compete successfully in both dressage and jumping events. (I am thinking of horses in the higher levels of competition; on lower levels there are quite a few.) This, in a way, may suggest that there is a vast discrepancy between dressage and jumping. But this is not really the case, since in other places one may frequently see horses which successfully compete in both disciplines. For example, during the CDIO in Wolfsburg, in June 1971, the former international open jumper Ajax (Sweden) placed tenth in the Grand Prix de Dressage under the ex-show jumper Ulla Hakanson.

Let me offer a blanket statement to this legitimate and interesting question: Dressage and jumping are not only compatible but are, in fact, complementary. Let me substantiate this perhaps bold statement.

During my European equestrian education I was never made aware of anyone of sufficient expertise who did not agree that dressage and jumping are, in fact, compatible. As far as I am aware, all the great equestrian authorities agree with this tenet. Therefore, I feel comfortable in knowing that my book will not reflect my personal opinions only.

Equestrian experts agree that there is only one basically correct way of riding in sports competitions. To be sure, this way of riding was not originally developed for this purpose. Today, however, in most industrialized societies, the horse has ceased to be a beast of burden and means of transportation, and consequently its development is shaped according to sporting needs. These needs are similar to those of the past as far as the mental and physical development of the horse is concerned. As was the utilitarian horse of the past, the sports horse of our times must be athletically well developed and, in general, considerably improved over its natural state.

The one basically correct way of riding is often called the classical riding form. The rather pompous term "classical" is justified by the fact that the origins of this way of riding are found in the writings of the Greek Xenophon, who lived some twenty-three centuries ago. Something that has endured that long, even if it happens to be an equestrian tradition, deserves to be called "classical."

Even more relevant to our topic than the antiquity of the classical riding form is the fabulous wealth of accumulated knowledge, all of which is based on the infinite wealth of past equestrian experience. It promotes ideals, goals and methods that have proven most effective through centuries of trials, errors and contests. In the past two thousand years everything has been tried, feverishly debated, keenly contested and daringly experimented with. Millions of known and unknown equestrians strained their minds and bodies to find out what should be done, how it should be done, and why it should be done in order to achieve the most desirable results with their horses.

Basically, this is what we have inherited:

(1) Ideally a person should become an equestrian because he loves and respects horses and feels a need to dedicate himself to their well-being. Therefore, the goal will be to develop the horses on their terms, at their natural pace, through their natural tendencies and by natural means, in order to unfold their natural talents to the utmost degree. The role of the equestrian is that of an educator. He will always be guided by empathy towards his horse.

(2) The goals of classical horsemanship are guided by the ideal of

developing a horse that will live long, in good health, and will stay consistently useful and happy while serving his rider. This fundamental goal can best be achieved by a concurrent and gradual development of the horse's physical and mental potential.

For our contemporary sporting purposes a horse should be developed physically to move evenly, in correct balance, zestfully and straight in all his natural gaits. He should be able to lengthen (extend) and shorten (collect) his strides without losing balance while maintaining an even rhythm. Therefore, he should neither run nor slow down but rather shift his center of gravity to maintain an even rhythm in bold impulsion. The horse should be able to carry his rider with a minimum of exertion and without any stress. He should conserve his energies by his improved athletic ability, which consists of the development of correct muscles and the strengthening of his joints. He should have, as a consequence, a relaxed elastic movement resulting in a comfortable and harmonious ride. In short, he should become an athlete of great strength, yet so coordinated and supple that outstanding performances will appear effortless and poised.

Mentally a sports horse should be aware and obedient. Trust in the rider results in relaxation, which in turn develops into obedience. Kind, perpetual, reasonable, consistent and sufficiently strong communication will increase the horse's attention span (hence further educability) and awareness. The physical and mental development of the horse should proceed hand-in-hand, reinforcing one another, and should show a tendency to gradual improvement.

(3) The methods of classical horsemanship were developed to serve the ideals discussed and to achieve the fundamental goals described. They are based on a harmonious understanding between the horse and the rider. Such understanding can be achieved only by constant communication between them. Meaning is introduced into these communications by the rider, who perceives and perpetually evaluates his horse's responses. He also responds to the horse's communications by meaningful, consistent, gentle but sufficient aids. Because the rider reserves the initiative to create desirable changes, he is in command.

Specifically, the methods of classical riding are based on patient, gradual, yet systematic and consistent plans for improvement. The instruments of communications for the rider are (1) his weight (position of torso), and (2) use of back muscles (flex-relax). Both of these are communicated to the horse through either the rider's seat (two seat bones and the crotch) or his knees and thighs. These communications areas must remain stable and never shift position. (3) His legs (always contacting the horse's sides), and (4) his hands (only as an extension of the torso's activities) communicating with the horse's mouth.

All three contact areas — seat, legs and hands — must affect the horse all the time and be in harmonious coordination. They must become more and more refined until the horse grows (physically and mentally) to understand their "whispering" rather than to expect their "shouting."

The results of classical horsemanship will manifest themselves in consistent, enduring athletic achievements, near or at the top of the horse's natural potential.

This is a brief outline of the ideals, goals, methods and results of classical horsemanship. At the same time they are also the ideals, goals, methods and results of dressage. Classical horsemanship and dressage are synonymous and the terms are used interchangeably throughout the world. And none of these principles, I am sure you will agree, contradict those involved in jumping! Furthermore, none of them can but greatly improve the development and career of a great jumper.

The Three Faces of Classical Horsemanship

Classical horsemanship today promotes three phases of competition. They are (1) **the Combined Events, (2) Stadium Jumping** and (3) **Dressage.** *World Championship titles as well as Olympic Medals can be earned only in these competitive phases. International riding competitions are also limited to these three phases and their various sub-categories.* Most horses one sees in any of these three competition phases have been trained in accordance with the principles of classical horsemanship.

The outstanding horses that compete internationally share certain characteristics both physically and mentally regardless of the area in which they compete. In other words, an outstanding horse could almost invariably compete successfully either in Combined Events, Stadium Jumping or in Dressage. Any horse with good conformation and proper upbringing may well be suitable for competing in any of the three international events; it is his training, his specialization rather than potential and talent that will determine the area of their competitive participation.

The skill of jumping best develops without the undue burden of the rider. The three year old Hannoverian Stallion, Atilla is shown in gymnasticizing over small jumps. They develop in the horse confidence, a sense of spacial judgment, attention to the task. But most importantly, free jumping allows the horse to develop his jumping skills undisturbed and therefore in his natural rhythm. In both of these pictures, perfect style in jumping is shown by this young stallion who carries the genes of some of the finest jumping sires in the world.

Photographed by
Mrs. Susan Derr Drake

Riders who wish to specialize may be guided in the selection of their horses by the following guidelines, provided the general suitability of the horse has been established: (1) *A horse with exceptional beauty and elegance, offering outstanding natural balance in motion, will be particularly suitable for dressage.* (2) *A horse that shows outstanding jumping ability and has an exceptional sense of rhythm, timing, observation and courage, will be a good candidate for stadium jumping.* (3) *A horse that shows stadium jumping ability and also has robust health, excellent legs, stamina, courage and great gallop will make an excellent prospect for combined events.*

Jumper, Dressage or Three-Day Horse — Foundations Are The Same For Them All

Horses that are selected for athletic careers should, ideally, receive identical basic training for a period of three years after saddling. Should specialization occur too early in a horse's development, the horse will most probably never deliver a truly outstanding performance.

As the purpose of this discussion is not to relate in detail the proper athletic founding of a horse I will merely state that, in the opinion of experts, a horse that has been saddled as a three-year-old should be trained until it reaches the age of six years with one goal only — its general development. During these three years the horse should be moved over open country, be exercised over cavaletti, and also jumped over single and combined fences from both trot and canter, and be gymnasticized on the flat. All these activities, with the exception of the actual flight over the fence, fall into the category of dressage gymnastics. In short, as long as the rider is in total control of his mount, he is dressaging him. It is only during the time when the horse is in actual flight over the fence that the rider exchanges his control for fluent accompaniment, offering the horse a complete freedom from interference. Consequently, the correct foundation of a horse's training is laid through dressage! The proof of the pudding is in the eating — a well trained horse must compete to prove himself.

From age four to six, depending on the development of the horse, his training should include participation in competitions. The most appropriate form of competition for this period of training is the Combined Events, since this is the only event that contains all three phases. Specialized experts will evaluate the horse's gymnastic development in the dressage arena; others will judge his handling himself in the open country. And, finally, he will have to prove himself in the stadium over the fences.

Since Combined Events are offered rather infrequently — due to lack of facilities, great organizational burden and high cost — the horse may be shown during this period of its development more frequently in both dressage and stadium competitions.

The main objective of this period is testing and evaluating the horse's progress. The horse should be moving with a great impulsion. While showing zestful forward urge he must at all times remain under the rider's control. He should perform with energy yet without showing stress and strain. He should be supple both longitudinally and laterally, able to shift his center of gravity in order to extend or collect his strides (longitudinal bending) as well as make controlled transitions from pace to pace. He should be able to bend in his entirety from side to side on arcs (lateral bending), to execute curbed lines without losing balance or impulsion.

Mentally, the horse should be alert and obedient. He should be aware of his environment, of his rider's aids and of his own body. He should render himself to the rider's aids. He should allow the rider's aids to "run through him" and control the position and activity of his body without strain.

Undeniably, these physical and mental attributes are necessary for a well founded jumper, and are only achieved by proper dressaging!

At The Age of Six, Decide on Your Horse's Specialization — If You Must

At the age of six, generally, horses may become specialized by continuing to compete in only one of the three phases. At this time their athletic development will allow such a high level of performance that perfecting it will require specialization. There is seldom time and energy left for either the rider or the horse to continue competing in all three phases. Riders and horses, however, who have the time and energy to spare, should continue to specialize in the diversified competition, the Combined Events.

Only outstanding horses are worth specializing, for others will not show outstanding results regardless of the effort. At the time an outstanding horse is being specialized he ought to be able to do the following:

COMPARISON OF THE "CROUCH"
All Weight in Hind Quarters

A — Take-off for a seven foot stone wall
B — Levade at the Spanish Riding School.

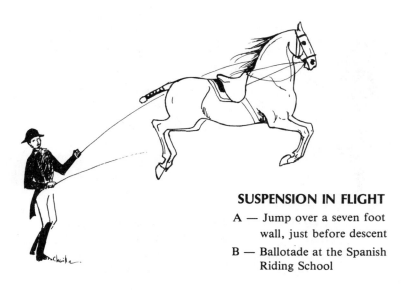

SUSPENSION IN FLIGHT

A — Jump over a seven foot wall, just before descent

B — Ballotade at the Spanish Riding School

Jumping Competitions Are Decided By Action Between, Rather Than Over The Jumps

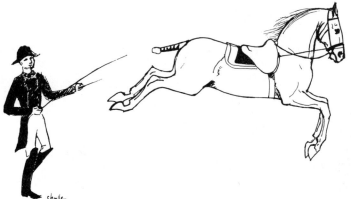

DESCENT — Shifting of the Center of Gravity to The Forehand

A — Jumper preparing for landing
B — Capriole at the Spanish Riding School

(a) Successfully compete in the Third or Fourth Level AHSA Dressage Test.
(b) Compete and place on four-feet high jumping courses.
(c) Complete successfully the Intermediate Level Combined Events Test.

If the horse is not capable of performing as suggested, then he has either serious athletic limitations, was incorrectly founded or has an incompetent rider.

Now let me comment on the continued compatibility of dressage and jumping, after specialization has taken place.

The Three-Day Horse — A Living Proof of Compatibility

Horses and riders who continue to compete in Combined Events internationally, in World Championships and in the Olympic Games, have perpetually demonstrated that serious dressaging promotes outstanding jumping performances. Within three days they prove time and again that a well trained horse can elastically "dance through" a dressage program, then, the next day, go over a strenuous and speedy cross-country course with solid jumps and show stamina, courage and impulsion, and, on the third day, jump a stadium course with considerable finesse!

Riders who specialize in jumping sophisticated stadium courses are all aware that the fences are not the determining factors for success! What leads to success in stadium jumping is how the horse is brought to each fence, how he departs from fences and how he responds to his rider on the flat between fences! The results of stadium jumping competitions are decided primarily on the flat, and only secondarily by the flight over fences. Riding a jumper to success is done on the flat. The flight and the subsequent clearing of the fence is determined by the rhythm of the horse, the correct length of his strides, the degree of his impulsion for push-off, his undisturbed attention and concentration, his use of the correct musculature, the correct bending of his joints and his yielding to the rider's commands, allowing the rider to ride him to the correct take-off points, at the correct impulsion, in the correct stride (collection-extension) and the correct level of flexion. These requirements for proper flight in jumping are all worked out by dressaging. Never will indiscriminate and perpetual jumping of fences prepare a horse for great achievements in the jumping stadium.

Jumping Is Only An Extension of Dressage

In short, jumping is an extension of dressage. It is one of the "figures" in dressage. There is not much difference in preparing a horse to take a fence correctly or to perform a piaffe correctly, for doing either requires identical physical and mental development. They both require a total and harmonious control by the rider. Jumping is, essentially, a dressage movement. A stadium course is, basically, a dressage test. Of the two tests, dressage and jumping, the latter is the more difficult. Jumping a course calls for faster responses and coordination, more radical shifts of position in order to maintain harmonious unity.

Then why is it that so many horses jump courses successfully without having been properly dressaged? First of all, because of pure luck. Secondly, because for a while even mistakes can lead to superficial success. And, finally, because people can afford to ruin horses and dispose of them while their careers are still in their infancy.

The Classical "Airs Above The Ground"

The ultimate in dressage is demonstrated by the riders and horses of the Spanish Riding School in Vienna. At that institution the "airs above the ground" are still taught to horses and shown to spectators. At the same School and also in the Grand Prix de Dressage Test, the other sophisticated dressage movements are displayed by horses. These movements are no more than demonstrations of the ultimate physical and mental achievements of an athletic horse. They are merely gymnastic exercises which, however difficult, are possible when a horse is developed correctly, in accordance with the general principles outlined in this book. Jumpers, much like dressage horses, will show extension and collection. They will show pirouettes at the canter. They will sit down on their hindquarters at the moment of take-off, much like dressage horses do when performing a levade. Jumpers will take leave of the ground and suspend themselves in air much like dressage horses do when performing the capriole or ballotade.

Thus, even at the level of the greatest specialization, the horse that jumps a high obstacle will have to use his body in a way similar to the horse performing haute ecole movements in the Spanish Riding School. They are both talented athletes, developed correctly to display their highest inborn capabilities. This is, indeed, the task of the true equestrian, the full development of the natural potentialities of the horse. Whether he displays the results of his artistry over fences or on the flat ground is a matter of taste and temperament.

3 Submission to the Rider Through Longitudinal Flexion

Gaining The Horse's Attention

Horses instinctively pay attention to all stimuli in their environment. That behavior is part of their natural "survival kit." They have keen senses, especially smelling and hearing, that aided them through milleniums in taking notice of approaching danger. Once danger was monitored by these suspicious senses, the powerful, speedy runner took flight in defense. Horses, that pay little attention to their riders and much to everything else in their environment, behave much like their ancestors did in nature. Let such behavior serve as a warning that the horse is getting ready to take flight.

A horse that is inattentive to the rider is simply untamed! Dressage is an untranslatable word precisely because it denotes more than training. The term also describes taming!

When a rider begins "dressaging" a horse, he is coming into contact with an untamed animal that heeds the commands of natural instinct. The most important initial task is the taming of the horse. Even after the horse is tamed for the purposes of human use, we continue to encourage further submission to human will; resulting ultimately in unquestioning obedience. From the untamed natural horse, to the totally obedient horse, the road is a long one, and to travel it takes wisdom from the rider.

The most fundamental result of taming is the replacement of inborn instinct-dictated reactions in the animal by rider-inspired reactions. Such results depend on two prerequisites. One is the earning of the horse's trust. The other is the horse's understanding of which reaction is desired by each request of the rider. These are in sharp contrast to the horse's unthinking, unfeeling, instinctively coded reactions to environmental stimuli.

The trusting horse will submit willingly to his rider's wishes. He will obey joyfully his rider's commands. Trust, resulting in such submission and obedience, must be earned by the rider, for it can never be demanded or cajoled. A rider can earn the trust of his horse by being kind, understanding, patient, reasonable and, above all, consistent in his actions. In short, people can earn the horse's confidence only by those methods that will earn them the trust of other humans.

The horse's understanding can be developed through educational principles that are found in human education also. Intelligence cannot be given through education. It is an inborn ability. Yet it can be awakened, encouraged, sharpened and put to desirable use. Intelligence has much to do with discipline. It can be utilized to replace random, unpredictable actions by consistent (therefore predictable) and focused activities. Such desirable mental developments depend on increased attention span, in short, the ability and willingness to concentrate.

Precisely this concentration is the epitome of the manifestation of all taming. Concentration is the very capstone of all that has gone before into the building of foundation and structure. Submission, obedience, trust, awakened intelligence, zestful curiosity all result in the end, in a horse concentrating on the wishes and commands of his rider. Once this mental development has been achieved, once concentration upon the rider replaces random reaction to environmental stimuli, then the horse is tame. The tame horse will never fidget, prance around, and be preoccupied with other stimuli than those initiated by his rider.

Stretching to Flex

The lowering of the horse's head and the stretching of his neck are very important tasks during the early stages of his training. Therefore, your concern with this aspect of the training is wise and commendable. Even later, throughout the horse's career, he should be capable and eager to stretch first forward and then gradually downward as he is being encouraged to assume relaxation. Whenever the rider commences a "free" movement, that is free walk, free trot or free canter, the horse should stretch his neck forward, continue to extend it with an outstretched head, then gradually lower both. While in competitions only free walk is asked for, during work periods the free trot and canter should have an important place as an effective rewarding device.

We must remember that when aiming at stretching the horse's neck, we also desire the stretching of his back; without the latter, the former cannot occur. I will now offer some techniques as to the stretching of a horse, his back, and head.

Basic to all stretching techniques is the ability to slow down the horse. Horses, that carry their necks and heads up, drop their backs down, and move with stiff joints are usually moving much too quickly. Many horses when slowed down, yet aided in rhythm to maintain active engagement in the hindquarters, will lower their necks and relax their backs.

The slowing down of the horse should be done by the rider's weight and back muscles, never forgetting the importance of the shoulders in adding weight to the seat. The rider's hands (and the reins held in them) should be merely cushioning extensions of the torso.

The hands could do a variety of things in coordination with the body in order to relax the horse's back and neck and lower his head.

The hands can stroke the reins. The rider takes both reins in one hand, putting the middle finger between the two reins and holding the palm upward. The reins must be even, conduct a mild feel or invitation that is stroked backward and upward. The reins are slowly stroked between the fore and middle fingers and the middle and ring fingers from the horse's crest towards the direction of the rider's chin. Once the reins run through the fingers of one hand, the other must be ready to contact them way down at the crest of the neck to assume stroking. Taking the reins from hand to hand must be done without losing contact with the mild pressure on the mouth.

This stroking activity stretches the reins initially by repeatedly lengthening the distance between the horse's mouth and the rider's hands. However, soon the horse will react to this invitation by lengthening with a quick "dipping" of the head down. From then on, especially if the rider can continue to slow down the horse, he will start to pull the reins through the rider's palms and stretch forward and down.

In short, at first the rider invites stretching by inviting on the reins from a close contact, releasing them to a long contact. Then, as the horse relaxes with these mild, even and sensibly active reins, he will stretch the reins by pulling them through the rider's fingers. When that has happened, it will be up to the rider to decide how often he wants to repeat the stretching. As the horse accepts the reins through this exercise, soon the rewarding attitude of "being on the reins" will be assumed by the horse. After that, stretching should be cultivated only during transitions from canter or trot to the walk.

Another method for lowering the horse's head and neck and inviting him to accept the bit can be described as follows: The rider should post the trot and hold the reins as close to the horse's mouth as can be reached without strain. Then he should elevate the reins directly upward, bringing the hands as high as possible towards the rider's face. In such a case the bit leaves the bar of the horse's mouth and is invited against the skin of his lips, working upward at the corners of the mouth. As it is natural for horses to react to any pressure by pulling the opposite way, they will "dive down" on the rein soon after it has been inviting them directly upward.

As the horse plunges down with his head, the rider should be ready to follow deep down with his arms. That is done by lowering the arms, if necessary, until the fists are down along the sides of the horse's neck. As soon as he has come up with his nose, however, the reins must begin to elevate with that rising nose. This is quite a gymnastic effort by the rider and should only be done if the rider has such a balanced seat and firm knee contact that the horse will never be disturbed by these vast changes in the rider's arm position. It is very important to maintain an even and soft contact throughout the exercise. That is rather difficult as the horse's head will go from very high to very deep and back to high at first. Yet the reins should never slack, nor should they pull when the horse finally dives down. The rider's seat must remain upright, his legs steady, regardless of where those arms must follow, from invitation to the deep cushioning of the dive.

A third method that encourages the horse to accept the rein contact and lower his head could be performed as follows: the rider should "fix" his hands by pressing his fists against the inside of his thighs. That will bring both reins down and slightly outward, away from the horse's neck. The reins will be low and steady as if they were side reins, yet kept sensitively active in maintaining mild contact. They will be

Photographed by Mrs. Sandra Gardner-Baker of Walnut Creek, California

This is Chrysos, a young Westfalen stallion, selected in Germany by the Author, imported and owned by Dr. Mary Contakos of Danville, California. Here he is ridden by Ms. Gwen Stockebrand. This team has won many important victories. The picture demonstrates the full longitudinal stretching of the horse. Flexion should be, and in this picture is, merely a by-product of correct stretching of muscles and ligaments. A well-stretched, "tall back" shown here is the key to flexion elsewhere.

Without it, the locomotion of the hindquarters cannot be communicated to the balancing apparatus of the forehand. The bridging span of the back creates the "one horse" which can move in his entirety, rather than the "shattered horse" moving in bits and pieces. Ease and confidence displayed by the horse's movements, allows this rider her supreme elegance.

spread wide towards the rider's knees. Many horses who cannot relax to hyperactive reins will find this gentle "frame" acceptable and will yield to it at the poll and jaw. As soon as that happens the rider should oscillate the inside rein, maintaining contact only with the outside one.

The oscillation of the inside rein simply means that it should be gently stretched forward, opened or released forward, so that the horse can stretch forward and down to seek contact with it. The oscillation should be tiny, not a dropping of the rein into a visibly hanging position.

As the horse is relaxing into this "side rein," steadiness of the reins, and as he is actively seeking contact on the inside, oscillating rein, the rider should reward him by lengthening both reins by about an inch. It is as if side reins had been re-adjusted to a longer neck. This lengthening of contact should proceed step by step as long as the horse remains on contact. The moment the soft contact chewing stops, the horse's nose stretches out and his neck stiffens, it should be taken as a sign that the reins have been "dropped" and that they no longer communicate because they have been released too far.

The fourth method I want to describe is the least "tricky" one of the lot and used most commonly by accomplished riders. The first three methods are good vehicles for riders who cannot yet harmonize their aids, do not yet offer rhythmic aids and cannot yet contact the mouth with steady hands. In short, those methods described above are to compensate often for the shortcomings of the rider by the technique.

Ideally, a horse can be relaxed to the bit by asking him to stride deep under towards the center of gravity, yet to wait for that stride with the bulk of his front. The rider must drive the horse, yet make him understand that he is inviting the front end to wait until the hindquarters catch up.

With proper coordination the horse will surely understand that if he shortens his body, he can carry the rider in comfort. He will bend the joints of his hindquarters, will arch his neck and bridge the two ends with a high, full back that swings. The rider will contact on a short rein that is held in normal position and will begin to drive. As soon as the horse responds to the driving by speeding up, he will half-halt and insist on a slow rhythm. When the horse is shortened, the rider will yield minutely with the inside rein first and continue to drive. Gradually, the reins will be lengthened again, yet only so far as to be able to forestall speeding up. The horse will gradually understand driving to be meaningful in shortening his body rather than as a sign to speed up. He will lower and lengthen his neck, and yet without lowering his back will stay in contact by reaching forward to seek the rider's hands.

Flexing Longitudinally

"The horse on the bit" is a misleading expression, yet it is one we are accustomed to using, and by consent pretend to understand, in spite of its mischievous suggestion that it has to do with the rider's hands exclusively.

Being on the bit may well be the most important concept in classical horsemanship. Only a horse that contacts and accepts the bit and moves on the bit is in an athletically correct position. Using a human analogy, let me suggest that there is a great difference between people who are moving about in a grocery store buying mustard, for example, and those working out in a gymnasium. Both are moving and are engaged in some mental activities, but only the one working out in a gymnasium is improving himself physically and mentally. He will show muscle development and skeletal coordination that one cannot acquire by shopping for mustard. Likewise with horses; just in moving a horse around, the rider traveling, the horse covering ground without using himself properly, no improvement can take place. Let me suggest that the horse on the bit is the only horse rendered athletically, gymnastically workable and improvable. Therefore, the horse has to be on the bit before any dressaging (gymnasticizing) can take place.

Being on the bit has to do with the total horse. When a horse is on the bit his skeletal position as well as his use of his muscles changes. To be on the bit connotes relaxation, suppleness (of muscles), elasticity (in joints), elegance and obedience and that, in short, is both the foundation for and the substance of all dressage work. A horse on the bit is one that is longitudinally flexed, thereby becoming a shorter horse, capable of moving deeper under its weight with the hindquarters and lifting the weight up rather than pushing it forward. This longitudinally bent horse is in a physical position to fulfill the tasks called for by its rider, and therefore will be able to surrender to the rider's will and become obedient rather than subservient to force.

To put the horse on the bit requires a degree of collection (however minor, initially) and, once achieved, continues to serve the purpose of

more intense collection activities. Putting a horse on the bit and maintaining him there — that is, rendering a horse athletically workable in
order to improve him — can be done only by observing the classical
principles of horsemanship. *The principles of riding can never change.
Only the techniques of carrying these principles out might be slightly
altered to suit the individual horse's needs, attitudes, disposition and
developmental level.*

A horse on the bit is: a horse longitudinally bent *(flexed);* a horse
submitting to the rider's aids *(on the aids or ahead of the legs);* a horse
in an athletic position.

With these synonymous phrases I can better explain the condition
that is commonly called being on the bit. When a horse is longitudinally
bent, he becomes a shorter animal, being able to stride deeper under a
more compact weight, consequently having a chance to lift, rather than
push that weight. In this position the horse bends at the poll, arches his
neck (however mildly initially), relaxes his belly muscles, elevates his
back and bends the joints of his hindquarters more intensely when in
motion. When the horse is thus bent, he becomes attentive to the rider
who encouraged him to so bend, and he finds the position more comfortable for carrying his rider. He becomes calm and pleased. He will
find it easier to carry the shortened bulk with his more relaxed muscles
and will be eager to further obey the rider's aids, as he found them helpful. He will now respond to "whispering" rather than "shouting" aids
of the rider's legs, weight and hands. He will feel supple and easy to
command. The horse will be in an athletic position; that is, attentive,
coordinated, relaxed and flexed.

For this reason, when the horse comes to the bit, there is that feeling
of *"what a different horse!"* As if by magic, all the difficult things
become simple. It is as if a deaf and dumb animal has become percep-
tive, conversational and intelligent!

Only a horse on the bit is workable by the classical riding principles.
I repeat, *principles of riding never change!* However, the techniques
of riding may slightly vary according to the horse's individual needs.
That is why being on the bit means always the same thing, yet there are
several ways in which to achieve the position.

The horse has to be invited to accept the bit always from rear to
front; that is, by primarily driving rather than restraining aids. It is interesting to note that being on the bit always denotes a certain level,
however minor, of collection! The moment a green horse has stepped

deeper under his weight, lifted himself somewhat off the ground (suspension), elevated his back, lowered his neck and bent at the poll, he has collected! From then on, the degree of collection will be gradually increased with gymnastic training. As the muscles of the horse become more supple and his joints more elastic, he will carry more and more of his weight on the hindquarters, lightening his forehand. His body will shorten, he will suspend higher in his movements and become slower yet more elastic in his actions. All this starts with the first moment of infinitesimal collection called accepting the bit.

There are several ways in which a horse can be ridden to the bit and only a rider with diversified experiences will easily find the most suitable way for the particular horse he is working on. Basically three fundamental ways are used to put the horse on the bit.

1. A horse that is moving above the bit because he is crooked needs only to be straightened and he will step up to the bit instantly.

2. A horse that is running because he finds his rider not a weight but a frightening burden will need to be slowed down through repeated half-halts in order to go to the bit. Often riders, traveling victims on their furiously rushing charges, will yell back to the instructor in the center, "I cannot slow him down." The vicious circle of running horse, panicking rider losing balance, horse sprinting yet faster forward like a wet bar of soap leaping forward from tightening legs as the rider falls further behind the center of gravity, can hardly be stopped. But lo and behold, the rider comes to the center and halts to ask how to slow down, exactly the way he slowed to the halt to ask the question! All horses can be slowed down through half-halts, the rider indicating a desire to walk. Just before the horse walks, the rider is to relax the reins — without losing contact, however — and allows the horse to slowly trot on. This, if repeated, will convey to the horse that he may trot, but slower, and he will relax, find his balance, feel a more harmonious rider accompanying him and will gently accept contact on the bit.

In this instance, basically the rider went from contact, to restraining, to contact on the reins. On such a horse, it is essential to slow down the motion (even at the walk) to the point where the horse renders himself drivable! As long as the rider must travel, hand on and cannot put his legs on his horse's sides, the horse will not come to the bit.

3. The lazy, weak or tired young horse will often go behind the bit, rejecting contact by overbending his neck, tucking his nose in, head

hanging with profile behind the perpendicular line to the ground. He will appear relaxed but will continue to push, rather than lift his weight onto his forehand. On this kind of horse the rider must forcefully drive while finding contact with the bit as far back as he must, even if the horse momentarily will "wipe his nose on his own chest." When the bit is presented to the horse, forceful forward driving (even with touches of whip), will entice the horse to start pulling the reins forward, stretching his neck. At once the rider must lighten (make pleasurable) the contact. In short, here the rider forces contact by presenting the bit relentlessly to the hiding horse. Then he drives until the horse becomes so active with his hind legs that he will need to extend his neck. Then, and only then, the rider's hands lighten (but not drop) the contact, which is now maintained on the horse's initiative.

The three basic varieties of putting the horse on the bit most commonly refer to horses that were not started correctly. These horses are the most commonly known objects of instruction. However, the green horse will need none of these methods if started correctly from the beginning! Let us briefly outline how one proceeds with such a green horse.

The weight of a horse standing under the rider will be distributed two-thirds on his forehand and only one-third on his hindlegs. In motion, originated in the hindquarters and received by the forehand, the same proportionate weight distribution will prevail on a green horse. Therefore, if a green horse is only driven (or allowed to run) without controlling him by a light rein contact (and even half-halts), he will shift as much as three-fifths of his weight onto the forehand! This by all means should be prevented, the goal being, of course, that as the horse develops proportionately more and more of his weight be carried by the hindquarters.

To begin with, walk the horse at a slow, even pace with long, generous strides along the walls of the arena. Wait until he lowers his neck, reaching toward the ground with his nose (elevating the back) and at that moment offer lightly to contact the bit (find contact on the reins) and in a minute release contact and continue a free walk.

Repeat the contact on the reins for longer and longer periods of time, planning to release (yield) the contact only when the horse's neck is deepest in its downward search (his back stretched highly). As the horse learns that he will be rewarded by lightness when he elevates his back and as he builds his confidence in the rider's hand, which never confines him or discomforts him with unusually long periods of contact, he will begin to seek the feel on the bit as soon as the rider invites him by contacting the reins.

Gradually, still at the calm walk, the horse will relax his neck muscles, yield at the poll and jaw as soon as the rider presents the bit to him with his light contact on the reins.

Now begin to work on a circle, usually on the left hand side, with a diameter of about 16 feet (quarter width of dressage arena). Bend the horse with the inside leg behind the girth, but not too far back (to avoid pushing the hindquarters out) and keep the inside rein at its original light contact (as it was on the straight line). Allow the outside rein to mildly strengthen its contact. This strengthening will occur if the outside rein is held exactly as it was on the straight line. Because the horse, by bending on a small circle, will become longer on his outer side, the contact on that rein will necessarily strengthen. Note that this effort will supple the horse's muscles on the outer side rather than, as commonly misunderstood, on the inner, hollowed side! As a result the horse will now step deeper under the weight with the inside hindleg, slightly elevate his neck, relax at the poll and jaw and mildly arch his neck on long and generous contact and move in an ever so mild collection.

After the horse has been working on the bit at the walk and on circles on both hands, continue with a combination of exercises:

Contact at the walk, as described. Then trot and immediately ride the 16 ' diameter circle at the trot. Make sure your inside leg bends the horse and the outside leg guards against drifting with the hindquarters out. As you are returning to the wall do a transition to the walk. Repeat the exercise but only when the horse is calmly walking on contact and not before!

Again walk on contact, trot and immediately ride a half circle (16 ' diameter), returning to the wall on a straight line (changing hand) and walking upon reaching the wall. Soon the horse will remain steadily on contact with the bit both during walk and trot and transitions from one to the other.

The young horse's initiation to the steady acceptance of the contact terminates with the final exercise of riding a figure-8 pattern. This is ridden so that each circle of the figure is 33 ' in diameter, thus placing the figure-8 over the width of the dressage arena, changing direction at the center line. (For wall support, best to do it at the end, not the middle, of the arena). Walk on

Photographed by Susan Sexton

Ms. Gwen Stockebrand riding Bao in an extended trot. You can easily see the "hands of a giver rather than that of a miser." This lightness through the reins allows the horse to perform in self-carriage, without "the fifth leg" on which to lean. The rein eluding tensions, offers the horse unencumbered progression through space. Only a horse in self-carriage can move in his entirety and develop all his muscles as he "strides through to his bit."

contact, supple and bend the horse onto your first circle, then trot. Walk reaching the center line. Supple the horse to the other circle, wait until he surely bends to the arc of that circle and only then trot. As soon as you reach the center line, walk again. Repeat. It is important to understand that the rider must wait at the walk until the horse bends on the arc of each circle before trotting the circle. When this last exercise is done with steady and light contact between rider's hand and horse's mouth, the horse is on the bit and the foundations for serious dressage work had been laid!

The effort to put the horse on the bit should start within days after the young horse has been mounted by his rider. When pursued correctly, as outlined above, with utmost patience, lightness of contact and a great deal of rewarding, the horse should have achieved the last stage within two to four weeks! If a green horse is not correctly started and encouraged to carry his rider in the athletic position (longitudinally bent, on the bit, on the aids, in balance, etc.), the likelihood of his becoming an "evergreen" will be sadly increased.

Riding Towards the Bit

One can forever, without wasting time, consider the issue of riding the horse forward toward the bit; that is, the matter of longitudinal flexion. Indeed, if one can consistently produce longitudinal flexion on any horse with any sort of problem, one is really a rider! That is what riding is all about: *the on-going, perpetual process of sending the horse forward toward the bit.* This suggests the great secret: the horse never *arrives* on the bit; he should never take hold of it, pull or hand on it, should never use it as a crutch, as a fifth leg! The secret is the continual sending of the horse toward the bit, for only through the resulting longitudinal bending can one achieve the proper position and attitude (muscularly relaxed and skeletally balanced) in which the horse's gymnastic development can properly take place.

When one drives the horse forward towards the bit, the bit should ever so slightly elude the horse's "arrival" on it, his taking hold. This allows the horse to *step forward without fear* of hindrance by pulling (and the accompanying pain). The horse's forward (but not running) thinking very much depends on his courage in working towards the bit. The bit must represent to him a suggestive and resilient opening, a yielding and elusive communication, rather than a literal contact. A tense, restraining, pulling rein results in an open jaw, tense neck and back muscles, and ugly, apprehensive, stiff, pussy-footing strides.

This brings to mind that the name of the game is *self-carriage.* It is we, dressage fanatics, who are supposed to be the upholders of the classical tradition of all-with-the-seat-and-legs-and-nothing-with-the-hands. We are the promoters of beauty through freedom and impulsion. We are the ones who do not ride with strength but with understanding through natural and proper communication. We seek to ride a horse who lacks pain, is happy! Now, all of these goals depend on *yielding, elastic rein contact!* Read about it even in the FEI Rulebook!

When the reins restrict, they should be part of the half-halt (the action of the lower back and legs: primarily driving while secondarily restraining for balance) and be totally lacking in power and rudeness. It should feel as if you were drawing a violin string through a cube of butter, nothing more, and yet get the result!

Now that softness and sensitivity have been established, we must consider strengthening the horse to ride him towards the bit, and to do so we must think primarily of slowing the horse. I have noticed that most horses understand the leg aids in only one, incorrect way: go ahead (usually fast and tensely). Instead, the horse should, early in his training, understand and *trust* the leg to mean something other than, "Hurry up." So slow your horse down. (Yes, you can. You manage to stop him to get off at the end of a lesson.) One can only teach a slowly moving horse the notion of moving away from leg pressure sideways with all or part of his body. That is precisely the reason for teaching turns on the forehand and haunches from the halt! (I disapprove of it, but . . .) Later, when one introduces and teaches shoulder-in, leg-yielding, or any of the two-track movements, *slow the horse down.* Horses who hurry cannot learn *engagement* (bending of joints), cannot relax for fear of losing balance, and must often *counter flex* in self-defense. Thus one sees those terrible demonstrations of stiffness and paralysis, all in the name of "suppling exercises on two tracks."

When a horse moves slowly, one can move his front end (shoulder) or hind end (haunches) to one side, flex him, by design. When one's horse is crooked without permission, one straightens him by the *very same methods used to bend him.* If, for example, he is moving with his haunches always to the right, apply the aids to produce a haunches-in left on a straight horse. That is all, but it is not all that easy. Because your horse is crooked to the right, he may momentarily straighten but soon snaps back to his crooked position. Repeat the exercise, for with each straightening you induce changes that will ultimately reduce the snapping back. Liken it to uncoiling a spring: you loosen it gradually until you have a straight piece of wire in your hand. The horse cannot do it all at once; he needs repetition and time. If he had the properly developed musculature (the ability to stretch and contract on both sides), he would not need straightening. Crookedness is a manifestation of uneven development, first in the muscles and later, if not corrected, in the joints as well. So one must be very patient in straightening the horse and wait for proper development that only comes with time.

QUESTION: Why are Third Level rides scored so much lower than the preceding levels were? What is wrong with horses on Third Level?

ANSWER: I came away from my judging assignments with many observations concerning the "crisis at Third Level." I believe that judges have a primary responsibility to uphold the correct principles of classical horsemanship. That, in fact, is the essence of their duty! Should judges become victims of fashions and fads, should they be willing to compromise, even an iota, what has been correctly pursued for centuries, the art of dressage could disappear in a generation.

Dressage, being a *living tradition,* survives only so long as those cultivating it have the passion for its purity. For living traditions cannot be assimilated through books and films only; they live through their practitioners. If we read about and watch dressage but do not practice it, the art could disappear. Yet the gymnastic principles of dressage as well as riding techniques and even the very style of dressage riding are often being compromised by either ignorance or complacency.

Rewarding (recognizing!) that which is correct and punishing (without pity) that which is false is the primary function of judges. They are not only responsible to the contestants in the show they might be judging, but also should serve the art they evaluate. The rider merely represents the ideals the judge is there to uphold, rather than "reward or punish" the rider (as a person) per se!

I believe that not only *what* is being said but also *who* says it matters. Those contestants who hold dressage (rather than ribbons) dear will appreciate a judge who scores without mercy to the rider but according to principles. Such a competitor will appreciate comments that will help him abandon possible wrong directions in his riding in good time for facilitating a splendid recovery of the horse and a golden future to the rider. For the serious rider is dedicated to the art of dressage and will accept Machiavelli's dictum, *"Il guerda el Fine"* (guard the end; i.e., the end product in the long run is more important than temporary successes). Ultimately, the rider who contributes significantly to classical horsemanship is the one who "makes it" and not those who gather hundreds of small victory ribbons. Who would not trade an Olympic gold medal for a hundred blues won at County Fairs?

Thus, we arrive at the issue that conscientious judges find few acceptable Third Level rides. Therefore, their percent scores remain low for that level. Well, why?

The Training, First, and Second Level tests follow one another in a comfortable rhythm of tiny steps, a steady progression upward. In those three levels, one needs a horse with three good gaits to show in horizontal balance, maintaining good rhythm, to prove that he has accepted the aids and works with relaxation and pleasure under the rider. Often riders who show Training and First levels already do all the Second Level exercises in their daily work. For sure, those who compete on any of the three levels will testify that their daily work includes quantitatively more and qualitatively more sophisticated work than the tests call for. In fact, during these early stages of training the tests are, indeed, simpler than the daily work should be.

Not so at Third Level. The gymnastic evolutionary distance between Second and Third Levels is far greater than that dividing the first three levels from one another. In fact, the Third Level test represents a *different gymnastic concept* altogether than had been required previously. There is so much "big news" on Third Level that it appears rather seriously and suddenly *dressage* (if done properly) as opposed to the all-around hackish look of the preceding levels.

At Third Level, both collection and extension are required in all three gaits. (Grand Prix does not call for more!) Sophisticated lateral bending exercises are called for by the volte (good enough for Grand Prix!) The two-track movements include demands to displace both the shoulders and the haunches and that in rapid-fire succession to prove the pudding by fluency. Also, requirements call on the rider to find the medium mode in all three gaits and demonstrate them over short distances, yet distinctly enough to differentiate them sharply from both the collected and the extended modes! Thus, the constant modulation of the horse's base from lengthening to elevation (shortening) is required to be shown with fluid efficiency. To top it off, the demands include engagement exercises.

Well, we know what is demanded, if we read and ride the test. But what makes all these demands possible? *Suppleness and elasticity! Those are the items tested at Third Level;* that is what the Third Level test is all about!

At the Third Level, the horse should show the ability to *stretch and contract* his musculature, thereby enabling him to lengthen and heighten his strides. He must make taller steps with more distinct rhythm and confidently accurate striding (being airborn without fear of losing balance). He must be able to shift his center of gravity towards the haunches and begin to lighten the forehand for taller carriage. The Third Level, if done right, is a rather beautiful test and so "dressagy" in look that it carries inherent spectator pleasures (riding pleasures too!) similar to those experienced while watching the Grand Prix.

Yet, who would walk a mile to see Third Level? Few, because in Third Level disguise we often find the real life duplicate of General Sherman's bronze horse at the corner of Fifth Avenue and 59th Street. There, holding down one corner of Central Park, strides the most uncomfortable of bronze horses with his outstretched neck, wide-open jaw straining with anger at the bit, the very image of stiffness and agony, frozen into monumental permanence! Well, that sort of entry in Third Level justly makes the knowledgeable spectator feel as if he is being rubbed down with sandpaper.

Riders go wrong by forgetting that only that which is *built from the haunches forward towards the bit* and moves freely through a vibrating back succeeds. Collection cannot occur by pulling on the reins; cannot be cajoled by lifting the horse's head up, shortening his neck, or any other hand-riding method; and a horse cannot move when being held in front and pushed from behind, only when being yielded to when driven from behind. *The name of the game is self-carriage!* That is the goal!

Riders should remember that plus one and minus one beget zero: pulling on the horse and kicking him simultaneously create nothing but a tense, confused, alarmed horse with an open jaw, rigid back, and fast and pushing but mincingly short steps. The antithesis of the elastic horse we wish to create!

When horses rise with the forehand (lighten), they do so by rocking upward at the withers! *Not* by having the poll held high by demanding and rude hands that artificially shorten the neck (and pain its muscles). They can work upward with the withers only when the haunches have engaged. Horses can engage at the haunches and elevate their forehand *only* when they use their back and neck muscles correctly: fully stretched, completely relaxed, and vibrant. Remember that the total lightening of the forehand is the levade, and there the

Photographed by Hillair Carthine Bell

Ms. Hilda Gurney riding Keen in training session at the Medium Trot. The most important mode of trotting, the Medium Trot fathers both the collected and extended trot. Here, well engaged and magnificent for its "up hill energy" the Medium Trot shows that while the horse must extend his stride enough to reach beyond the hoofprint of the forehand with his hind leg, he also must maintain a higher, more composed neck position and offer less than full extension in stride and body in order to keep a greater upward bounce. This incredibly energetic trot is the germination of the slowness and grandeur that is Passage, the ultimate collection sitting back to Piaffe and the stretched out resonance of bursting energy resulting in extension.

Both of these extremes, total collection at Piaffe and full extension, are fathered by the much practiced medium trot (as seen on opposite page).

True extension develops only after collection is possible and practiced. Here everything is fully stretched as Keen is extending when Miss Hilda Gurney asks for maximum lengthening of both the strides and the body within the necessary longitudinal flexion.

Photographed by Susan Sexton

*Ms. Gwen Stockebrand riding Bao at the Passage. The most majestic develop-
ment at the trot, the Passage is a slow, solemn yet energetic, collected trot.
Maximum suspension between strides makes the horse impressively tall in appearance. In nature Stallions display themselves in this movement while mares
perform it as they circle their foals when feeling threatened. A challenge, a
display of energy and splendour, pride and hauteur matchless in most other
creatures. When tamed and called for by the rider, this eloquent pace is
the Passage.*

withers rock back. But the horse never lightens the forehand by being
pulled up at the head. *Everything comes from behind,* so let us leave
the head and neck alone.

The horse should "playfully" assume collection in self-carriage and
collect from the rider's lower back influence and rise in front of him
towards supple reins. The collected horse feels short and tall and as if
losing rein contact, by being so incredibly light precisely when collecting. *Collection is forward suppleness, not retardation.*

The few riders who approximate the truth in riding pass into Fourth and higher levels. Few, all too few! And that is why, once again on Fourth Level and above, one can see respectable performances. The Third Level is the *crisis level*, the one where dozens of riders fail, the eye of the needle through which none of the thick threads may pass.

So let us remember that at Third Level, *dressage arrives,* steps up to you, and quietly says, "You may pass only by doing right with your horse whose locomotion is in the haunches and whose beauty displays itself in the playful self-carriage of the forehand." The rest of the riders can stand in the stirrups, haul in the mouth with the reins, look down upon the creature whose head hangs, whose mouth gapes open, who wipes his nose in his chest, who minces his stingy strides in the rhythm of an eggbeater and forges forever onward into rapid oblivion.

The Meaning And Purpose Of Collection

The term, *collection, may denote two different meanings.* In one sense, collection is a relativistic term. In that sense it refers to a change in the horse's pace relative to whatever his pace was before. Thus in this sense, any time a horse moves taller and therefore shorter and slower than before, he is "collected" relative to the working, medium or extended nature of the gaits preceding the change. In this relativistic sense of the term, each rider collects the horse, even the youngest and the greenest. For even on the very first occasion a horse is ridden, he will have to be slowed down, even halted. Yet even at this "primitive" stage of collection, by merely slowing the horse, the essence of true collection presents itself as the horse *shifts the center of gravity toward his haunches.*

In another sense, however, the term collection is absolutistic in its connotation. In that sense collection refers to a specific mode of executing the basic paces, walk, trot and canter. The meaning is absolutistic because the standards that define collection in the paces are absolute and recognizable to those who understand that level of equitation. In fact, collection in all three paces is so specific that it is recognizable by the horse, by the rider and by knowledgeable observers.

The Characteristics Of Collection

1. *The haunches lift higher above the ground* and therefore, become coincidentally shorter, thus slowing progression but *not rhythm*. The hip, stifle, hock and pastern joints rotate supply and with great animation. However, the majority of the lifting action remains the assignment of the hocks. That is why all exercises strengthening and animating the activity in the hocks aid the development of collection.

2. *The leg supporting the horse's weight on the ground will sink* as the joints in it will yield softly to the weight in them. Like a compacted coil spring, the strengthened joints of the horse allow for sinking in order to cushion the strides for the structure above it and to propel the horse with greater force upward; for a coiled spring will propel more forcefully than would a rigid support. A truly supple and collected horse, therefore, will feel soft-striding yet springy, enabling the rider to aid and accompany his movements effortlessly. Therefore, supple horses inevitably appear elegant in flight with an effortlessly composed rider in the saddle. The feeling one gets watching such supple performances is that the horse carries his rider as naturally and effortlesssly as he carries his own skin.

3. *The strong and supple joints of the haunches will be used with great accuracy* and therefore economy. An effortlessness should accompany the most difficult tasks and there is a feeling of playing rather than working at the movements.

4. *The croup is lowered.* In addition to the supple use of the haunches the horse will be in the habit of fully flexing and elevating his back. Habitually carrying the rider with stretched and swinging back muscles, the horse enables himself to eventually lower his croup. For the back muscles that are stretched and that vibrate will also strengthen and carry the rider effortlessly, leaving additional strength for pushing the croup further under to shorten the total bulk of the horse. This compaction of the body also allows the center of gravity to move further back, thereby perpetuating itself.

5. As the center of gravity is shifting backwards *the forehand is liberated from its task of supporting* the majority of the composite weight (of horse and rider). Lightness and elegance of carriage occur as the forehand can be displayed rather than burdened.

6. *The horse will become shorter* yet taller-moving. He will fully stretch his back ligament and musculature over his topline but into a keener arch. His shorter mass will, of course, be easier to support for the haunches and easier to lift upward.

7. *The shoulders will move more freely* because they must no longer take a supportive role in the movement. (Ultimately in levade there will literally be no weight on the forehand). Consequently *the knees lift so high as to raise the cannon bone into a position perpendicular to the ground.* As a result the *withers will rock (bounce) upward with each stride* (rather obvious during passage work). Coincidentally, because the horse's neck and head happen to be in front of all the elevated forehand, *the neck will arch high and the head will be carried in the highest possible position.*

8. *The horse's profile will appear vertical (perpendicular) to the ground* as he will continue to flex towards the bit. He should continue to carry his head with the neck muscles emitting from the withers area and from which muscles he can hang his head down. If the head is supported by the lower neck muscles emitting from the chest area, the carriage is incorrect and the horse's head appears to be supported by being "shelved up" rather than "hanging down."

The above enumerated elements of collection, of course should occur simultaneously and are mutually supportive of their unique roles. They enforce one another, perpetuating and improving the degree of collection as a result of the interplay of these elements.

As these symbols of interacting collection occur we must remember that collection develops gradually and slowly. Based on the stretching and strengthening of muscles, the rotation and suppleness of joints are furthered. These combine into creating the accuracy of motion that represents economy of energy. The gradual gymnastic work which emphasizes relative collection will eventually succeed in creating absolute collection. That is why we should now concentrate on ideas that serve as means to the end (goal) of collection.

As much as driving the horse forward is paramount, every day's work should include episodes of collection. When collecting the horse, *do it through half-halting* and always approve accommodation by an elastic, give and take, rein-contact. *Never lose rhythm,* yet considering that most riders rush their horses in the mistaken belief that they are getting impulsion, do slow down to give your horse a chance "to sit around on the haunches." Relative to whatever forward driving goes on in the general effort to activate the haunches, the rider must also periodically shorten the horse's strides. Most often gymnastic riding goals are pushed in the wrong ways. *Extension comes from collection* and not the other way around. Thus, as one collects to gain extension (seeming opposites), one may do many things other than collecting in order to perfect collection.

Let us suppose that your goal includes developing collected paces but your horse is not yet ready to produce truly collected strides. You may practice many different exercises that perfect collection, but not yet ride your horse in collection.

The greatest enemy of collection is the misguided belief that the horse's front end (neck and head) should be lifted high by the rider's hands (reins) in order to lighten the forehand. The simultaneous shortening of the horse's neck produces pain and consequently resistance and false carriage. When superficially perceived, a collected horse may strike some people as being distinguishable by its elegantly arched neck and high head carriage. They do not realize that this is not the cause but rather the by-product of collection. Collection takes place in the haunches because it depends on the horse's ability to engage the joints in his quarters supplely. The misunderstanding that by raising the horse's head one can collect the haunches is analogous to putting the cart in front of the horse. In other words such belief is based on a confusion of cause and effect — confusing the symptomatic result with the fundamentals that caused it.

Let us examine an analogy. You want to sweep some crumbs into a dustpan. As you sweep the crumbs with the broom toward the dustpan, you must recede with it slowly in order to gather the crumbs. The ratio of the speed of the receding dustpan to the speed of the vigorous broom approaching is the key to the success of picking up all the crumbs efficiently. Both of your arms are working to get the crumbs collected into the dustpan. Both move the crumbs forward. One arm with the dustpan is "tempting" the crumbs to arrive by receding from them, while the other arm with the broom is "urging" the crumbs to go forward into the pan. This activity suggests collecting something in that it is pushed forward towards a receptacle that is not stationary but yielding. The collection occurs without anything ever stopping the motion of the crumbs forward.

Similarly, we collect the horse's energies that generate in his quarters. *We cannot shape the horse, only his energies.* We cannot collect him by shortening his neck, twisting his jaws sideways or lifting his head up; that would be reshaping the horse by force. We cannot carve or cast his body. We cannot shape him in his stall. *We can only ride the horse's energies into collection but never his bulk.* The energies are supplied by the haunches and shaped by the half-halts of the rider. The rider is the transformer of energies received from the haunches through the back. Energies absorbed (and understood) are fed back to the horse in a modified form.

To find and feel the correct ratio between driving the quarters and restraining the progression of the forehand without tensing the rein contact, is the art of collecting. The half-halt is not so named in vain, for half of that aid should ask for a halt and when the horse is responding by gathering itself towards the halt, the other half of the half-halt sends him forward as if the rider changed his mind. The horse cannot understand the command to collect unless at first the aids are emphasized. He should be asked to "come back" on his haunches and when he almost halts he should be "restarted" by the continuation of rhythmic aids. As all half-halts are resolved by yielding, do remember that after the transition to collection is performed the horse must continue in self-carriage.

The most severe problem with collection occurs when the rider thinks it to be resident in the horse's neck and head carriage. *We are trained to manipulate by hands and verify the results by sight.* We always "fix things" with our hands and grope to balance and steady and grasp to feel in contact with whatever we are doing. We watch intently and visually "feel" things happen. These acquired attributes hinder us in riding in general and collection in particular. Riders find the horse's neck and head easily accessible to the aids, for the hands through the reins maintain a physical connection with the head of the horse. The reins represent many powers through leverage and pressure that can cause pain to the horse. Through the reins the horse's head can be lifted, turned and manipulated. Thus, the horse's head becomes a "doer's paradise" because as soon as the hands "do" the horse's head visibly reacts. Manipulation checks out visibly.

The haunches, on the other hand, cannot be directly touched and manipulated. We have not yet invented (and hopefully never will) a mechanical device that would lift the horse's hind hooves and enable man, through straps or something, to jerk them forward or upward. We have our seat and leg influences acting on the horse at his middle (back and sides). Those areas are distant from his haunches which are, of course, behind and below the areas we directly contact with the seat and legs. There is no actual, physical connection between the rider and the horse's haunches. Yet we must clearly communicate information to the horse that will affect the action of his haunches precisely.

To achieve a sensitive communication process with the horse takes a long time of consistent and insistent aiding. *The horse's acceptance of the aids must be diversified and his submission to the aids well confirmed* in order to collect effectively. The driving aids of the legs and seat are vague to the horse because they are conceptual aids! Having no direct physical force acting on the areas they address, these aids will only be obeyed by the horse after he makes the conceptual leap of understanding their intentions! Thus, we must first convince the horse that when we do something with our legs to his sides, we really wish to affect the action of his hind legs, his source of motive force. To transfer sensations felt at his sides and through the saddle to mean action in his legs is a conceptual leap for an animal.

When the rider's leg actions are ignored by the horse's haunches, the conceptual leap has not occurred and the meaning should be emphasized by the use of the whip. The whip is the "spark" that jumps a thought from the rider's mind to the horse's mind (from a live battery to a dead one?). The stimulus of the whip invigorates the haunches and as instinct suggests flight, the haunches become active. The horse then begins to understand that the legs' demands must energize the haunches.

However, the instinct to take flight might create a new challenge. The horse might misinterpret the driving aids (particularly when supplemented by the whip) as a wish by the rider for more speed, and turn to running. *Speed is the enemy of impulsion* and engagement. By speeding the rhythm of the footfalls, strides must become short and the motion choppy and tense. Impulsion depends on slow but ample rotation of the joints which thereby allow economically efficient strides — long, ground-gaining strides.

The horse is on the aids when he submits to driving aids without rushing from them. Upon receiving leg aids a well-trained horse will either engage or bend (which is based on engagement). He should never run from or jump from the legs. For only a horse with "staying power" will lengthen or collect his strides in rhythm and bend rather than drift sideways away from the legs with a stiff body.

The half-halt is indispensible for producing these results. Therefore the half-halt is a near synonym to dressage riding.

More On Collection And Engagement

When driving the horse forward, one must discourage it from running faster by the necessarily frequent and skillfully applied half-halts. The horse's understanding of the leg aids should become more sophisticated as time passes and training progresses. Instead of resulting in speed, in effect the faster rhythm of footfalls, the horse should learn to differentiate the various effects of the rider's legs and produce appropriate reactions — running being the only inappropriate one. Correct reactions include either *lateral bending or engagement* (increased longitudinal flexion).

The rider must use both legs for riding all the time. When bending the horse they both fulfill highly important roles. Never can a rider bend a horse "with the inside leg" only. To bend a horse, the rider uses steady, continuous *outside leg pressure* in order to push or press the horse's quarters inward. That "curling" of the part of the horse behind the rider is done with the outside leg slightly behind the inside one but so as to have the heel flexed down. This positioning of the outside leg to the rear is accomplished by pressing the knee downward and dropping the outside hip, the power then coming from the well-stretched calf. The *inside leg* of the rider *has a double function.* On the one hand, the inside leg is placed just behind the girth, in the normal position, to define the area *around which* the horse is to bend. On the other hand, the inside leg *provides the impulsion* necessary for bending.

When moving through corners (arcs) and curves the horse should be bending and therefore use his hind legs in slightly different fashion from one another. A laterally bending horse will step with his hind legs toward the hoof prints of the fore on the same side! Often one can see stiff horses crossing with the inside hind leg under the body toward the hoof print of the outside fore, as if in a leg yield, the outside hind leg, of course, spinning off the curved pattern outward, all together. A properly flexed (curved) horse, however, will track correctly with his hind feet, because he uses them slightly differently. The outside hind leg will do slightly lower but longer action to accommodate the horse's longer (stretched) outside, skimming closer to the ground with its hoof and rotating lower with the hock, but longer at the stifle. However, the inside hind leg must make a larger forward rotating motion at the hock, to produce taller, more engaged action on the inside. Hence the important role of the rider's inside leg action — to increase the impulsion but not speed on the inside by aggressive rhythmic aids! The horse in bending contracts (shortens) its inside but also *shifts the center of gravity to the inside,* both of these causing the vital need for increased inside hock activity.

Imagine an analogy in human terms: stand up on your right foot and lift your left knee high with both hands clasped around it. You will realize that with your left knee lifted high (analogous to the horse's left hock) your body will develop a bending posture to the left. Note also that your balance is perfect in spite of standing on your right leg alone because your left knee is high up and your torso is contracting on the left and stretching on the right. Thus bends the horse in fine balance, your inside leg driving his inside hock into the proper behavior.

Only this kind of activity with the legs will produce proper and consistent lateral bending in the horse. Lateral bending is paramount to arriving at collection. One never gets collection by riding in collected paces; collection is developed by means other than collection itself. All riding is made up of many means leading to the desired ends. Therefore one achieves a Grand Prix test not by riding a Grand Prix test every day starting with the green three-year-old and "drilling" it into him. This analogy, far-fetched enough to be grotesquely comical, makes its point strongly. We do not get passage by riding passage; we do not get collection by riding a "collected" trot on an undeveloped horse. One of the many means, indeed one of the most important means, to collection is the riding of proper bends! When bending, as mentioned above, the horse must use the inside hock differently than it uses the outside hock. That differentiation "collects in" from behind the horse's inside leg; bending is unilateral (one sided) collection, and a most important building block in producing genuine bilateral collection — equal on both sides.

The shoulder-in, being one of the finest suppling and therefore collecting exercises is primarily concerned with the intensification of the horse's bending *through the mobilization of his inner hock.* That is why the pulling of the inside rein during a shoulder-in is its very negation. For the whole movement is primarily addressed to the inside hock and that then must not be inhibited in its action potential by a restrictive inside rein. Through the shoulder-in the rider can "sweep the horse's inside hind under" by doing the exercise in mirror images until strength, courage in lateral balance, etc., add up to that perfectly soft and harmonious result when *both hind legs sweep under*, as if they *both* simultaneously do the shoulder-in, *but now on a straight track. Behold collected trot!*

The ideal dressage horse, that moves foward with minimum effort producing maximum impulsion efficiency on a straight line, is developed through the means that include much bending. For through bending is the horse elasticized so as to make it possible for it to move straight and efficiently, much like the medieval sword makers of Bagdad, Toledo, and other centers who tempered their steel until they could show them in the marketplace with blades bent to a full circle. The blade which bent to the circle either way, was the blade so tempered that when straightened it chopped off heads with the greatest efficiency. The supple and flexible sword when straightened wielded the maximum efficiency!

Only the horse that can collect — its haunches inward and under — can efficiently extend. When such a horse extends (whether to the medium trot or to full extension) it will give the rider a feeling that the horse is sinking down behind while climbing a staircase with its front end — two steps at a time! The animation and freedom of the forehand makes the horse dance upward "tilling the air". The animation and the effortlessness of this kind of motion has such a hypnotic effect on the horse that it feels as if it could maintain this activity eternally! The horse finally becomes self-propelled, self-risen in the front, in full flight upward and onward with so much kinetic impetus that the rider becomes a mere supporter of the action by accommodating it as a harmonious passenger. The feeling is that the horse rides itself through the rider, who merely lends his weight as a medium of balance and stability through which the horse can run its energies unencumbered.

An arched neck does not by itself denote a horse on the aids. Being on the aids helps to become part of the momentum of evolution towards collection (out of which comes extension) and engagement. A curved neck, an arched neck, an overbent neck, a broken-at-the-third-vertebra neck, *any neck is not ridable!* The neck is symptomatic of what the haunches are doing and very few of the arched necks are telling a pleasant story.

Through bending and particularly correctly performed two track movements, the horse will assimilate the correct meaning of the rider's "collection leg aids." For instance when the horse understands that during a shoulder-in the rider's outside leg pressure prevents it from speeding up or "uncoiling" to evade (by straightness), and the rider's inside leg supplies a rhythmic impulsion aid inviting the hock to action, then the horse will understand leg aids. Being on the aids is essential to gymnastic development. Being on the aids means the horse monitors the leg aids correctly, neither refusing them by rushing away nor by stiffening. When the rider's left leg calling makes the horse engage his left leg to a larger, smoother rotation, then the message has gotten through. Then comes the time the rider can call with his legs and the horse will produce the fireworks in the haunches that signal engagement available; energy ready to lift high or long, but never to run!

About Engagement On The Aids

Bringing the horse to the aids is primarily done by the driving leg aids and only secondarily with the concurring seat and derivative hand aids as they all work together in a system. The *HORSE CANNOT BE ENGAGED THROUGH THE HANDS;* not because I think it wrong but because it is physiologically impossible. This is not a matter of style, emphasis, method or taste. It is a fact of objective physiological data.

When the horse is properly *ON THE AIDS THE NECK WILL COINCIDENTALLY ARCH* and the poll will flex as part of the total longitudinal flexion. On top of the spinal column of the horse, following its entire length, runs the *CERVICAL LIGAMENT.* That ligament should at all times be fully stretched. When it is fully stretched, not only will its elasticity and therefore activity (swinging) increase but it will elevate the horse's back or spinal column. To elevate the back one ought to "pull down" the cervical ligament on both its ends; that is have the horse "tuck under" his haunches and push, forward-and-down, his neck *simultaneously.*

That is why just "showing the ground" to the horse, in effect lowering his head, is not enough without at the same time driving his haunches under him; for the ligament, and with it the back, will fully stretch and elevate only when *BOTH ENDS* of the ligament are approaching the ground!

When the haunches engage more, and oft times the whip must be used to insist on it, then the biceps femoris muscles visibly press the stifle farther forward and upward (a major function) while lifting hocks higher in their rotation (a lesser function). These muscles, running roughly on the back side of the horse's rump, are observable at the walk, trot or canter as the action that "tucks the haunches under," that is pulls the back end of the ligament tight. The front of the ligament, as it is attached to the horse's skull, can be pulled tight simultaneously by riding the horse's head forward and down. Without this activity the horse is physiologically incapable of carrying the rider properly and developing gymnastically.

When the back has been elevated, then the horse can balance himself and relax those muscles that are furthering effortless locomotion and carriage. Thus the correctly stretched horse, and remember this is attained by a driving rider, will "hang his head" from the muscles running at the top of his neck or crest and emitting from the withers, the splenius primarily and the semispinalis capitis secondarily. The horse will then no longer need to support his head carriage by "shelfing it up" with the muscles emitting from his chest (brachiocephalicus) and look as if he grew a goiter. Needless to say on the longitudinally-flexed horse, also called "on the bit," all other muscles will also automatically relax and move with a great deal of flexion or stretching to create ample, loose, effortless locomotion. These relaxed muscles can be observed "playing" in ripples under the fine summer coat of a correctly moving horse.

The greatest hindrance to driving the horse properly is from riders stiffening their legs. Gripping the horse with tight legs or pressing on his ribs inward, tightly holding him with the heels, are all incorrect leg positions and deny aiding. Riding with the seam of the boots is a bad habit held over from times when the rider needed to grip in order to balance himself. Often "quietly elegant legs" are confused with gripping, tight leg positions. The horse cannot monitor tight legs as aids and will sour to the pressure which he will interpret as another "necessary evil."

Just weight on the horse's sides will be tolerated much like he tolerates the weight in the saddle, but gripping legs never modulate and therefore never "converse." In human terms tight gloves do not communicate what gently squeezing hands can. Tight legs also induce pain and discomfort much like tight shoes. In fact with the passing of time the pain induced by both tight shoes (for humans) and tightly gripping legs (for horses) will sharply increase and approach the intolerable level.

In the preceding chapters I have written about the incorrect use of the rider's legs, including the rhythmic upward "scratching" of the horse's sides by rocking the toes down in the stirrup irons and scratching the horse with the heels creeping upward. I do not want to repeat these things, nor the advice on how to learn the correct pushing aids which totally depend on the free, relaxed rotation of the ankles; the toes either rotating or swinging in-out, first visibly while learning, then invisibly.

Rhythmically repetitious, forward pushing aids are the only legitimate driving aids. They of course, also coordinate with the proper functioning of the buttocks and the muscles that partake in driving. Such aids are very effortless and feel light — burn no calories — and the horse reacts to their companionship by lively paces! While learning correctly driving aids or teaching them to the horse the frequent and consistent use of the whip is very necessary. The horse must react to these rhythmically light and harmonious aids and if he "forgets" to react, you must "jump a spark to his batteries with your cable/whip!" The whip serves as the spark (perhaps lighting bolt!) that connects the rider's mind and will to his horse's mind and consequently submission. It is much better to settle the attention-to-the-aids issue firmly than to nag at the horse for fourteen years!

Never forget that the effective aid is not exhausting to the rider and not souring to the horse. Never forget that the horse is capable of flicking a fly off his skin and therefore can tune in to the lightest aids if *THAT IS WHAT YOU TEACH HIM.* Do not forget that the horse can and should pay attention to the rider *ALWAYS* while working, but should also be given frequent rest periods. The horse's ears should not "listen" by pointing forward but should be relaxed and slightly slack towards the rider in a position of submissive listening. High eyes should not focus forward nor roll sideways in observation of all others but rather look "as if in a daze with an inward vision." As soon as the horse is "off the aids" tune him back with the whip!

We can ride neither forward nor sideways by physically dislocating horses with force. That is, we cannot push them around. Regardless of how much power you use (actual calories) you cannot *FORCE* the horse to do anything. No amount of strength can compel the horse to do anything. The simple reason for that is that the rider is not on his legs! No more can you force a horse in any direction by physical muscle power than can your ear lobes force you to change your course or pick up impulsion. Thus, muscle power and force will not ride the horse for you, only aids will and they might as well be light and harmonious.

The horse has the neurological aptitude to react to very slight stimuli. He has the mental aptitude to perceive for a sustained period of time very mild stimuli and differentiate between them. He has an excellent memory. Force and power will only stiffen the rider. Sensitive aids will result in exquisite communications. If a horse pulls on you, remember that it takes two to pull! If you unpull — yield one rein at the time — the horse cannot and will not pull. Horses will learn anything. They will learn to gymnasticize with you on light communications just as easily as they will learn to do the same by harsh communications.

To increase the horse's attention to the leg aids, two track exercises are the most valuable. For when inducing a crossing of one hind leg by your leg action on the same side, you communicated to the horse that action way up on his ribs has to yield results way down at his hoofs. Two track movements have terrific gymnastic value. Nothing else "brings the horse into the aids" more firmly than obedience to the two track aids.

To build the horse from behind is no idle chatter. It is a physiologically predetermined compulsory position. Now only remember that it can be done as soon as you succeed in gaining the horse's attention to your forward driving aids. As soon as the horse accepts your legs without rushing but instead by demonstrating "staying power" — tolerance for the leg's conversation — he should produce upon the lightest inducement, results of slower but larger rotation of the haunches. Nothing can be developed from the head backwards. It is your job to teach him your legs; tolerate no compromise. The way is forward and upward in a slow commodious rhythm.

The alternative method for collection is of course through "longitudinal engagement activity." First of all you must feel the pace your horse is supplying and harmonize with it. This is most evident in the trot but the same applies to walk or canter. Go along, follow, move with, dance along, passively agree to feel what he supplies from the haunches. This is a short but diagnostic period during which you are a listener monitoring that which the horse offers in the concept areas of relaxation, submission to the aids (flexion), balance, rhythm and impulsion. Only after understanding what your horse is doing, feeling it to the point of going along with it, can you begin to produce a change.

The goal of aiding is always the "disturbance" of the status quo. You cannot disturb something you cannot even monitor and understand. Once you understand, however, you can ask for a change according to need. Maybe a deeper flexion with higher back carriage. Improved impulsion or rhythm may be the most important need. Once you have harmony with the horse and have discovered his rhythm and impulsion you can, for the first time, set about to improve on it! You must now begin to ask for longer or taller steps than those he volunteered. That is, you should lengthen or shorten the horse's base (i.e. begin extending and collecting).

Now as you work on the paces by lengthening and shortening the base, alternate between the two modes. Extend the pace to the ultimate the horse can offer in PURE RHYTHM and then collect the pace, without slowing the rhythm, as much as you can. It is important that your horse "go ahead full stretch" instantly when asked (remind him with the whip) and to "come back" to you when half-halted into collection. The wishy-washy, gradual sequencing of these exercises or the gradual development into and out of these extensions and collections, can annul the whole gymnastic value. The horse must pay attention to the aid, which should be sufficiently marked for him to react to correctly. At first your aids may have to "shout"; use the whip to make sure he is extending right now! And then use the hands — PASSIVELY RESISTANT BUT FIRMLY (connected to seatbones) — with the torso planted squat down so as to "shout at the horse" to come back into collection. With every repetition the aids should become much more refined because the horse does understand! Just do not take "no" for an answer on the first few sequences. He will very quickly learn what you mean and put a lot of "fireworks" into the pace by engaging himself and submitting to the engagement aids and by not running from them.

Yet another aspect of collection and resultant extension is done on the 20 m. diameter circle. That is the most important pattern (gymnastic, too!) on the way to Grand Prix. By the way, one can build a horse in an arena with that dimension. I am not recommending that type of confinement but it was used in the last two centuries with success (Empress Elizabeth of Austria rode in a 20 m. diameter circular blue tent and on a very high level). On the 20 m. circle you should "settle" the horse into a medium trot.

When you ride a medium trot, you are inducing a ground-covering superiority in the trot, for the horse's hind legs must pass over the hoof-prints of his fore. In that sense the medium trot is an "extended trot" with modifications. In the medium trot however, in contrast to the extended, the horse is not allowed to stretch his neck fully forward and therefore some of the shoulder action of the horse is kept "in reserve," not allowing the horse to fully extend in the shoulders. Thus, the medium trot is ample in length but not fully extended to the horse's outmost stretching ability. The taller neck position and taller but shorter use of shoulder action "composes" the horse in the medium trot into a very energetic and elegant movement that is engaged behind but produces height of steps and a distinct lightening of the forehand (bouncing the withers up, lifting the knees higher). The medium trot is the "bread-and-butter" exercise on the way to Grand Prix. Without the medium paces the proper muscular development producing the proper skeletal rotation just cannot develop. The Grand Prix is much born by development in the medium paces, with ample mileage spent staying with it. The 20 m. circle is that fortunate gymnastic tool (pattern) which, being a continuous line, allows the "perpetual flow" of motion rather than the corner-to-straight rearrangement of the horse's balance and rider's aids.

To the medium paces' development the sense of "perpetum mobile" is highly important. Riders often feel that much driving for medium paces is detrimental, hard work. Remember that just a century ago in Paris, London, Vienna and the world's other metropolises, horses were medium trotting across capital cities, carrying their passengers to dinners, dentists, theaters, and shopping, maintaining the pace for miles, clock even, on pavement yet and day after day! Your horse can do it, too.

The medium trot has the distinct signature of great engagement and impulsion in the quarters (stepping deep under the forward) combined with a slow but commodious motion of the forehand as if to "wait" for the arrival of the haunches. That relative restraint in the forehand in relation to the keenness of the haunches defines that wonderful forward yet bouncing upward motion that gives the feeling of the horse rising in front of the thighs and sinking behind the seatbones. Through that only comes the internationally qualifying paces.

The passage is, of course, born out of the medium trot. Both the strength and the technique needed by the horse for passage comes forth from medium trot work. Once the horse is ready for it, often a bold half-halt into a medium trot can make the horse collect into passage.

The medium trot as contrasted to full extended trot can forestall any mistake on the horse's part in misinterpreting driving aids for meaning speed or tilting the weight onto the forehand.

I hope you will begin to engage your horses by using the three fundamental methods I have recommended here: to put him on your aids and teach him what your legs mean, use the bending and two track movements; to mobilize him and confirm his balance use transitions from longer to shorter pace; to stabilize his rhythm and put mileage on his muscular development and skeletal proficiency ride the circle at the medium pace.

Engagement And Daily Riding Strategies

Engagement is a concept which has two closely related meanings. In the general sense, engagement occurs when *the rider succeeds in shifting the center of gravity backward* toward the haunches of his horse. It also occurs every time *the rider succeeds in making the horse do better than before* in whatever he is being asked to do at the time. As the process continues, the rider is *perpetually seeking to shift the center of gravity backwards and perpetually demanding a finer output* from the horse. Thus, the final and specific definition of engagement appears. In the definitive sense, *engagement refers to maximum output by the horse in performing any gymnastic exercise asked of him.* That, of course, presupposes that he is supple and elastic and capable of shifting his center of gravity toward the haunches as well as maximizing his athletic output all the time.

Now that the concept has been stated and defined, let me elaborate at leisure in order to further clarify the subject.

Shifting the horse's center of gravity towards his haunches should remain a perpetual effort in the rider's daily work. The horse's center of gravity is "naturally" on the forehand, as the bulk of his chest (rib cage), forearms, neck and head are far heavier than the bulk of his quarters. Thus, a horse at the free walk will have three-fifths of his composite weight over his forehand. With considerable imagination (which is rather useful in all learning), we can propose that the horse is like a builder's "level" and has a bubble in him floating forward or backward to show us when he is "level" or horizontal. Imagine your horse this way as you ride and "feel" for his center of gravity or, rather, cultivate the "center of gravity of his motion." For you *cannot shape your horse, only his energies!* If you propel him energetically enough that he supports more than half of his weight with his haunches (taking more than half off the forehand), you are engaging your horse.

Obviously, in working for this kind of engagement, the most useful daily exercises are the transitions. Both types of transition — from pace to pace and within a pace (going from a more collected to a more extended trot while keeping impeccable rhythm) — will shift, however temporarily, the center of gravity of the horse backward, toward his haunches.

There are two curious things you may want to note. First, going from extension or potentially faster pace to collection or potentially slower pace (e.g., from trot to walk) shifts the center of gravity backward more easily than the reverse of the process. One could call this "shifting gears upward." Yet, if you manage an upward transition with the center of gravity staying in the haunches, you gain greater gymnastic value because of the more sophisticated engagement of the horse. Second, the center of gravity will, by necessity, have been shifted backwards more efficiently if the horse is bent into a lateral movement. Thus, doing extension-collection-extension exercises on a 20-meter circle will have a higher gymnastic yield than doing the same along the long walls of the arena.

Demanding of the horse that he do better than before is the indispensable job of the rider for every minute spent in the saddle. This implies that the rider has concentration and focus which allows him to sense, feel, know every moment while in the saddle, what his horse's performance level is. To feel what the hindquarters are doing, to monitor the energy level and its forthcoming supply all the time. To be accurate in monitoring and, indispensably, to be punctual in reacting to any moment of slacking on the horse's part. This is the attitude of a "taskmaster" who demands performance from the horse not only on the level now being volunteered, but always just a little better!

Engagement is based on uncompromising focusing of the horse's energies. (It is presumed that the rider has acquired the correct seat and aids, without which there is neither stability nor close enough contact to control the situation.) Whatever the horse is doing at the moment, the rider should ask him to do it better. In short, the rider's continuous task is *maximization of the horse's output.* If the horse walks, there is surely a better walk that could be gotten. If you are bending your horse on a circle, there is surely room for a better, more continuous bending and at a better impulsion than what he is just now doing. If you extend the trot, there could surely be a wee-bit longer stride. In the half-pass, the closing of the legs could surely be deeper if you could (as you should) bend his torso more intensely and accelerate his tempo sideways. "Ad infinitum" one could continue to catalogue the rider's perpetual effort to do better than before.

Interestingly enough, horses are not only willing and capable of producing greater quality than before, but they can learn that there is consistency in this demand and will habitually put out more as the time of training progresses. Then when you have a "weaker day" when the "flu is going around," you can still compete on a horse which is accustomed to putting out a great deal of performance because he has consistently been asked to do so. *The rider does a favor to the horse by demanding because a horse which moves with maximum efficiency will have minimum effort (wear and tear).*

Maximum performance of all the gymnastically important exercises with minimum effort is the ideal task of the fully developed dressage horse, as shown on the Grand Prix level. Years spent shifting his center of gravity towards his haunches and years spent maximizing his efforts from moment to moment will have him the perfection of balanced coordination, elasticity and suppleness on which this performance is based.

Therefore, on the highest levels of gymnastics we look for a horse who can perform, to the ultimate extent of his natural abilities, each task called for at its maximum level. For instance, if an extended trot is called for, he will extend his trot to such a level as he can reach with his particular conformation and still remain in perfect rhythm and balance (including straightness). But the same horse, when asked to perform the piaffe, will not be expected to show his engagement by extending his strides to their outmost conformational limits. Quite to the contrary, his engagement will be proven by the total lack of advancing over ground while remaining active in trot-like motion (piaffe is really a passage in place, not a trot in place). Similarly, while a well-engaged half-pass is evaluated on the depth of crossing of the legs — a result of outmost bending in the spine, or lateral suppleness — which then produces a highly airborne, sideways floating with great cadence, we do not desire a similar crossing of the legs on the straight wall or at a medium trot on a circle. In short, what is the sign of great engagement in one movement is not the sign of engagement in another. For engagement is evaluated by the performance of the *essence of each gymnastic movement.* So, if the essence is length of stride, then it would be the length of stride which would be evaluated to measure engagement. But should the essence of the exercise be the lowering of the haunches, then that will be important in determination of the degree of engagement of the performance.

Engagement is the ultimate goal of dressage riding — the horse that is *willing and able to maximize the performance of any task with minimum effort.* Those riders who consider it their daily coaching duty to command their horse to do better and to step under more than ever before will go to the top.

The following diagram is a visual expression of the hierarchy of engagement work:

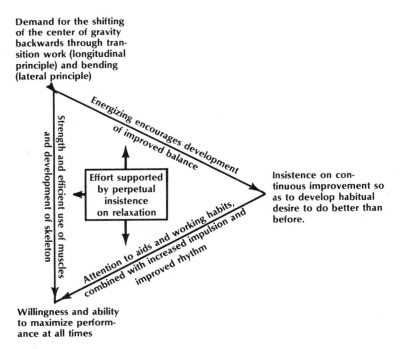

Demand for the shifting of the center of gravity backwards through transition work (longitudinal principle) and bending (lateral principle)

Energizing encourages development of improved balance

Strength and efficient use of muscles and development of skeleton

Effort supported by perpetual insistence on relaxation

Attention to aids and working habits, combined with increased impulsion and improved rhythm

Insistence on continuous improvement so as to develop habitual desire to do better than before.

Willingness and ability to maximize performance at all times

 # Lateral Bending

The Two-Track MOVEMENTS

For the sake of simplicity, remember that the two-track movements may be put into two groups:

1. The *shoulder-in* (or *shoulder-out*) all by itself. This is the only two-track movement where we ask the horse to bend toward one side, yet expect him to continue moving in the direction of the other side. For example, when performing a shoulder-in to the right, the horse must continue to move in the direction of our left hand and knee.

2. The *haunches-in (haunches-out)*, the *half-pass* and the *pirouettes*. All these movements belong to the same group because in all of them the horse is asked to proceed in the direction towards which he is bent. The aids, therefore, are basically identical in these movements. They differ only in intensity, both at the legs and at the reins,because the mildest bending is required in the pirouettes to allow more turning activity (minimum muscle, maximum skeletal and balance displacement demanded); the half-passes demand more bending and bending at the haunches in demands most (with maximum muscular stretch and minimum skeletal displacement required.)

There is one important aiding feature relevant to both of these

The half-pass left at the trot ridden by Ms. Gwen Stockebrand on Bao. A fascinating moment captured by the photographer showing the wonderful impulsion propelled by a powerful engagement of the haunches. The hind legs wide showing how much ground is covered when engagement is really bold. At the same moment the right forehand is crossing over the left, showing how this exercise is wonderful for liberating the shoulder action, making brilliant extensions possible as a consequence. The perfect harmony of a relaxed rider, as seen on this picture is the greatest asset for the horse in his chance for such a well-engaged performance. The rider truly "aids" rather than hinders the effort.

groups, that is to all the two-track movements: do NOT aid with the seat. That is, neither shove forward with buttocks nor gyrate sideways with the lower back. Stay perpendicular, lean neither forwards nor backwards. More importantly, hang neither inward nor outward, trying to push the horse away with the torso. Do not stiffen and raise one shoulder or look down. In short and once again, sit PERFECTLY straight and upright in order to REMAIN RELAXED and give your horse a chance to work relaxed! In two-track movements the all important aids are the legs, but the leg aids have no chance to be effective, unless the seat is PERFECTLY ANCHORED, for the leg aids are felt by the horse only in proportion to their RELATIVE STRENGTH and that depends on the steadiness of a deep anchorage at the seatbones. Let us not forget that we cannot displace nor bend a horse with our legs unless they are supported by a perfectly steady seat. The reason for this is that we are on top of the horse and not anchored on the ground!

Any straight but flexible object can be bent only when it is affected at a minimum of three points. Place your riding whip on a table and try it. The whip is a particularly good instrument of analogy to the horse as it has a heavier, less yielding (flexible) butt end and a rather wiggly, highly flexible thin end (comparable to the horse's neck). Now try to bend it until it bows in continuum; put your thumb on one side of the whip and your forefinger and little finger on the opposite side. You will see you can bend the whip. Using two hands, you can place three fingers against the whip the same way but at even more appropriate distances to pursue the analogy with the horse.

What will this experiment demonstrate to you? That the horse must be BENT AROUND (but not with) the inside leg which remains the rhythm-keeping impulsion leg also; that is your thumb. On the outside of the horse you bend him with the outside leg supplemented with a much lighter effect on the outside rein!

Now try out the mistakes with your fingers still working the riding whip:

1. Push the whip only with the thumb, that is, the inside leg; it will remain straight yet navigate sideways: a leg-yielding but not a *shoulder-in*.

2. Add the pulling of the inside rein to the pushing of the inside leg and you get a straight whip with only the wiggly thin front of it "neck bending" yet the straight torso of the whip rushing away sideways

Both of the above create an EVASION of the bending! The horse may go sideways, will rush sideways, but he will never bend, tax his inside hind legs, bend the joints of his legs, stretch the muscles on his outside and contract the muscles on the inside. However, if you bend the horse WITH the outside leg, AROUND the inside leg, supporting him with the OUTSIDE rein, you will get bending; as a consequence you will also get balance (rather than hurry) and as a result you will get a valuable gymnastic exercise!

So it will become clear that in the shoulder in, the haunches must be "pressed inward" in spite of the fact that the shoulder is taken off the original track and is moving on an inner track away from the wall. The outside rein should be as steady as a violin string (neither stretched nor slack for in neither case is there music). The inside rein supples and is rendered resilient to encourage forward progression, particularly the deeper stride forward and across. The inside leg is rhythmically active, but not too far back and pushing, for that straightens the horse and hurries him sideways evasively.

In the *pirouettes, half-passes* and *haunches-in* the bending mechanisms remain the same but here the horse must travel in the direction to which he is bent. Therefore, the outside leg assumes a double mission: it bends the haunches as well as encourages sideways displacement, so it must work double time over the shoulder in effect. Yet the inside leg remains identical in function, proposing the area AROUND which the horse must bend (therefore should remain behind the girth but not far back) and SUPPLYING the impulsion. The feeling is that the rider "receives" the horse with the inside leg and keeps his timing. The inside rein continues to encourage resiliency and is suppling, "opening" in tiny rhythmic movements rather than busying itself tightening and falsely neck-bending the horse.

When teaching two-track movements, slow down to communicate the idea that you want a short horse on its haunches, for when the horse has eventually understood the movements and capable of performing them, it has to do them in proper collection. Under no circumstances tolerate the horse running away from the leg aids; ride in contact ALL the time at least with the legs; otherwise, the horse may sprint at their unexpected use. That is the whole idea of contact riding in dressage as opposed to other modes of horsemanship. You must slow the horse down and place the legs BEFORE asking for two-track movement. Once on the performance track, bending and collecting a horse that is nervous about the legs will result in failure.

Precisely for that reason we ask for two-track movement AFTER corners, presuming that the rider USES the corners to begin intensified bending BEFORE the two-track performance.

All two-track movements can best be divided into two major categories. In one of these is shoulder-in, the only two-track movement in which the horse *does not* bend in the direction of his progression. In the other category are all other two-track movements, grouped together because in all of them the horse bends *towards* the direction of his progression. Thus the *haunches-in*, the *half-pass* and the *pirouette* are included in this latter category.

We should also remember here that the *shoulder-in* and *haunches-in* have twin counter parts: *shoulder-out* and *haunches-out*. Beyond this similarity, they further resemble one another in that they emphasize the displacement of either the front half (*shoulder-in* and *out*) or the quarters (*haunches-in* and *out*) relative to the line of progression. Thus they are emphasizing control in the interest of *straightening the horse and moving him correctly forward*.

Are there any similarities relevant to all two-track movements?

Yes. Maybe the most important, from the point of view of the horse's gymnastic development is that *the horse must bend continuously and evenly along his spine.*When his bending is not continuous, but rather emphasizes the easily navigable neck position, the horse will evade bending in the rest of his body. In fact, the horse's disobedience to flexion is his offer of an exaggerated neck position, which should not fool the alert and knowledgeable rider.

In all two-track exercises *the horse's balance greatly improves* as he learns to cope with new sensations in the displacement of his center of gravity. Furthermore, we greatly *improve the horse's flexibility* (manifested in longitudinal flexion) *as he stretches on one side but contracts his musculature on the other side* (making himself elastic). As these movements combine the balance displacement (moving sideways) with the bending (flexing muscles) their joint effect *strengthens and therefore elasticizes the horse's joints*. All these elements will add up to a *more powerfully* moving horse, with greater *expression manifested in cadence of movement* and of course the *grace* resulting from a well-balanced, strong animation.

Yet there is additional value in the two-track exercises from *the rider's point of view*. Those exercises are the most valuable in cajoling the horse's *submission to the aids*. They increase his attention to the details of receiving different aids on either of his sides. As you well know, in two-track movements the rider must aid differently on either side. The refinement of the *aiding language* between horse and rider through the two-track exercises may be likened to the first excursions into conceptional abstract conversation by someone just learning a foreign language.

Pursuing the ideas of comparison through similarities, are there things the rider must always do regardless of which two-track movement he pursues?

Yes, and they are well to be remembered: for the success of two-track movement greatly depends on the accuracy and correctness of the rider's aids. First of all *the rider's outside leg should always be positioned further back than the inside leg.* This outside leg (on the horse's longstretched side) must be pressed back and down at the knee, while keeping the heel down. If the heel lifts up and the lower leg approaches a horizontal position, the positioning of the leg is incorrect. It becomes ineffective. If, however, the outside leg is correctly positioned back, it will fulfill its major function of *keeping the horse's haunches bent.* Coincidentally, this outside leg positioning answers another question often asked.

On which seatbones should the rider be sitting most heavily during two-track movements?

There is no option when the rider aids correctly! In fact, the outside leg being back and bending the horse *puts the rider's inside seatbones inevitably more adhesively down and forward* as it should be. In fact, the outside seatbone may feel as if it has somewhat risen up into the buttock muscle and left the saddle in favor of doubling the weight into the inside. Thus, *the rider always sits on the inside seatbone which is at the horse's hollow* (or short) *side.*

Is it possible to find similarities in the action of the rider's hands during two-track movements?

During two-track exercises the horse must cross with one hind leg in front of the other. On the side on which the horse's hind leg crosses over, the *rider's hand must supply* (yield) *the rein* in a gesture of *opening the gates to forward progression.* Crossing with a hind leg is not all we hope for. We ought to get a well engaged crossing: one with a tall, yet deep. hugely rotated gesture and not one intimidated by a frozen hand.

The curious thing about this is that during a *shoulder in the inside hand of the rider must yield* (as that hind leg is crossing in engagement!) In all other two-tracks it is *the outside hand of the rider that permits the engagement by yielding.* The hand opposite the yielding hand remains in charge of *the rein of reference* (against which the yielding may make sense) *and is stable, light but in perpetual contact* (and control!!)

What is the guide line for good suppling hands?

Suppling must mean yielding! When a rider misinterprets suppling as a chance to pull back on the jaw (introduce pain) and then push it forward, he is mistaken. Suppling must *totally relax the already existing light contact* without any restraint preceding it. Do not "jaw back" on the horse or "saw" or "rock" the rein to get a "give" out of the horse. Simply try to lose contact with one side of the rein *without visibly slacking the leather.*

There is more to suppling. When it is artfully done, it *is done in rhythm with the horse's stride!* The rein should act exactly *at the time when the horse's hind leg lifts off the ground on the side of the suppling rein.* The steadiness of the rider's seat and aids, the sophistication of their quietness cannot be overemphasized. To establish the "feel" for suppling and "supporting" on opposite reins much depends on the rider's ability to be correctly anchored and using the *aids as a system.*

Which leg of the rider should supply the rhythm and the impulsion when basically both are used for the bending of the horse?

On the horse's long side (outside) *the leg is steady and positioned back.* On the short side (inside and hollow) the leg is in the regular (so called girth) position. The *impulsion is always supplied with the leg on the horse's inside* (hollow, contracted side). That is the reason that during the shoulder in the rider's inside leg, curiously enough, must take care of *both the crossing of the horse's inside hind leg and the impulsion.* However, in the other two-track movements, the *impulsion leg* (being on the inside) *will not be responsible for the crossing as well.*

As a teacher have you any further advice?

First of all, when aiding a horse in any two-track movement, *help him improve his balance by staying in balance yourself.* Leaning to either side denies the horse the chance to either understand your aids (frustration) or stay in balance (fear). The *rider's spine should remain perpendicular to the horse's spine.* Therefore try to ride toward a mirror; for even under coaching riders do not seem to believe they are tilting to one side.

Also, remember that you can never shape the horse; only his energies! When in two-track, you are giving your horse a sophisticated new "shape" which can only be sculpt correctly when the horse supplies sufficient energy to be shaped. *Never give your horse a shape! By allowing his impulsion to vibrate through his entirety, he will look his best and inevitably be gymnastically proper.*

How does one effectively develop the lateral movements after shoulder-in?

Few are the occasions when the half-pass, the pirouette (turn on the haunches) and haunches-in are properly performed. In the AHSA tests all of these movements are asked for. These three movements are more intimately related than the ordinary relationship that is necessary in all correct dressage riding, where no exercise is meaningful without its being in context with those preceding and following it.

I will suggest strategies for the development and relating of the half-pass, pirouette and haunches-in. There are, first of all, important similarities of purpose.

The primary purpose of these exercises is the engagement of the hindquarters of the horse. The result expected is increased ability to collect by the horse's acceptance of more weight with the hindquarters.

The second important purpose is to improve the horse's lateral balance. Collection refers to improved longitudinal balance and is the primary purpose of these exercises, but not to be underestimated is the secondary purpose of lateral balancing. This results in the horse's ability to displace sideways his center of gravity.

While the first two purposes concentrate on the entire horse's center of gravity (skeletal balance), the third purpose of the exercises is the suppling of the musculature. Therefore the correct bending of the horse remains essential, for this is what will stretch his muscles on the outside and relax those on the inside.(This goal is reiterated, since it has been pursued earlier with single-track lateral movements and the shoulder-in).

The fourth purpose is that of increasing the horse's mental obedience and adding sophistication to his harmonious coordination.

The relationship of the movements of half-pass, pirouette and haunches-in is the core of my thesis.

The half-pass can be performed in all three paces — at the walk, trot and canter. When developing it, the order of training should proceed exactly in this order, from the potentially slowest to the potentially fastest pace. Obviously both collection and balance are easier for the horse to achieve when his bulk is travelling more slowly.

The pirouette can be performed only at the walk and the canter. Some riders pirouette at the trot with their advanced horses by performing a piaffe during which the horse rotates around its hind legs. This movement is not called for in any test and is seldom done but for the purpose of lightening the horses's forehand, creating more engagement, and improving balance and obedience at the piaffe.

The pirouette at the walk should be taught much sooner than at the canter. Between practicing the two together, years may pass. Pirouette at the canter is proof of the highest collection in that pace and therefore the most sophisticated of canter exercises. Pirouette at the walk is much simpler and should be practiced at the early stages of training to introduce the horse to the idea of increased engagement.

Haunches-in can again be performed in all three paces and again may be introduced in the order of walk, trot and canter. I do not recommend its practice in canter since most horses have a tendency to canter with their haunches-in, and the rider must spend considerable effort to straighten them. Insisting on a haunches-in in canter would therefore add to rather than diminish this natural tendency to move crooked in canter. However, with some horses, late in their development, when they respond to the rider's aids immaculately and when they are straight in canter, the haunches-in might be introduced as a preparation for the pirouette! Particularly useful is the haunches-in ridden on a circle, which is being gradually diminished until a pirouette occurs.

The positioning of the horse is very similar in the three movements: the horse should be continuously bent along his spinal column toward the direction of his progression; the horse should be crossing with his outside legs in front of his inside legs; the horse's center of gravity shifts to the side toward which he moves. Because of these similarities, the rider's aids are placed in an identical position for all three exercises and only the degree of aiding might alter according to necessity.

Because the horse is using both his skeleton and his musculature in similar ways and because the rider should aid all three exercises the same way, one should develop a strategy of going from one to another of these movements whenever possible.

Here are some strategies for teaching and practicing the half-pass, pirouette, and haunches-in, including some combinations of them.

With a young horse, you may start a half-pass down enter line (see Fig. 4-1) for a few steps. When you lose control of the flexion or he gets tired, go straight. Then repeat a few steps, always going straight periodically to re-establish control and help the horse learn his balance. With more advanced horses the straight steps help the rider in adjusting his aids, correcting his seat and paying attention to his inside leg staying in contact with the horse.

Performing this two-track exercise on the center line (Fig 4-2) will appear as a haunches-in exercise, although the rider should be aware that he could consider the same a half-pass if he imagines the center line to be the diagonal of another, imaginary manege! Worth noting here, however, is the fact that the haunches-in and the half-pass are very similar but not identical, insofar as the horse should be bent slightly more during the haunches-in and therefore will cross with his legs less deeply than in the half-pass where the crossing should be deeper but the bending less exaggerated (a minor difference).

Fig. 4-3 reinforces the training device that a half-pass across the diagonal is simultaneously a haunches-in along the wall of another imaginary menage.

Fig. 4-4 shows the strategy of developing a good pirouette with the aid of haunches-in. Pirouettes are seldom satisfactory in the shows I judge because of lack of understanding that they are based on control of the horse's haunches, rather than the pulling around of his head and restraining his forward urge. During the pirouette, the horse should be performing a haunches-in, with outside hind leg crossing over the inside hind leg, and should maintain his rhythm and bending. His forehand should merely be guided over an arc. The pattern and strategy illustrated will visually emphasize the idea of controlling the haunches rather than the head!

Fig. 4-5 shows a slightly different variation of a pattern than Fig. 4-4, but one that has the same educational value for both horse and rider.

Fig. 4-7 shows the mirror exercise of the haunches-in, which is of course, the haunches-out. It differs from the haunches-in only insofar as the choice of walls is concerned. The haunches-out you see in the drawing, when moved to the opposite wall, would be called haunches-in. Here we must note, however, that haunches-in is easier to perform

Strategies For Teaching The Half-Pass Pirouette and Haunches-In

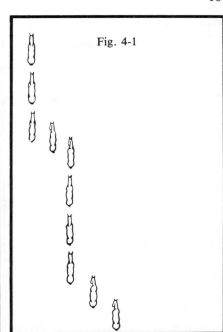

Fig. 4-1

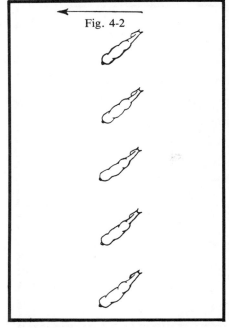

Fig. 4-2

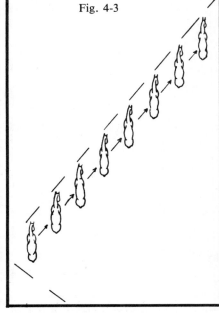

Fig. 4-3

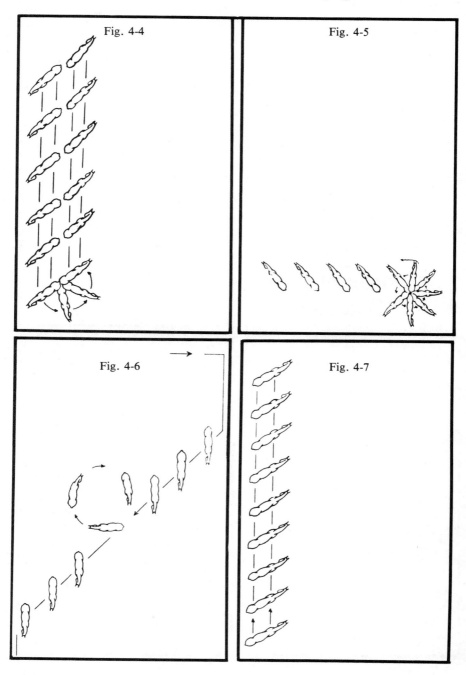

Fig. 4-4

Fig. 4-5

Fig. 4-6

Fig. 4-7

because it begins with the bending of the horse already established in the corner preceding it. When a haunches-out is performed, the horse first has to be counter-flexed, which demonstrates more sophisticated control.

When the horse moves on the center line with his haunches displaced, on two tracks, we may call the movement either haunches-in or haunches-out depending on the hand on which the horse traveled before the exercise started. For example, a horse traveling on center line with haunches to the left will move in haunches-in if it was started from the left hand side, while the horse performing the identical movement but having approached it from the right hand side will be in haunches-out.

Fig. 4-6 shows that when a young horse loses his bending or rhythm or both, they can best be re-established by riding circles after a few steps of half-pass (or haunches-in) and then continuing with the two-track movement.

Exercises like those illustrated can be invented endlessly. The combination of patterns that help develop both the horse's understanding of what he ought to do and his physical ability to do it can be enhanced by patiently varying the patterns and combinations that build the half-pass, pirouette and haunches-in movements.

P

R

U

V

Major Stages Of Canter Pirouette

This is an excellently photographed sequence on the major stages of a Canter Pirouette. Of immense educational value is the opportunity to observe Miss Hilda Gurney riding Keen.

S

T

W

*Photography for sequence
appearing on these two pages
by Hillair Carthine Bell*

*Pic. P: The preparation by collecting the Collected Canter even more until it is
a School Canter.*
Pic. R: The half-halt and School Canter manifesting.
*Pic. S: The haunches under, the horse "sitting" the center of gravity shifted to the
haunches allows the horse to raise the forehand. The rider's seat deep and torso taxing
to accommodate the new center of gravity way behind.*
Pic. T: Forehand rising into the turn as a miniature "rearing."
*Pic. U: All legs off the ground, horse airborn a magnificent moment, demonstrating
that there is still the wholesome basic pace of a canter, clear in beat, impulsive and
powerfully engaged. Nothing "stuck to the ground" but all in flight: as it should be at
the canter!*
*Pics. V & W: Completing the pirouette one can observe the significant role the freedom
of the shoulders play in this most sophisticated movement. During the pirouette the
horse demonstrates the highest degree of collection possible at the canter.*

The Basic Paces and Their Development

How Are The Different Paces Of The Horse Related?

The different paces are the walk, trot, canter and backing. The halt is not a pace because it is a period of immobility. Yet it concerns us as being part of the "natural horse," and during the halt the horse must maintain his forward attitude, being ready to move off zestfully into any pace.

Now that new terminology is used in connection with the trot and because there are a greater number of differentiations within that pace than in others, I would like to create the logical order among the various kinds of trots:

In order determined by length of stride (most to least): *extended, medium, working, collected, passage, piaffe.*

It is worth noting that the "working" trot is no longer necessary when the collected and medium trots have been established. With proper development these should replace the working trot.

In order determined by period of suspension (most to least): passage, extended, medium, collected, working, piaffe.

All two-track movements are shown with the appropriate (to level

113

of development) collection. Note that while the shoulder-in and shoulder-out increase the ability to perform a brilliant collected trot, the half-pass helps the development of a brilliant extended trot (by developing hip and stifle joints and freeing the shoulders). Development of collection, in most cases, is easiest in the trot and by far the most difficult at the walk. The highest degree of collection in the different paces is demonstrated at:

> *Collected* walk - for walk
> *Piaffe* - for trot
> *Pirouette* - for canter

Extensions in all three paces are best demonstrated in the pace done in extension, rather than through figures (such as pirouette above).

In most cases when the natural walk of the horse is poor, his canter will be poor also. When purchasing a dressage prospect, the walk should be scrutinized most carefully, for the improvement of that pace is the most difficult and sometimes impossible. The trot pace is the most easily improved.

While in both the canter and the trot there are periods of suspension, there is none during the walk. While in both walk and canter we ask for pirouettes, we do not perform the same at the trot. The changing of leg order is unique to canter (flying changes) and is not called for, or possible, in the other two paces. While in trot we call for lack of spatial advancement (piaffe), we always advance in the other two paces. While we perform shoulder-in and shoulder-out at both walk and trot, we do not perform the movement in canter. However, one may ride a "plié" in canter, which is an increase in the lateral bending of the cantering horse and invites his inside shoulder to track inward directly in front of the inside hip (for suppling, straightening and elevating the shoulder, thereby freeing the forehand).

Why Is The Walk A Neglected Pace?

Of the three basic gaits, the walk is the most difficult to improve. Therefore, when a rider selects a horse for gymnastic purposes, especially for dressage, he should take good care to select one with a good natural walk. A good walker can be recognized as one moving forward zestfully as if approaching something desirable; he will move with even (four-beat) foot-falls. He will carry his weight with ease, lifting up rather than pushing with well-bending joints of his hindquarters, striding deeply under his perpendicular line of gravity and with a freely extended shoulder reach. His ribcage will swing gently from side to side (like a rocking hammock) demonstrating a relaxation of his musculature, an important sign of the walk being effortless.

Most horses when free and at leisure move about slowly looking for forage, going from mouthful to mouthful seldom on a straight line, rather by side stepping, turning, halting and looking about. Horses will walk only when approaching something of interest. Often, however, instead of walking, they will take flight at a canter or trot when something disturbs their leisurely foraging.

Man for centuries encouraged the development of a good walk by gently herding young horses towards pasturing and watering places. Development of the natural paces of a horse should take place during the first three years of its life, before the added weight of saddle and rider are introduced onto the back. Without this early correct upbringing a horse will often be saddled as a poor natural walker.

Many riders neglect improving the naturally undeveloped walk for various reasons. I feel that for many riders the walk is a derogatory gait. This feeling may not be a conscious one. Yet we realize that as novice riders we all began sitting the horse only at the walk, that being the slowest, smoothest and therefore the safest gait. We may continue to associate the walk with these early equestrian experiences of insecurity, victimization, stiffness, discomfort and agony.

Some skilled riders are simply bored with the walk. Yet those with thorough understanding of dressage and courage for artistic detail will find it intriguing and challenging. I, for one, even believe that "warming up," achieving initial relaxation, should be done at the walk before any trot work commences. However, the majority of riders seem to value the trot as the primary pace for initial relaxation and will relegate the walk to periods of rest. Worse yet, riders resting their horses in walk will not demand the correct gait from the horse but will compromise for any slow creeping movement.

In short, we did not fall in love with the art of riding by being lured to walk. Exhilaration comes easier at the trot and canter as the horse moves faster and more energetically in those gaits. Had we desired to creep along at a slow pace we could have saddled oxen!

At the walk there is no period of suspension as in canter and trot. This major distinction is the key to the difficulties encountered while attempting to improve the gait. The walk is also the potentially slowest of the three basic gaits, thus aggravating the rider's problem. The walk is earthbound; the beauty of the trot and canter depend both on the quality and quantity of their suspensions. We gymnasticize our horses to increase the strength and suppleness of their joints and muscles; our purpose is to enhance their ability to perform a variety of modes in suspension. While we can ride our horse for improved flotation in suspension at trot and canter, we are denied the same opportunity in walk.

Aids are based on changing currently existing balance and harmony. In the slow, earthbound walk such aids become difficult, for the horse, never totally leaving the ground or progressing with speed, is quite capable of accommodating unbalanced situations with ease. Subtle changes in our aiding system may simply be ignored by him.

How Can We Improve The Walk?

Two major dressage principles contribute to the improvement of the walk.

1. The horse develops in his totality. While a broken down piece of machinery may be repaired by fixing the malfunctioning part, a horse can never be improved by attempting to work on the faulty part alone. Therefore appropriate gymnastic work at the trot and canter will remarkably well contribute to the development of the walk.

2. Never the *quantity* but rather the *quality* of aids will improve the gait. Therefore a sluggish walk will not improve by vigorous kicking. Aids too strong for comfort or too rapid will also fail to encourage improvement. The most effective aids will be comfortably gentle, exquisitely coordinated with the horse's movements (hind legs). No gait requires more "feel" than the walk!

The rider can improve the walk through correct aiding and also by logical gymnasticizing:

The rider's legs should be adhesive to the horse's sides. To an observer they should appear as if they were painted there with heels down to increase the strength of the calfs without stiffening them. Invisible pressures with these legs will always be in rhythm and harmony with the horse's movement, will coordinate with seat activities and will have proper strength without inhibiting punitive measures. A deep knee position and well pressed down heels that can best be achieved by merely touching and resting the toes on the stirrups will maintain quiet legs.

The rider should, with quiet legs, insist on keeping his horse parallel with the path of progression. Often the walk fails to develop properly because the horse can evade the rider's sloppy leg aids. Only well attached legs can ensure that the horse will not step off the line of progression with one of his hind legs and that he will progress with equally long strides with both hind legs.

The rider should always be aware of the activities of the horse's hind legs; otherwise he cannot influence and control their activities. Only steadily attached legs can increase the feel of the seat as well as the legs themselves in knowing where the hind legs are and what they are doing. When the left hind leg is striding under the rider's weight, his left leg will be pushed out on the filled up side of the horse's ribcage, while his right leg will sink in on the other, hollowed side of the ribcage. On the horse's full side simultaneously the rider's seatbone will be elevated, while on the hollow side his seatbone will sink. Riders should train themselves to feel the horse's strides by closing their eyes periodically and calling out "right and left" to indicate the side on which the horse's hind leg is striding under the weight.

Both the position and the impulsive activity of the horse's hind legs can be influenced only when leaving the ground and carried forward. Thus a rider can push the left hind leg of the horse back onto the line of progression or forward into a bolder stride only when the left hind leg is leaving the ground. Should the rider fail to detect that instant or should his legs be too far from the horse for pressure, the momentum for improvement will be lost. Loosely hanging legs — haphazardly banging, kicking, nudging — are meaningless annoyances that may disrupt the horse's rhythm. They cannot possibly synchronize with the horse's activities in his hindquarters and they can never be on time for aiding.

For communication, the seatbones are the most important contact in riding. With the help of the tailbone pointing perpendicularly down into the saddle, the seat should be kept perpetually in the saddle while riding dressage. Not only are the activities of the torso communicated through a deep seat, but it also serves to stabilize the legs and allow their independent aiding. A balanced, deep, independent seat is prerequisite to all successful riding.

The middle of the torso (abdomen and small of the back) should always be relaxed and supple. The rider should "sit tall," that is, have his front stretched longer than his back. Yet an overstretched front, resulting in the tailbone leaving the vertical and pointing slightly backwards, will stiffen the torso. The deep seat depends on the suppleness of the torso. Unless the rider's middle can absorb the horse's movements, no pressure with the shoulder's weight can be applied, nor can the back muscles influence.

The back and shoulder areas effect riding by their weight. As mentioned above, their weight becomes effective only through a supple middle, for otherwise the seat will often become light or fall, beating irregularly on the horse's back. In order to serve their useful purposes, the shoulders should be well back, shoulder blades flat in the musculature, and chest elevated. The effect of the weight of the upper torso is often called the "seat aid." This is a misnomer. We must be aware that the seat merely communicates the aiding of the shoulders, and will not in itself wiggle around or shove the saddle, but rather stay steadily distributed over the saddle's surface. The seat also includes the thighs that should be stretched well down toward a stabilizing deep knee.

The hands of the rider should be relaxed. The upper arms should hang naturally downward without any muscle tension. The elbows should help stabilize the hands. The lower arms should effortlessly reach forward toward the horse's mouth. The most active ingredients of the hand aids are supplied by a supple wrist and the fingers. In order for these to be effective the rider must close his fingers on the reins and ride with a closed, rounded fist. The tightening of the fist and the fingers' invitations on the reins should be the only activities for inviting the horse to slow down his front, and the relaxing of fist and the fingers to encourage him to lengthen his front.

As the horse is nodding with his head during a walk, the wrists and fingers should accompany his nodding movement in order to cushion the feel of contact. The wrists and fingers should assure the steadiness of contact revealed by a taut rein. Their function is similar to the tension spring of a tape recorder which by a little needle keeps the tape running always taut, never allowing it either to slacken or to snap.

What Are The Modes Of Walking?

The walk is a pace without suspension, the horse having either two or three feet simultaneously on the ground. Yet when performed with regularity, one should hear four distinct and even footfalls on the ground. The order of footfalls will be as follows: right hind, right fore, left hind, left fore. The legs should lift (not push) off the ground and reach freely forward, with generous, unhurried strides. The rhythm of the footfalls must remain the same in all modes of walking; only the length of the strides will change.

The free walk will be volunteered by a balanced horse as his most comfortable walk under the rider's weight. The horse will carry his rider with a stretched, elevated back. He will stride energetically, with comfortable, elastic, even strides. He will be straight (in lateral balance) and neither hurried nor sluggish, looking purposeful (in longitudinal balance).

The rider should never drop his horse into a free walk but rather liberate him into it through stretching. By momentary strengthening of all the aids, including the rein contact, the rider will perform a half-halt. Then, by yielding his fingers and wrists while continuing to drive, the rider will invite his horse to "chew the reins out of his hands." The action will be gradual and continuous as the horse stretches his neck and head first forward and then downward. Abruptly yanking the reins downward or only lowering the neck without the forward stretch first are both incorrect activities. However, when correctly stretched, the horse will lengthen his strides evenly to accommodate his now longer frame.

The horse, once stretched to the free walk, should be encouraged to move straight. The rider's seat, legs and hands will guide him to do so. At the free walk the reins should not be totally abandoned and held at the buckle. Rather, they should be stretched to the utmost still held by the horse on light contact in his new, stretched position. Thus, the reins will remain a secret guiding instrument of straightness at the head and neck. Yet no neck reining should ever occur. The substantial weight of the head and neck should not be allowed to fall sideways, for in that case his body which follows will have to meander after it in support of its weight.

The rider's head and shoulders should be floating above the long and supple movements of the abdomen and small of the back which are to absorb the rhythm of the free walk. Shoulders should never fall (tilt) backwards in an attempt to drive for longer strides.

The rider's legs will not only maintain impulsion and encourage long strides, but will need to guide the horse on a straight path, catching the horse's attempt to deviate from the straight path with his hindquarters.

The ordinary walk serves as a point of reference when speaking of other modes of walk. At the ordinary walk the horse must submit to and comply with the rider's aids. He must be longitudinally bent into an attitude shorter, therefore taller, than in the free walk. He will walk with his hind legs into the hoofprints of his forelegs. An athletically suitable horse, moving at the ordinary walk, on the aids, striding correctly as described above, will cover a distance of 330 feet (100 meters) per minute. The ordinary walk must be developed on a measured path with the aid of a clock. The rider should retain the "feel" of the walk when it is the required 330 feet/minute output and insist on performing it at that rate. All the aids are at the rider's disposal to regulate the walk until this goal is attained.

At the collected walk the horse will stride with higher, consequently shorter, steps than in the ordinary walk. As a result of shorter, higher stepping, his frame will be shorter from head to tail. His hindquarters will be engaged and lowered, thereby carrying less weight on the forehand and elevating the neck and head. The essence of a collected walk is in the high and energetic activity of the hind legs and not in the shortening of strides. Therefore, driving is the most essential ingredient of its creation.

The rider will have to drive into half-halts to make the horse understand that he is to elevate his steps rather than extend or hurry them. The rider will feel as if progressing uphill, for the horse will lower his croup, lighten his forehand.

The aids must be in perfect harmony with the horse's hind legs. The legs must aid into the hollowing side of the horse, folding under the sinking ribcage. The rider's body must be well stretched from the seat up to keep the spinal column straight (the neck is part of it!) for the performance of half-halts, and from the seat down, stretching the knees, calfs and heels, for synchronized leg aids.

At the extended walk the horse should stride longer, therefore lower, than in the ordinary walk. His hind hoofs will print past the hoofprints of the forelegs. Consequently, he will have to lengthen his neck, creating a longer frame. As with collection, extension is a matter of degree.

Again the most important element of aiding will be the drive.

The legs should drive with stroking movements, yet without leaving the horse's side, in order to drive forward in exact harmony with the horse's hind leg as it leaves the ground. Too often untimely driving aids create undesirable short, hurried steps.

The hands must remain in contact with the horse's mouth. Yet the feeling at the hands is an opening of the reins, "pushing" them forward, encouraging the horse to keep contact.

In conclusion:

1. The various modes of walk must be performed in identical rhythm, the footfalls remaining in the same even four beats.

2. All other modes of walk are relative to the ordinary walk. Free, collected and extended walk represent degrees of alterations on the ordinary walk.

3. The horse develops in his totality. All gymnastic exercises other than the walk will contribute to the improvement of it.

4. The gymnastic accomplishment of a horse is measured by how greatly he can lengthen or shorten his strides while maintaining an even rhythm, in good impulsion, well balanced and always paralleling the path on which he moves with his spinal column. To "coil" and "spread" your horse, making him an elastic accordion that never loses the rhythm of its tune, one must create an elastic horse interested in the aids.

5. Have a positive attitude towards the walk.

6. Rest your horse in canter and trot, too. Yet when resting him at the walk, insist on a free walk on loose but not dropped reins.

7. Use smooth aids that are synchronized with the horse's movements. Keep well stretched legs perpetually working within the horse's musculature in order to remain subtle, harmonious and rhythmic in your aids.

8. Be aware that as your create relatively higher (collected) or lower (extended) strides than the ordinary walk, the horse's frame becomes accordingly shorter or longer. Therefore, never think in terms of slower or faster steps.

9. When riding, close your eyes often in order to develop a keen feel of the horse's hindquarters. The visible part of the horse (head and neck) is only symptomatic of the activities of the "invisible" parts (hindquarters and back). We must ride the "invisible" areas, for the head and neck serve to balance the hindquarter's activities.

What is the Difference Between Medium Trot and Working Trot?

In the past, the "ordinary trot" was often required in lower level dressage tests. This trot has also been discussed in some of the most reputable equestrian literature. The ordinary trot, however, is no longer required in dressage tests but needs mention in my introduction to serve the purpose of contrasting with it, as standard, the working and medium trots.

The ordinary trot is usually offered by a horse that is suitably built for sports riding. When a horse with suitable conformation is allowed to carry his rider in a comfortable trot, on light aids and in open country, he will offer a so-called ordinary trot. That trot will approximate the horse's natural (unimproved) movement under the rider's weight. The average horse will cover about 220 yards per minute at this ordinary trot.

The working trot differs from the ordinary trot, naturally offered by the green horse, in that it must show additional effort. This effort (that is, improved impulsion) makes the horse work beyond the trot he would offer when no demands are placed on him by the rider. A horse performing the working trot should perform a rounder motion, due to added (increased) engagement at the joints in his hindquarters.

The working trot enables the horse to maintain his balance through the corners of a dressage arena and to remain balanced on larger arced lines, such as a circle. Due to the increased mobilization of his joints (skeletal improvement), he will be able to develop those muscles that foster increased bending. As a result, in addition to improved balance, lateral bending will also increase.

The working trot is asked for in lower level dressage tests because in a test a rider is expected to show a certain degree, however small, of improvement over the naturally offered, ordinary paces. The very readiness of a horse for testing must be demonstrated by these improvements in the gaits, balance and suppleness. Thus, even in lower level dressage tests, to demand "working" from a horse is reasonable. Without his ability to work with his joints, he could not correctly perform the geometric patterns of the test; for those patterns demand improved balance and suppleness.

The medium trot is a pace between the working trot and the extended trot. While the working trot may still be highly individualized, the medium trot should represent (demonstrate) more uniform standards of appearance. Depending on conformation, horses will perform highly diversified working trots. They might all be working; i.e. engaging in the trot, and in spite of that look different in their effort, as the individual horses will represent different breeds and different conformations.

In the medium trot, however, the horse is expected to show a lengthening of his strides, greater power (impulsion) of locomotion and, as a result, an improved carriage. The tempo (ground covered within certain time unit) of the medium trot is greater than that of the working trot. The horse carries himself in a shorter position, his neck somewhat higher and, in spite of lengthened strides, also strides higher off the ground. In short, the medium trot should show greater suspension than does the working trot.

During the dressaging of a horse, the working trot is achieved sooner than the medium trot. Care must be taken that in both, the rhythm of the horse remains immaculately even and without much visible aiding. Both the working and the medium trot benefit from frequent transitions from one to the other during daily riding. Initially, posting the medium trot may be helpful in the horse's understanding that the length of his stride must increase. While sitting, the working trot may enable the rider to keep the rhythm of his horse while working him toward improved impulsion.

In summary, remember that both the working trot and the medium trot are improvements over the voluntarily offered ordinary trot which is not a "show quality movement." The working trot may be more individualized (according to breed and individual conformation) while the medium trot is more uniform in its execution. The working trot clearly demonstrates increased engagement at the joints with resultant improvement of balance and therefore execution of laterally bent patterns. It also demonstrates that the medium trot must be bolder than the working trot, showing a longer stride (greater tempo) and a prouder carriage than did the working trot.

How is the Extended Trot Developed?

A well-pronounced, expressive extended trot alternating with collected trot can well be the highlight of a dressage program.

What is an extended trot? It is a trot during which the horse swings his legs as far forward from the hips and shoulders as is possible by his conformation. The legs act as pendulums, suspended from the hips and shoulders, swinging freely forward while the hoofs remain relatively close to the ground, describing a generous, even arc.

It is a trot full of impulsion during which the horse's hindquarters, acting as the motor, push the horse forward in rhythmic elasticity and with full force. This greatest power of locomotion is communicated to the totally outstretched forelegs by a relaxed and swinging back. Its importance lies in the full lengthening of the strides as opposed to continued short strides with increased frequency of beats, which is rushing.

In compliance with the horse's ground-gaining, powerful movement forward, the horse's body floats longitudinally through the air. His carriage becomes extremely steady and his front hoofs print the ground where the imaginary line extending down the forehead and nose will pierce the ground. The horse's forehead and nose, in profile, may be stretched slightly forward from the perpendicular position. Under no circumstances should the profile point toward the chest, going behind the perpendicular position.

There are two common faults seen at the extended trot.

1. When the horse is held too tight on the rein he will be crowded, cramped and restrained in the front. In such a case the horse cannot use his back to develop and communicate (transfer) the locomotion of the hindquarters with a swinging back to the forelegs. Consequently, the front feet will step on the ground behind the point indicated while in the air. The effect will be similar to boxing or "goose stepping."

2. When the horse goes behind the bit and his forehead is behind the perpendicular (to the ground) line, in profile, he is not moving forward but is resisting and evading the movement. His weight shifts to the forehand and while his strides may become more frequent and rushing, he will not fully lengthen them. Since the horse can stretch his forelegs only as far out as a straight line from his face to the ground, he cannot step out far enough to accommodate any extended strides of the hind legs, hence extension will not occur.

How to create an extended trot? In order to increase the tempo of the trot, the rider increases the drive with the legs, also increasing the pressure of his seatbones (by using the small of the back), while continuing a steady, even rein, which yields as the horse's stride lengthens.

Driving with the legs may be done by simultaneous pressure of both legs or by alternating leg pressures, using each leg separately at the time when the horse pushes forward with his hind leg on the corresponding side. I personally believe the simultaneous leg pressure system to be both easier and more effective. To apply alternate leg pressures effectively, the rider must be most accomplished in coordination. Even then it can easily produce a swaying effect, so that the horse will not travel extremely straight, but will sway from side to side. This side to side swaying will shorten the strides and disrupt the general harmony of the horse's carriage. His back will remain slightly rigid and strained. Needless to say, the transiton into the next movement will be impaired. A horse moving on a straight line in walk and trot uses both sides of his body the same way. Therefore, I believe that simultaneous aids on both sides communicate more effectively and produce better results.

To increase the driving potency of the seat, the rider can increase the seat pressure by filling his lungs with air, holding the air in, which widens the chest, and flexing (tightening) his back and abdomen muscles. Meanwhile the seat must continue to follow the everlengthening swing of the horse's back which results from the lengthening strides.

The aids must be firm but calm and should be repeated until the horse will step with his hind legs forward under the center of his gravity with full power. It is crucial to keep an even two-beat rhythm. Should any violation to the clarity of beat (evenness) occur, the horse must be taken up to a shorter trot, comfortable enough for him to recover his balance.

The desire and willingness of the horse to go forward can best be built on long, straight lines, which if lacking in outdoor space, can best be found on the diagonal of a small arena. However, as the horse becomes willing to perform this powerful movement, extensions can be produced on any shorter, straight stretches. The horse, which is not able to naturally carry himself and his rider in the extended trot, may find the shorter stretches easier at first.

As the horse increases his tempo by stretching into extensions, he will freely swing his legs, like aforementioned pendulums, from the hips and the shoulders. At the beginning this movement will result in the lowering of the neck and head position. It is not considered a fault and should not be corrected by tightening the rein. As the horse matures in this movement and becomes capable of keener engagement of his joints and muscles, his balance will improve. With that improvement, the head and neck position will automatically come to its ideal place. A horse moving with impulsion and in balance will inevitably present the correct neck and head position.

Often Asked Questions:

What are the Most Common Mistakes in Creating an Extended Trot, and How Can the Rider Correct Them?

Never gather or invite a horse into a tighter rein. Do not always drive with the legs by banging on the horse's sides. If that action seems necessary, it is a sure sign that the horse has not been properly prepared for the extended trot. The forward urge is still missing and the horse is not yet ready to fully use his hip, stifle, hock and pastern. Do innumerable transitions to improve the forward urge (with light but sufficient aids) and do lateral bending exercises for further strengthening of joints and muscles.

If the horse responds to your aids by extending but with stiff spread hind legs, he lacks strength, and his joints are stiff. Continue lateral bending exercises and longitudinal transitions.

If the horse creates "goose steps," like the soldiers of the old Prussian army, with forelegs stiffly kicking up, showing the bottom of his hoofs, then the horse is rigid in his back. His back must be made to swing long to communicate the impulsion from rear to front. Proceed to strengthen the back muscles by cross country work, cavaletti work, jumping from trot and climbing. To limber up the now strengthened back and invite swing, proceed with longitudinal transitions and try extensions while posting.

It can happen that the horse will strike a canter when asked to extend the trot. When that happens, determine which one of the following three major reasons caused the canter and remedy it accordingly.

1. The horse strikes the canter as a result of exuberance and too much forward urge. In this case, drive the horse straight and forward in canter until he is calm, balanced and yielding. Then take him quietly up to a regular, balanced trot and repeat the aids for the extended trot.

2. The horse strikes the canter because he is crooked. He may only canter with his hind legs and continue to trot in the front. He will fall on his shoulder as a result of losing his balance. In such a

case, take the horse back to trot instantly but gently, straighten him and ride him forward to a lesser degree of extended trot that could be performed on a gentle serpentine line.

3. The horse strikes the canter as a resistance to extension. He will curl his neck, go behind the bit (spit it out), switch his tail, or elevate his neck and head (empty his back). He is cantering resistantly, evading the rider's legs and seat aids. In this case, continue to drive the horse forward at the canter until he quietly stretches his back, lowers his neck, stretching it forward. When that is achieved, however long a time it may take, only then take the horse back to the trot and repeat the aids for extension.

The greatest enemies of extended trot are inability to fully lengthen the strides, and uneven leg order. Riders must realize that the extended trot may not develop because of their own shortcomings. The above essay presumes the rider to be both skilled and sensitive. Riders must guard against extensive and unwarranted use of spurs. They must have hands willing and able to yield generously. They must have a balanced and supple seat. Riders who still bounce in the saddle, lose their balance, need to grip the horse with their leg to remain in the saddle or pull on the reins to ensure a false sense of security should not yet try extended trot with their horses.

When posting on the outside diagonal, do you feel the inside seatbone tap the saddle more firmly than the outside? Or vice-versa?

Posting on the outside diagonal at the trot is the correct way of posting. When posting the outside diagonal, the rider's seat rises when the horse's outside hind leg is on the ground and his inside hind leg in flight forward. The rider is reached by the saddle (and thus gets seated) when the horse's inside hind leg touches ground and his outside one is suspended. If the rider sits correctly while posting on the outside diagonal, she will feel the inside seatbone tap the saddle more firmly than the outside one, indeed! The reason is that the rider touches the surface of the saddle when the horse's inside hind leg touches the ground. At that time the two bulks, those of the rider and the horse, meet with each other for a moment, the rider's bulk being lowered, the horse's being stabilized on the inside. The resultant feeling is a stronger pressure under the inside seatbone.

This feeling may further be exaggerated when trotting on an arc, whether it is a simple corner or a full circle. For when a rider bends a horse correctly onto an arc, he will not only use his boots to do so but will also use his torso! While bending a horse onto an arc, the rider's shoulders (and consequently his hips and seatbones) will parallel the position of the horse's shoulders. As the inside shoulder of the horse "falls" slightly behind the further advanced outside shoulder, so must the rider harmonize by retarding with his inside shoulder relative to his outside one. This is the position that makes the imaginary line which connects the rider's shoulders point exactly to the center of the circle. All "feeling" riders can testify that when one rotates one's torso in the manner described above there will be more weight developed over the inside seatbone. When an instructor correctly suggests that one should weight the inside seatbone when riding on a circle, he should add that the weighting is induced by the correct shoulder position of the rider, that being the inside shoulder's rotation backward.

I have always been taught to change at X when coming across the diagonal. When executing an extended trot rising, would it be improper to change before starting across the diagonal?

Yes, it would be improper to change the posting diagonal at the beginning of the diagonal while extending the trot.However, your reasoning, in general, is correct: changing the posting diagonal at X is disturbing the balance of the horse that is performing the extended trot. Therefore, the proper way to do it is to change the posting diagonal at the end of the diagonal, when you are arriving at the opposite wall.

There are two reasons for this strategy:

1. To change the posting diagonal at the beginning of an extended trot would upset the horse's balance more than it would by changing at X, where at least he is already in the "swing of things." At the beginning of the diagonal, when you stretch the horse's body and lengthen his stride, he has to adjust to a new balance. The rider should not add to the difficulty of this task by doing things with his seat.

2. As the horse arrives at the end of the diagonal, however, he is once again "collected back" (relatively speaking) to a more comfortable and more familiar stride. For this reason he will find a change in

the rider's posting diagonal easy to accommodate without losing his balance or blemishing his rhythm. Furthermore, the very act of changing posting diagonal, that is remaining seated for one stride in order to rise on another, may contribute to a successfully smooth collection through the seat aid. At the same time the horse should be re-bent (laterally flexed) to the new direction, and changing the posting diagonal then, when the horse is laterally flexed again, can contribute to the success of the bending too; his inside hock will be invited at the right time to swing under and carry more weight.

I have long awaited a clarification by judges (on forums) or test writers of this very question. I, for one, was taught to change position always at the terminus of the diagonal, not only when extending! I understood the logic of this strategy to be the same as I have explained above. I realize that at the time you travel over X you arrive on the "new rein," but as the horse is required to be arrow straight on the diagonal, from the point of view of his balance he does not change rein until he reaches the arrival corner!

Is a trot which is difficult to sit a powerful one and thus good, or is it something which can be improved with training?

A trot that is difficult to sit is not necessarily a good, powerful one. Nor is a soft trot one that is inferior.

A rough trot, difficult to sit, is rather a sign of rigidity. There are two kinds of rigidity. One is result of stiffness in joints and muscles; the other could be caused by unfavorable conformation.

If the rough trot is a result of stiff (ungymnasticized) joints (hip, stifle, hock, pastern) then dressaging (gymnasticizing) will not only improve it but will eventually eliminate it. However, if the rough trot is a result of a conformation problem then it will continue to stay that way, with some mellowing, despite gymnasticizing. Typical conformation problems that cause a rough trot are: (a) short, direct pasterns (perpendicular), (b) direct and wide shoulders, (c) an extremely short and heavily muscled back combined with low withers. When conformation creates the rough trot, the horse will eventually soften, because problems on a green horse are further aggravated by stiffness in the joints and rigidity of the musculature.

In general, I would advise against horses with a rough trot for the following reasons:

If it is a conformation problem, the horse will not only be unpleasant to ride for years, but will have a tendency of breaking down sooner than another with good conformation doing the same tasks. A rough trotting horse is not only jarring to the rider but similarly jars himself, "sledgehammering" his own joints, resulting in easier breaking down under stress. After all, we dressage horses to make them elastic for their own sakes! We ride to improve horses! A horse that cannot be improved for his own sake is not worth the human effort.

If roughness is due to stiffness of joints and rigidity of muscles, however, the horse can be infinitely improved. Yet, why would a rider, who has a choice in determining which horse to select, want to start with a markedly stiff one? Such a horse will just stretch the training timetable unnecessarily and will handicap the performance schedule of an ambitious competitor. Also, before the horse improves, the rider will have a long period of unpleasant rough riding. It may even damage the seat of the rider, introduce stiffness and contribute to irritable temperament.

In short, try to work with a young, green horse, who donates to your efforts a good conformation and natural elasticity, and you will not only be ahead of the game in terms of training, but will find pleasure in your daily riding.

Have you ever heard of "talk" with the outside rein (half-halts), when cantering?

I have a bit of resistance to the expression "talk with the inside rein." However, we must never quarrel over terminology, but rather trust that we can understand each other in spite of words. One should never just talk with any rein, really! I often judge riders in competition who do oscillate, tremble, play, jitter and fuss with one or both reins in order to engage their horse's attention or bend his neck. Unfortunately, they get both results: the horse fidgets on the rein, including at the restless halt that follows, and the horse "breaks his neck" far behind the poll, while continuing to evade with the hindquarters. That kind of damaging "talk" with the rein I strongly disapprove of!

However, I presume you mean half-halting correctly with the outside rein during canter. Right? Indeed, I recommend that a rider use the outside rein to half-halt with during canter! Again presuming that the rider sits correctly during the canter, his inside shoulder (torso), elbow, therefore hand and rein, will be in an advanced position in comparison with the corresponding elements on his outside. Therefore, generally speaking (unless correcting special faults), the rider's inside rein is "feeling forward" into the horse's bounding movement. The purpose is to encourage ever deeper (freer) strides for the horse's inside hind leg. This ensures the impulsive, generous, round, free canter we desire.

However, the outside rein, on the outer hand, controls the activities of the horse's outside hind leg (rein of opposition). As each canter bound commences with the outside hind leg touching the ground (after the period of suspension or flight when no legs were on the ground), the length of the canter bound is determined by the length of the flight. Collection and extension of canter can best be regulated with the outside rein (provided it is a mere extension of the workings of the rider's seat, as it should be). As the inside rein's job is to follow the horse's head movement (in tiny circularly yielding movement), allowing it to balance forward impulsion, it is doing the job of creating the roundness of the movement. The outside rein, on the other hand, must regulate how long the canter leap may be! Indeed, it must half-halt into the movement to do so.

The length of the horse's canter stride can best be determined at the time of his suspension (flotation). If you want to shorten the stride (and make it correspondingly higher: collect), you must shorten the distance of his flotation and bring his outside hind leg sooner to the ground. That can be done well with the half-halt on the outside rein. Obviously, the half-halt has to be performed at the right time, that is when the horse's inside foreleg leaves the ground to join the other three legs, already suspended, in flight.

As far as other paces are concerned, an exhaustive answer would take much space. However, in brief, let it suffice to say that when the horse must be ridden on parallel aids — that is, in rein-back, at the walk and trot on straight lines — both hands must perform half-halts (as a result of even use of back muscles and shoulder position). On arcs, however, at the walk and trot, just as at the canter, the horse is on "diagonal aids." Therefore, the half-halt should be performed on the outside rein, too!

Accuracy of circles on the counter lead at canter seems difficult since the horse's spine does not follow the arc of the circle.

The counter-canter is an exercise that helps perfect the horse's balance, strengthens the back muscles behind the saddle, and establishes utmost obedience to the rider's aids: thus it effects the horse's skeleton, musculature, and mentality. It's worth noting that all three of these attributes are very important for jumping horses also.

In counter-canter the hind legs of the horse must continue to move toward the hoofprints of the forelegs, exactly as when cantering on the "usual" lead. When performing the counter-canter on a circle (or arc) the hind legs must still continue to move toward the hoofprints of the front legs. The hind legs must track on the arc of the prescribed circle and under no circumstances deviate outward from that pattern. Nor should the forelegs track off to the outside of the prescibed circular arc. In short, both fore and hind legs must stay on the arc of the circle.

As the horse must maintain a continuous but mild flexion towards the lead, at the counter-canter on the circle he will not parallel the arc of the circle with his spinal column. Rather, he will be counter flexed, yet so mildly that while maintaining his balance in collection only his head and neck will be slightly bent away from the circular arc to the outside.

There are several frequent mistakes that must be avoided.

The horse may cross-canter or change lead when asked to perform the counter-canter on a circle. To avoid this, make sure your aids are strong and correct — outside leg back, inside leg just behind the girth and insisting on maintenance of bending to the lead, lightly contacting outside rein steadily offered but never pulled, inside rein following horse's head movement and yielding on every stride, which means fast but in the proper rhythm (outside and inside refer to the side of the horse's lead). Rider's shoulders must continue those of the horse; the one to the lead slightly advanced over the outside shoulder, allowing proper weight distribution and the continued sliding (driving) aid of the inside seatbone.

The horse may evade collection by deviating outward, with his haunches off the circular track, not following with inside hind leg towards the hoofprints of inside foreleg. To avoid this error, make sure the pattern of your ride is sufficiently large for the horse's development in collection. Ride a circle on the rein on which the horse's lead is (that is, right lead canter ridden first at a circle to the right) and notice the mild lateral flexion which should be continuous. Then track on to an opposite circle, maintaining the same lead but taking good care not to exaggerate the lateral flexion, particularly at the neck, which is easy to manipulate.

The horse may lose his balance due to a premature attempt or too tight a pattern, and hurry (faster rhythm or longer strides), as well as lean inward on the circle at counter-canter. In order to prevent loss of balance make sure you do not start counter-canter too soon on a full circle, and once on a circle that it is not too small. Make sure your weight remains on the inside seatbone and properly over the horse's center of gravity, rather than leaning out away from the lead (which means leaning in toward the center of the circle). That is, do not "fall away" from the lead to the outside, thereby forcing the horse to lean also in order to "catch up" with your falling weight.

The worst mistake of all occurs as a result of the horse being incorrectly flexed while counter-cantering on an arc. For instance, the horse on a left lead moving on an arc to the right and being bent to the right. In this case, when the horse is bending onto the arc on which he moves but is on the opposite lead, we cannot even call the action counter-canter, but must label it "on the wrong lead." We do this because the movement produces no gymnastic benefits (as listed in the beginning of this article). Cantering "on the wrong lead" contributes to the breakdown (rather than improvement) of the horse's balance, rhythm, collection, obedience, and strength. Few good jumps follow a turn performed this way. The rider who lands on the inappropriate lead should either change lead or collect the horse to a proper counter-canter with the proper bend before facing the next obstacle.

I want to emphasize that counter-canter, while improving balance and demonstrating collection and submission to the rider's aids, is most important for its strengthening a set of muscles behind the saddle. Only the counter-canter and the rein-back develop these muscles and force the horse to tax them. These muscles are important for lowering the croup and bending the haunches, and therefore needed for many high level gymnastic exercises. Therefore what the counter-canter, particularly on a circle, can develop, cannot be developed properly by any other exercise; it has no substitute. For this reason it is an exercise of great value when correctly done. This is also one of the reasons (along with improved balance) why counter-canter is a prerequisite for starting flying changes!

Remember that the counter-canter can be performed only with a horse that can perform the collected canter. That the patterns must be generous at first (never full circles) and become sophisticated only when the horse demonstrates proper balance. That the bending to the lead must be mild and continuous. That the hind legs must never be allowed to deviate in any way from the circle (as in the haunches-out), nor the neck to be sharply positioned away from the circle's arc. The horse's bend is proper only when the hind legs are allowed to follow into the hoofprints of the forelegs in calm and comfort. The bending will still occur because of the horse's musculature possibilities: slightly contracting muscles on the lead side and stretching them on the other. Never create flexion by stretching the horse's skeleton!

Some Advice on the Aiding and Timing of Flying Changes

While I intend to telescope in on the exact timing and correct application of the aids for a flying change, I will back up momentarily for a larger panorama. Both the horse and the rider should be ready for the correct execution of a flying change of lead at the canter. To be sure, horses will change leads on many occasions voluntarily, and often do so while jumping a course, during a polo game, or while working cattle under a western saddle. Often they do so improperly because they are "thrown over" to the other lead; that is, they change lead in desperation as they seek to re-establish their balance under a rider who grossly upset it.

The purposes of dressage, however, demand that we do only that which enhances the horse's correct gymnastic development. Only a physically and mentally well-prepared horse will react to adequate aids and with ease execute a useful act correctly. In dressage we do not do things under the ethic *"l'art pour l'art,"* but rather as a gymnastically sound and valuable act fostering the horse's development.

The rider is ready to perform the aids for a flying change when, in addition to a balanced and independent seat, he has acquired a deep and elastic seat. Once he has done so, he can best demonstrate his achievement by riding an extended trot. He should be able to drive and follow the extended trot without lightening the weight in his seat

Hillair Carthine Bell

*Miss Hilda Gurney, on Keen,
riding the Extended Canter.
Without frequent, bold extensions,
the horse as an athlete will not
develop properly. The extended
canter is much more important as
a means of gymnastic
development than is the extended
trot, which is an "end" (goal) of
gymnastic development. Before
any flying changes can be
developed the horse must do
outstanding work at the extended
canter, such as seen on this
picture: Relaxed, balanced,
rhythmic, impulsive and engaged!*

as he elastically absorbs the horse's movements. He will then maintain a light and even contact with the reins, show steady, relaxed legs staying along the horse's sides, and a perpendicularly upright position in spite of deep knees.

The horse is ready for the flying change if he can maintain elasticity in performing the extended trot, half-passes at the trot and a collected canter. The horse should also demonstrate his maturity or readiness by smoothly performing transitions from the canter to halt and from collected to extended to collected canter. While elasticity in the horse is detectable in many ways, I listed those movements and transitions that are most revealing or symptomatic of that condition of readiness.

The canter movement is comprised of five phases, the sixth being the resumption of the first phase belonging to the next canter bound. (See Fig. 5-1 for a better understanding of these phases.)

1. The outside hind leg starts the movement and remains on the ground while the other three legs are above the ground in suspension.

2. The outside fore and the inside hind join the outside hind on the ground, leaving the inside foreleg suspended.

3. The inside hind and the outside fore remain on the ground as the outside hind leaves it, and the inside fore approaches it.

4. The inside foreleg arrives on the ground, while the three others are suspended.

5. All four legs leave the ground, suspending the entire horse in flight.

The fifth phase, when the horse is suspended in air with all four of his legs off the ground, is that moment when the horse has the option to come down on either hind leg for the commencement of this next canter bound. Now it is up to the rider and his aids to determine whether his horse will commence the next movement on the original lead (on the outside hind leg again) or change leads, commencing the movement on the inside hind leg.

From the rider's point of view, only the last two phases, the fourth and fifth phases of the canter bound preceding the flying change, are of concern. He will have to prepare the change on the fourth and execute it on the fifth phase.

The rider must use diagonal aids during the canter; that is, his inside leg is positioned and is aiding differently than his outside leg. As always, during the canter too, the rider's seat must parallel the horse's

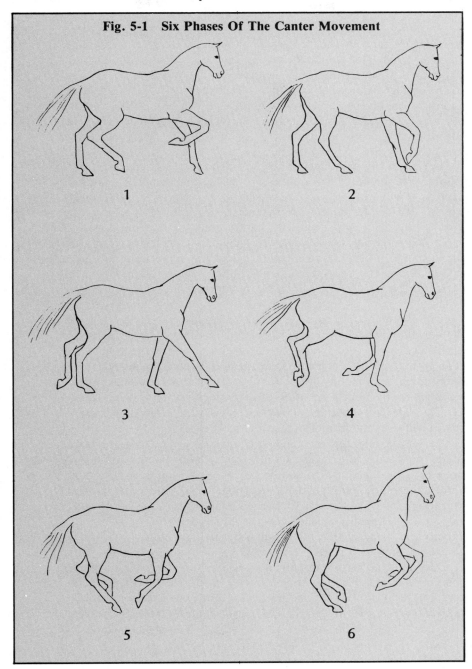

Fig. 5-1   Six Phases Of The Canter Movement

position. Because the horse's inside shoulder and hip move slightly ahead of his outside shoulder and hip, the rider's inside shoulder and hip must also be slightly ahead of those on the outside.

The correct seat during the canter places the rider's inside shoulder and therefore his inside elbow and hand slightly ahead of those on the outside. Because his inside hip also slightly leads over the outside, his corresponding seatbone, knee and leg will slightly lead over those same parts of his body on the outside.

The correct aids are related to the rider's diagonal seat and to the harmonies that the horse naturally offers during the canter. The outside hand is steady, offering a direct rein which determines the horse's length of stride. As that outside rein acts as a rein of opposition to the outside hind leg which begins the canter bound, it has the power to bring that hind leg down sooner or later (shorten or lengthen) after suspension. The inside hand is generous, yielding to the head movement of the horse, encouraging a rounder, more elastic action with the horse's inside hind leg. It will encourage impulsion by its generosity.

The rider's outside leg is steadily holding the horse's hindquarters in control and helps facilitate the lateral bending to the inside. It urges the horse on and forward with slightly stroking pressures. The rider's inside leg is positioned somewhat ahead, just behind the girth, giving a slightly nicking aid to create both impulsion and to maintain the longitudinal bending inward. The rider should synchronize the inside leg aid with the horse's elevation of the inside (leading) foreleg (phase 1). The rider's outside leg, however, should aid when the horse is suspended over the inside foreleg (phase 4).

The seat should feel as if it is anchored at the outside seatbone, (under pressure of the outside shoulder) while allowing the inside seatbone to float ahead on the saddle (as the inside shoulder floats and with it the inside hand yields). When felt by the rider, the resulting sensation is as if the horse is forwarded by the outside leg and the outside seatbone steadily pushing toward the inside knee.

Now the flying change. For aiding the flying change, we must be concerned only with phases four and five of the canter. In phase four, one can see the horse's outstretched foreleg on the ground, slowly slant backward as his body travels over it. With that movement of the receding inside foreleg of the horse, the rider's inside (forward) leg must slowly recede. It travels backward on the horse's side into an "outside" leg position. As a result of the rider having changed his leg position to that opposite of what it was, his entire seat and hand position should change along harmoniously.

In phase five, the horse is suspended above the ground and comes into easy harmony with the rider's new position. Being without anchorage to the ground, the horse can re-flex himself into a new lateral bend. By the time his flight is concluded, he will exercise the option of touching down with the opposite hind leg on the ground. The flying change will have been performed! Two words of caution:

1. Before asking for a flying change, produce an impulsive, collected canter with a somewhat exaggerated lateral bend in the horse. As you change your position and with it your aids during phase four, do it harmoniously so that during phase five you can once again exaggerate the lateral flexion to the opposite side.

2. I disagree with any advice to lighten your seat at the time of the flying change to facilitate an exuberant changeover, or even to extend the canter before the change. On the contrary, make sure your seatbones stay deep in the saddle with full contact, and in order to do so, stay very erect in the saddle. By bouncing forward, looking down, or any so-called "lightening" activities, you deny the horse the feeling of your having changed position in the saddle. Your seat is the most important contact area through which you communicate the change! If anything, then, collect the horse more intensely by running a half-halt through the horse just prior to the change of lead. Keep your head well up and even give your chin a slight upright jerk as you look from the old inside to the direction of your new inside. As you change your leg position, do it along the horse's side without leaving it. By kicking you will surely aid out of tempo!

In summary, remember that the timing for your aids is during phases four and five. The action of your aids can be synchronized by starting to move your inside leg backward at the same time as the horse's inside foreleg moves backward under his progressing body. The rest of your position (legs, seatbones, shoulders and hands) should follow as a consequence of your new position. Your seat and torso should remain relaxed and well stretched upright to allow the horse to feel your new attitude.

Why is it that a horse that can perform
the flying change of lead at the canter on every stride
will continue to make mistakes?

There has been some knowledgeable discussion in the past about the flying changes on every stride not being a natural movement, and that therefore they should not be included in dressage, which is committed to the development of the natural paces of the horse. I certainly do not wish to encourage or enter into debate on the "naturalness" of the flying changes on every stride but mention it merely to introduce the notion of how difficult the correct execution of that movement may be.

I think that the primary difficulty of that movement, as far as the horse is concerned, is its great demand for perfect coordination! In answer to the question asked above, while the flying change on every stride is not the "mostest" in anything like suppleness, collection, bending, balance, etc., it is certainly the movement that is "king" for the demonstration of immaculate coordination.

Flying changes of lead on every stride demand from the horse perfect balance, suppleness and collection but only as means to the end of demonstrating that he can use these elements to perform acts extremely fast in perfect harmony. The horse not only has to change the use of his leg order in seconds while floating in momentary suspension, but must also change his center of gravity with split second accuracy in order to remain straight throughout the exercise. An incredible athletic feat, especially under the foreign weight of the rider and considering that the rider may expect perfect coordination from his large mount but does not recognize the lack of it in himself.

Let us suppose, however, that the rider's balance and coordination are perfect, his timing and rhythm are accurate to the split second and the problem of making mistakes remains with the horse. I doubt, however, that such is the case when problems arise. But let us suppose we are dealing with a "perfect rider" and a horse that knows the flying changes on every stride, but "messes it up" in tests.

My suggestion is to repeat the exercise very often with the horse! Do it both on straight patterns (diagonals and wall) and also on a large circle with the diameter that of the width of the dressage arena (for balance perfecting). By frequent repetition one can best improve coordination. A movement whose very essence is coordination must, by definition be improved through repetition.

Most riders make the mistake, in cases of the horse's confusion during this movement, of punishing him. They either abruptly halt or punish the mouth some other way or spank him. When utmost concentration (from the horse) is called for in order to create perfectly synchronized coordination, any punishment is highly unreasonable and will create adverse effects. The horse will become tense, inattentive, and rushed; therefore, he will "mess up" his flying changes on every stride. By all means, do not punish when your horse makes mistakes during this delicately timed coordination feat. Patiently repeat!

Patterns and Figures Gymnasticize Horses

Daily Riding Strategies

Riding must first be in the head and then it will go into the seat. That is, *there is no successful riding without first knowing the right ways to go about it.* Not the *quantity,* but the *quality* of daily work will produce success. Good riding strategies are based on solid knowledge as to the physique and nature of the horse, the correct (tried and proven) methods for getting the best results from him, and reasonable, well-planned goals.

Riding goals fall into three basic categories:

1. *Long term goals* are the most general. Basically they include the hope of developing the horse's natural abilities to their ultimate extent, and of specializing him in the areas that give us pleasure, that is, in cross-country, jumping, or dressage, after proper founding in the rudiments of all three.

2. *Competition goals* are designed to meet deadlines — various calendar dates on which we hope to show certain levels of achievement by the horse. These goals give us time limits and serve as motivation for achievement within certain time periods.

3. *Daily goals* are the bread and butter of our riding. While they should be well planned, the rider must remain flexible about quickly adjusting these goals according to needs during the daily riding period.

Artists as well as human athletes work in a similar manner, and in their activities we can find parallels to riding goals. A painter will plan an overall goal of depicting various things on canvas. Then he paints for commissioning patrons and exhibitions that press him with deadlines. But as daily work continues he finds himself constantly adjusting to the needs of each particular canvas. When he begins, he has a general idea of what to paint and how to do it. Yet as he goes along he alters his composition, color scheme and texture in order to eventually achieve the fine artistic product he had in mind when he began.

Riders are often the victims of our cultural dictates. These include the notion that any change is progress. They also suggest that true progress can be depicted on a graphic line that proceeds onward and upward.

Preoccupation with change is contrary to good riding goals. For not all that is new is progress. That notion may serve the purposes of technological innovation and commerce, but adding new movements and figures to our daily work in rapid succession may result in a horse you lost way back when, and upon whom you force a false superstructure. This superstructure will indeed be new, but the horse will be merely a marionette on a string, performing conditioned and cued acts that are without athletic value. Should you make that mistake, your long-term, general goal of producing a horse that performs according to his natural abilities will have been lost.

True progress will take place only when something better replaces the status quo. That is, when there is genuine improvement rather than just change taking place in the horse. Therefore I invite you to consider an oriental (rather than our technologically-minded occidental) view on how to progress. Their view (particularly Hindu) can be depicted as a stretched out soft spring, viewed in profile as consecutive circles that loop through one another.

With this image in mind, you can see that I suggest riding strategies that involve constantly revisiting the places where you and your horse have been before. When things creep up wrong, I recommend that you take the horse all the way back "to the drawing board" and "redesign" him to his natural-moving and proper shape! *There is nothing more important in the message of classical training than that you maintain the natural beauty of your horse and improve on only his natural tendencies, and that you do that by natural methods and at the horse's own time!*

As you pursue the classical teachings of riding, therefore, you must have the patience and humility to change when your horse suggests that he cannot cope with the newness (for whatever reason). When you change, keep in mind that your horse begs for simplification, not complexity and newness (technology). In your daily work you must keep in mind that you want to remain a listening device, and when your horse signals stress, you ease up by revisiting the known ways, by pursuing the familiar, by reviewing the foundation. That will yield true progress!

While observing the workings of nature (we are part of it!) biologists discovered a long time ago that the development of the individual microscopically repeats the development of the species. The human embryo and fetus pass through developmental stages that recapitulate in brief the evolutionary development of the human species from the one-celled organism through fish, amphibian, etc. to the shape and complexity of a human adult.

In riding, daily work on any level must consist of a recapitulation of the total progress to the present time of your horse. Therefore, regardless of the gymnastic accomplishment of the horse, he will have to be started at the earliest level, relaxation, and briefly progressed through the more sophisticated achievements of balance, rhythm, elasticity, impulsion, to finally, cadence. If your horse is not fully trained he is to be worked up to the general developmental level of his current work, for example, only to the stage of perfect rhythm in all paces and transitions. There his daily work stops. Or maybe some embryonic probings at the next accomplishment level (elasticity) may be attempted.

Let us look at this daily repetitive diet of which systematic work consists:

Relaxation is indispensible for further achievement. It must be both physical and mental. On a green horse, that simple goal must be our all-consuming task for the entire riding period. But as the horse advances (improves, rather than gets gimmicky, fancy steps), we need spend less and less time and effort on relaxation, enabling us to go on to the more complex and sophisticated goals. Without relaxation the horse cannot render himself attentive to the rider's aids, accept the bit and listen to correct guidance concerning his balance.

Balance can only be achieved when the horse has relaxed all his muscles and carries the rider with a swinging (vibrating) back that is elevated. A balanced horse will be able to keep identical strides through straight and bent paths and will make transitions that are district, yet without impure steps.

Rhythm is the composite success of relaxation and balance at work. The horse moves with absolutely even strides in all three paces both on straight and curved patterns, fully attentive to the rhythmic and lateral (bending) guidance of his rider. His paces improve in purity and gain expression.

Elasticity occurs when the horse can stretch and contract various muscles in his body. Consequently he can move his joints in a round, supple, "oiled" fashion. As a result he can show (depending on development) proficiency in stretching or contracting his body, thereby lengthening or elevating his strides. Thus, he can show modulation in his paces, more or less extended and collected movements, without lengthening or elevating his strides. Thus, he can show modulation in his paces, more or less extended and collected movements, without altering the rhythm of his strides.

Impulsion is controlled energy, not rushing, tense exuberance. The horse's natural tendency to run, to move with joy and alertness are tamed by careful and gentle control. Impulsion must be based on the preceding four steps in order to be energetic (yet not rushing) movement supported by appropriate (relaxed) motion of all joints in the hindquarters. Effortlessness and abundance of energy without haste are the proof of this accomplishment.

Cadence crowns the work. A well-cadenced horse adds artistic elegance to effortlessness by moving with maximum suspension (flight) created by minimun touchdown (contact with the ground). A well-cadenced horse is so accomplished athletically that he uses his native talents with utmost economy and appropriateness. With the least expenditure of energy but the greatest application of control of his own body, he can now move with brilliance. That is the frosting on the cake!

Riding, because it is based on communication between two living organisms, must include not only "taking" by the rider but even more importantly "listening." The awareness of the horse's mental and physical state, indeed, should determine what and how much the rider may ask of his mount. Therefore the truly talented riders are labeled as having "feel," which is another term describing being a living antenna that picks up all communications the horse sends. The magic of perceptiveness, awareness, supplemented by intelligence, compassion and empathy by the rider, can induce him to proper actions, aiding and communications towards his horse. For a knowledgeable onlooker this becomes soon apparent: the rider, when left to his own devices, should "make sense" to the onlooker. A coach or other informed observer should always be able to understand what the rider is doing; even predict what he will do!

All too many riders, who are still lacking enough theoretical knowledge, expect from their coaches their money's worth of talking. Yet, most good things happen in silence. A noisy coach and one that dictates perpetually every move, produces riders that are incapable of tuning in with their horses and who merely receive verbalizations from the coach but no feelngs from their horse. The results may be disasterous: a dependency may be fostered between coach and rider whereby the coach is used as a crutch at best and an antagonist to resent at worst. In the process, the horse and his communications are sacrificed, the pleasure of riding unknown. Indeed, the intoxication of riding is not in the process of aiding or the process of talking to the horse, but rather in the thrill of monitoring his (hopefully) pleasant communications.

Not only need a rider be always and fully aware of the horse's well-being and his communications, but he must react to them with knowledge and insight. Knowledge comes both by practice (riding) and by coaching, reading, watching and discussing. More important, however, is the insight and wisdom gained by empathy towards the horse. Empathy, putting it simply, is the ability to put oneself into the position of another. To step into the other's shoes (horse shoes?), to leave one's own ego and enter that of another. Putting it another way, *think horse!* What do you think he experiences when you ride him?

We can start by imagining that our horse is in a state similar or analogous to that which we experience when dreaming! We are aware of situations while dreaming but do not know how we got into them. Nor do we have the power to extricate. We have pleasant, even thrilling dreams and also nightmares. They come about without us having much to do with them and when they are proceeding we have little to do with their control. Yet we react! We react, however, impulsively, even instinctively. We never react to the dreams rationally, logically. We can neither analyze them nor form a synthesis. We cannot manipulate them. But we remember them well. We react to these memories emotionally. We fear nightmares, we palpitate, sweat. Horses do too, when the rider gives them a nightmare!

Are horses smart or stupid? The argument goes on...uselessly. They are neither; they are in a dreamlike state. Are we smart or stupid when dreaming? Neither. We just know pleasure from pain; we know we are victimized by it. We know that physical discomfort brings on nightmares. An arm that went asleep makes us dream it has been amputated. Ride your horse a pleasant dream. Make him remember the thrill of it. How long should a dream last? How long should you ride? As long as it is pleasant, go on inducing your horse's dream. Of a nightmare, a few minutes are much too long!

Rationality is based on logic. Logic is based on synthesis and analysis. Horses have none. So do not treat them like people. That is why conditioning has a certain important role in riding: that which is undesirable must be promptly punished (not necessarily by beating) and that which is desirable must be promptly rewarded. Seldom does one see appropriate measures. Rather, one sees nagging. Repeatedly asking, never getting anything and letting it go with that, makes no sense to an animal. When you know the horse is wrong and will not make it right after repeated gentle cajoling, make a firm stand: make inattention or disobedience an uncomfortable experience. But be quick in making any cooperation much rewarded! When things go well, riders become mesmerized with awe and pleasure. That forbids them from taking both reins in one hand and petting with the other: an excuse for not rewarding. Well, keep both reins in hand, keep your fist closed around them, don't break the magic of your poise: but still tap his neck, just in front of his withers with that closed fist lightly; do stroke with your knuckles up and down ever so briefly. Always reward when things feel good and do it without breaking the magic!

When Does A Horse Deserve Punishment And What Form Should Punishment Take?

Both reward and punishment play an important part in the training of a horse. They are essential features of the aiding system. While rewards should be bestowed on the horse after he has complied with a request, punishment should follow disobedience.

Basically there may be four reasons why a horse does not perform what the rider has in mind: the rider's aid was not understood; the horse was not ready physically or mentally to comply with the rider's wishes; a sufficiently advanced horse, receiving correct aids, willfully disobeys them; or the horse evades the rider's influence by playfulness.

In the first two cases the horse is incapable of performing what is requested because the rider aided incorrectly or he overdemanded. In both cases the rider is at fault and no punishment is due the horse. In the latter two cases, however, the horse deserves some form of punishment.

General advice on punishment:

It should be always appropriate to the degree of seriousness of the horse's evasion or disobedience.

It should occur independently from the rider's mood: *never* punish because you are angry, irritated, impatient or revengeful. Only punish when the horse needs (rather than "deserves") it.

Punish instantly when evasion or disobedience occurs. The horse must identify punishment with the deed that provoked it. If you did not succeed in punishing instantly do not do so at all, for the horse cannot conceptualize and acknowledge belated punishment, which will lead to confusion and loss of confidence on his part.

Punishment should be limited to one effective act. It should never become a sustained beating.

Resolve punishment by making peace as soon as possible. First see to it that the horse complies with your wishes. Help him do so by requesting something basic that he can do well and use that opportunity to reward him.

Punish only with such methods as will not result in your loss of control over the horse. For instance, do not punish by riding your horse forward in a frenzy to a full gallop and end up being thrown or otherwise losing control of him.

Never punish through the mouth of the horse. You can ruin a horse's confidence in your hand and create mouth problems, retardation, alienation from contacting the bit.

Different modes of punishment:

1. *Punishment by omission* is based on denial (of rewards usually) and is the milder of the two. Repetition of aids when an exercise is not done properly on the first request denies confirmation by relaxation and yielding. It may include "boxing" the horse's sides

with boots used strongly and faster than the harmony of rhythm. Punishment by omission also means denial of rewards such as petting, stroking, resting the horse on a long rein, giving sugar, unsaddling, etc.

2. *Punishment by commission* is based on actively causing the horse displeasure and is the stronger (more dramatically effective) of the two. It may mean stronger, more forceful aids, demanding instant forward motion in an extended gait, application of the whip: once strongly without prolonged beating, or halting for a prolonged period of time without relaxing the aids. The latter is particularly effective with advanced horses when they evade through "exploding" or playfulness. As the rider is in most perfect control on an immobilized horse, the halt is most suitable to discipline the horse and communicate to him the demand for submission to the rider's will.

Punishment should always be done with empathy for the horse's level of development and the particular deed that provoked it. Young, inattentive, playful, happy horses should not be punished for periodic, mild frolicking. An advanced dressage horse, however, should not be allowed the same liberties.

How To Square A Halt

One can think of a number of reasons for a horse not squaring his halt. The remedy is varied according to the cause.

The horse is sloppy and develops sloppy habits. If that is the case, you should drive him more keenly forward in your work in general, and before a halt in particular. Never forget that one "does not pull up to a halt," but rather "drives forward into a halt." If just driving will not help, then touch the tardy hind leg with the riding whip after he halted in his sloppy fashion. Repeat that "magic touch" gently until he puts his foot into the right supporting position. If you have a helper on the ground, he could advance that tardy leg for you by using his whip from the ground.

If the horse halted out of balance because you interfered with the rein as you aided the halt, the remedy will have to be different. Many riders pull up to halt, even if gently, by applying the reins. Those who use one rein a little stronger than the other might get the kind of halt you describe. We inadvertently use one hand more strongly (right or left handedness) and the horse will stay behind with his hind leg on that side. He will understand it as a rein of opposition and will simply delight in responding to your aid. He will think that you want that hind leg slightly behind during the halt, for you actually communicate that wish, however inadvertantly!

If the hind leg stays behind due to relative weakness in its development, the remedy will be yet different. Humans too often support their weight on a stronger leg, resting the other while standing idle. Look at Michelangelo's famous statue of David. He stands *in "contraposto."* Horses will rest a weaker leg too. The longer they do it, the stronger the supporting leg will get and the more reluctant they will grow to use the ever weakening tardy leg. If such a case is the cause of your problem, you will have to strengthen the weaker leg.

Strengthening exercises for the weak, tardy hind leg may be as follows:

> a. shoulder into the weaker side;
> b. half-passes to the strong side;
> c. canter departs to the strong side;
> d. halt-trot transitions on a circle ridden on the weak side.

Do all of the halts when on the rail or circle when you are riding on the "weak hand." Precede your halts by two steps of shoulder-in.

Using a combination of these solutions would be the most advisable. I just separated the activities into different phases according to possible causes to make the explanations clearer and to offer some logic in solving the problem. In short, ride your strengthening exercises, then prepare a halt from two steps of shoulder-in. Yield the rein particularly on the weak side as the halt is performed. Then, if he still remains behind with that hind leg, drive it into place by a touch with the whip.

Teaching to Rein-Back

Willing and joyful submission while backing, eagerness in anticipation of the forward progression, coupled with fine collection without resistance give the pleasures of a good rein-back. The horse correctly performing this movement will lift his hind legs well off the ground. Indeed, any mental strain or resistance, any physical evasion or reluctance, will render the movement gymnastically useless and artistically worthless.

The purpose of a rein-back is to demonstrate the horse's willing submission to the rider's will and to gymnasticize him to utmost collection. The horse should never "back away" from the rider's aids in a rush, nor show timid reluctance by creeping. He should not evade the correct use of his body by dragging his feet or stepping sideways.

The correct rein-back is manifest in a relaxed horse, steadily on the bit, moving backward with even strides and in good balance. He will move with impulsion, using the joints of his hindquarters well for the carriage of his weight, which is shifted over a new center of gravity that is both toward the haunches and lower into the belly. His croup will have necessarily been lowered to achieve this. He will be a short horse because of the keenness of bending in his spinal column, because of the flexion of his supple yet strong muscles and because of the effortless, round usage of his well-strengthened joints.

The beauty of the rein-back rests with the expression of a forward urge in the horse, a zestful desire and readiness to resume forward progression in any pace commanded by the rider. All beauty in riding resides with the horse's yearning to move forward, and only during a rein-back and a halt can we show off his obedience to comply with our wishes that he not do so. Yet during both the halt and the rein-back, our horse should not be asked to relinquish his forward urge, merely to temporarily suspend the action without losing the expression of wanting to do so.

Once again we must reiterate the correct aids for the rein-back; for the desired correct movement depends on its two-fold ingredients: that the horse should be prepared physically and mentally and aided correctly by his rider. Presumably the horse is well prepared for the exercise. Then, let us look at the correct aids again. Before the horse can perform a good rein-back, he will have to halt correctly. Then the rider begins his aids.

Close your fingers well on the reins and steady your wrist. As a result, the top of your hand will feel as if you are squeezing water out of a good-sized, full sponge. Never pull backward with your arms if your fist cannot get a response. You surely held your reins too far back from the horse's mouth.

Shift the pressure of your seat from the tail bone to your crotch and thighs, rendering the back of the saddle lighter, but its front heavier for the horse. This "opens the gates" to backward progression. Never tilt your torso forward, ahead of the perpendicular, for that will make you rock out of balance both during the rein-back and at the departure forward.

Stretch your legs downward and ever so slightly backward and aid with them identically to the aids usually given during a forward walk: that is, relatively slow in rhythm and steady in a "breathing" pressure. These three aiding actions will result in the horse striding backward. The instant the horse lifts his legs to move backward, the above described aids will have to melt away into yielding aids as follows:

The hands relax but do not completely open. The feeling is as though a stretched rubber band were relaxed to its normal length, yet not dropped into a slack, hanging position.

The pressure remains unaltered, forward in the crotch and thighs, yet the back muscles relax simultaneously with the relaxation of the fists.

The legs do not push, yet should not lose contact with the horse's sides. Aiding and yielding should follow in a manner imperceptible to the observer who should see, particularly in the attitude of the hands, a perpetually forward urge to give the horse freedom from any pressure.

Avoid mistakes by paying particular attention to the following few ideas.

Make all your aids parallel aids; that is, do likewise on both sides. Do not aid with either your hands or legs on only one side of the horse at a time. Since the horse is required to remain straight and to use himself on both sides identically, it is only logical that you create the movement by aiding likewise. Reserve diagonal aiding for the occasions when your horse is evading you by stepping sideways. Then, but only then, you must answer him by also becoming diagonal in your actions.

Never overflex your wrists and bend them inward; nor should you push your fists forward, altering your wrists. The wrist position should remain the same, whether you "close the door to forward progression" during aiding, or yield in the movement. The wrists should be so positioned that the top of your hand should be a straight line, a continuation of your lower arm, forming one plane with it.

Make your aids tiny. You should look and feel tranquil. Your aids should be miniscule enough to go unnoticed by the observer; that is, aid by feeling your own muscles but not showing them.

Make your transitions soft by waiting for the horse's reactions while you teach him. In your hands you should have a feeling, when you close them over the reins, as if the horse recognizes the reins as rubber bands and he begins to stretch them forward against your palms. To receive that feel, the horse must be supplied with sufficient leg aids to stretch into the softly closed hands with proper flexion. As you yield your hands, the horse should relax his jaw in turn.

The horse will lift his hind feet with energy as a result of the above described aids. Particularly the yielding of the hand (relaxation of the fists), the lightening of pressure at the tailbone, and the rhythmical, adhesive legs will do the task.

How Can A Rein-Back Be Performed Without Pulling On The Horse's Mouth?

Reining back is a very important gymnastic development of the horse, but has also many practical applications in daily riding.

Gymnastically, athletically speaking, a rein-back will have the following importance:

It will tax, and therefore strengthen, all the joints in the horse's hindquarters.

It will strengthen specific musculature in the hindquarters. Importantly, those muscles that can lift with strength, and are not easily developed through gymnastics that involve fast locomotion. As an analogy it might help to note that the gymnastic (strengthening) value of push-ups *increases* as the speed of pushing up *decreases*.

It helps the horse understand and practice shifting his center of gravity backwards towards the haunches.

It helps the horse's facility in bending the joints of the hindquarters.

It is important to understand that the rein-back is done with the "parallel aids." That means that the rider must have his aiding (communicating) influence identically placed and identically performing on both sides of the horse, the reason for this being that we also expect the horse to use both of his sides identically when backing. The horse must be arrow straight while backing.

The rider may switch to uneven aiding only at times when the horse's physical attitude needs correcting and then only temporarily. When the horse deviates from a straight path of progression by pushing his rump off to one side, or bending his neck to one side, for corrective purposes and only temporarily, the rider must also deviate from parallel aiding.

When aiding correctly, there are always eight steps to be performed. These take place very fast and seem to be only one brief moment in duration. However, if any of the steps are omitted, no desired results can follow. Therefore, should any step out of the sequence be ignored, the entire sequence must be started again from the beginning, rather than continuing with the original attempt.

Look at the following table for understanding the correct aiding sequence:

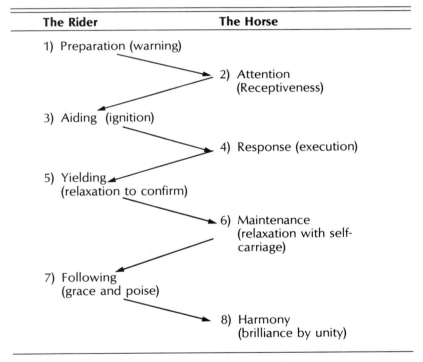

The Rider	The Horse
1) Preparation (warning)	
	2) Attention (Receptiveness)
3) Aiding (ignition)	
	4) Response (execution)
5) Yielding (relaxation to confirm)	
	6) Maintenance (relaxation with self-carriage)
7) Following (grace and poise)	
	8) Harmony (brilliance by unity)

Each of the above steps has to be separately repeated for each step desired reining back. Now, let us turn to the rider's actions that will produce a good backing down from the horse. That is, let me now answer the original question.

Preparation: The horse should be halted four square in perfect balance. He should be relaxed but attentive. He should be longitudinally flexed while halting (i.e., be on the bit and ahead of the legs). The rider should ever so mildly lighten his seatbones and put more pressure onto the crotch (and down on the stirrups). The rider should sensitize the feeling on the reins by slightly elevating and oscillating them.

Aiding: The rider should flex his back muscles and ever so slightly tilt his torso forward. He should invite gentle pressure on the reins, in order to "close the gate" to forward progression. This is done as the elbows come flush with the rider's spinal column, his upper arms hanging perpendicularly (his elbows pointing towards the hip joints) as the torso has tilted forward pushing the chest and abdomen ahead of the elbows. The legs press simultaneously for a "forward walk" command.

Yielding: As soon as the horse begins to lift his legs, the rider relaxes all his musculature: the back, the legs, and supples all his "holding" joints to render the bit "empty" of pressure. As a consequence, the rider's seat is refilling the saddle with the seatbones, and that readies him for blocking the backward progression as well as enabling him to re-state the "closing gate" contact on the reins.

Following: With a minute lessening of flexion in the rider's musculature and joints, he travels with the horse's movement in an erect, perfectly balanced position making the beginning of the sequence once again possible.

I fully recognize that the above description resembles a recipe, but I wish my readers to understand it rather as a do-it-yourself kit. In other words, trust your feelings about the horse's communications!

The major ideas to understand are that (1) there is a logical sequence to the communications and (2) it never includes pulling on the reins.

Inevitably, a green horse will attempt to evade. The usual reasons for that being that he has difficulty in monitoring your aids (wishes) and that it is physically taxing for him to comply with your wishes.

As soon as the horse evades, as shown by his becoming crooked or coming above the reins (emptying and stiffening his back), you must stop, straighten him out, or continue walking to bring him back on the reins before repeating the exercise.

When you teach a young horse to rein back, ask him to do only one step at a time. After each step drop the reins completely and pet him, making much of his performance. This strategy will not only make him understand and like what you want of him, but will also ensure that he cannot easily evade and move incorrectly. Then, gradually piece a sequence of steps together.

Transitions From Working Canter To Working Trot

Correct ground work is the guarantee that later advanced work, such as work in the collected paces, will succeed without being contested by the horse.

Therefore, create fluent, balanced, elastic, calm and obedient transitions from working canter to working trot which the horse can perform with ease and in accordance with her current physical development.

The most important thing for you to understand is that every change must be prepared. Only after correct preparation can you expect your horse to respond calmly to your aids for the desired change.

Here is some step-by-step advice offered with a word of caution not to take it merely as a recipe. Invest the process with your feelings. Digest the advice intellectually and then feel its proper practical application physically when riding.

Create a fine canter. Make sure the bounds are bold, round, and lift well off the ground. Make sure the rhythm is pure, clock-even, and that you take time for your horse to relax in this movement. In short, canter with correct impulsion, with even strides, on a relaxed horse.

During the canter your inside boot, inside hipbone and inside shoulder are positioned ahead of those corresponding on the outside. If you sit correctly, you simply parallel with your body the position of the horse's body. If you hold the reins correctly, short enough that they connect your back muscles with the horse's mouth, your inside fist will also be ever so slightly advanced over the outside fist, for the shoulder position will demand that.

Prepare the transition to trot by half-halting the horse. Essentially, that is an aid intensifying all the aids which are already in use; ask more jump from behind and as that energy is forthcoming invite the horse's front to slow down and wait for it. This will create a shorter horse, jumping higher, yet in the originally dictated rhythm. As the horse's attention is captured and readied for a change through these half-halts, the aids can soon be introduced. The most important effects of half-halts are a horse mentally readied to receive instruction to change and physically enabled to make the change as a result of slower forward impetus of the body mass. As the body is advancing a shorter distance forward, it should advance into greater suspension upward.

The above described desirable results of a good half-halt are necessary before a good transition can be executed. In the meanwhile, great care must be taken that the half-halts are soft and that rough interference with forward progression is avoided. The half-halts must be repeated on a green horse, often for a long time. They must "run through" the horse in order not to stifle him in the process!

Listen to the horse and he will tell you when the half-halts are successful. Then and never before is he ready for your aids to trot.

As always, aids must be coordinated and executed simultaneously on all points. Your legs must assume a parallel position on the horse's sides (as opposed to the outside one being behind the inside one during canter). Furthermore, the legs must begin to float rhythmically, indicating the brisk, dancing strides of the trot.

The inside shoulder must be brought back to a flush position parallel with that of the outside one. This movement of slight rotation at the shoulder will also bring the hipbone and seatbone back to properly parallel those of the horse at the trot. Automatically, the inside rein will gently invite back, reflecting its new position under that shoulder which was just brought back flush with the outside one.

As soon as the horse makes his first trot step, your entire aiding system must yield to produce the sensation of a harmonious satisfaction. It is essential that the horse be confirmed in his correct response by the rider's yielding all pressure of instruction. Most important of all is the instant yielding of the reins which have been ever so busy through the half-halts and finally through the aids! On a green horse, you can momentarily lengthen the reins to the buckle to dramatize your pleasure in his response.

Now that the trot has been created, you may feel that your horse is rushing. He is running after a lot of weight that has catapulted into his navigational area of head, neck and shoulders. At first, let that happen. For if you aided correctly and the horse rushes the trot, it is a sign that he is not yet safely balancing himself; that the center of gravity is still shifting against the horse's wishes, simply because he is physically not yet ready to manipulate it to his advantage. Do not punish him for it. With the repetition of the exercise and other gymnastic efforts, he will, eventually, be able to maintain his balance after the radical change in the use of his body which occurs when trot is assumed after canter.

If the horse is catapulting forward, rushing to catch up with his head, neck and shoulder weight, you resume half-halting, slowly and patiently asking for his front end to await the arrival of the hindquarters. As the horse's body gradually shortens, becomes more compact, he will be able to carry it successfully and in a comfortable balance.

In short, this is what should take place: a very fine canter must be created; after proper preparations through repeated half-halts, the horse is to be readied for a transition; bring on the transition with harmoniously coordinated aids that are correct indications of what you wish to create; as soon as a trot is achieved, yield your aids totally and merely seek to travel harmoniously as a reward; finally, reassert yourself through half-halts until not only any kind of trot, but the right kind is created.

You will soon realize that the elaborately described process which may take five minutes initially will soon be resolved in sixty seconds. However, this reward will be forthcoming only if you have the patience to perform your task without ever inviting tension or resistance in your horse.

In case you wonder how one knows when to aid or how often to repeat a half-halt, let the horse's relaxation be your guideline. If the horse responds to you without tension, you can commence to the next step prescribed. By repetition, not only will his understanding of your clear communications and his trust in their gentleness enable him to perform the transitions without fussing; the repetition will build his confidence in your reliability and patience and thus continue his physical development.

Tightening Circle
Without Losing Balance Or Impulsion

Let us say that you are, ideally, riding in a dressage arena. First ride a circle that has a diameter of thirty-three feet, the width of the arena. Make the center of the arena (letter X) the center of your circle. Make sure that the circle is properly arced and that the horse is moving on it properly bent throughout the length of his body. To aid you in establishing this proper circle, place a hub-cap at X to define the center of the circle. Put the letters E and B on the centers of the long sides of the arena. These are the only two points at which your legs pass the rail. Establish two other points on the circle where your line intercepts the center line of the dressage ring, and place two poles on the ground at these spots.

After you have established this circle and can move on it with a correctly bent horse in good impulsion, proceed to ride a spiral inward very gradually. Through spiraling inward, reach a smaller circle with the same correct bend and impulsion. Then spiral out again until you reach your original large circle of thirty-three feet diameter. The spiraling inward should only continue as near to the hub-cap in the center as you can manage to stay without losing either balance or impulsion. As soon as you notice either shortcoming, you should understand it as a sign that the circle is as small as the horse is capable of bending on without strain at this level of his development. Therefore, you should press no further. You should merely repeat the exercise after proper rest periods and refreshing, new movements.

In time the horse will be able to spiral tighter, to an even smaller circle. The ultimate goal, of course, is the circle called the *volte,* about eight feet in diameter. However, before the horse reaches that stage, there are several things of importance that warrant your attention during the exercise.

Make sure that you ride all circular lines (including circles and spirals) using diagonal aids. Your inside leg must be aiding for impulsion as well as bending the horse at the girth, or slightly behind it. However, the outside leg must be placed slightly further back, in the "canter position," to bend the hindquarters inward. (Note: bending, by definition, can only be done by the aid of at least two points.) The outside shoulder, seatbone and hip, on the other hand, must be advanced over the inside ones in order to parallel the shoulders of the horse. This torso position will also bring the position of the hands into an automatically correct relationship with the horse's mouth.

In addition, great care must be taken not to lean inward, like a motorcycle rider on a curve, and thus collapse the hip and waist. Obviously, as the spiraling continues inward, the aiding position has to be intensified accordingly. The line connecting the outside shoulder with the inside one, if continued in the imagination, should always be over the radius of the circle being described. In other words, the inside shoulder must be retarded enough behind the outside one so as to point toward the circle's center. As the circle is gradually squeezed smaller, this seat position must be exaggerated.

On the spiral, the horse should be moving inward gradually. This can best be achieved by the outside leg working as if giving the aid to elicit a travers (rump-in) in the horse. However, when enlarging the spiral, or reversing it, moving the horse outward in approximation of the original circle, the inside leg must ride the horse out as if giving the aid for a shoulder-in. Finally, I must add one more reminder about the aids for this exercise. When moving in an arc and tightening the spiral, there is more weight on the inside seatbone of the rider (identical to the travers). However, when enlarging the spiral to the outer circle, there should be more weight on the outside seatbone of the rider (identical to the shoulder-in).

It must be remembered that these exercises become meaningless as soon as the rider "cuts in" to make a smaller circle. That will happen invariably when the hands of the rider interfere. Therefore, the spiraling exercise must be performed with the boots and seat only. Also, any irregularity in the shape of the circle will indicate that the rider's position is wrong somewhere. Therefore, an unbending horse will merely "fall" inward on many-sided lines, rather than bending and spiraling in on a continuously curved line.

To recapitulate the salient points, let me repeat that you can best achieve smaller, more collected circles through spiraling exercises. You should spiral inward only so far as the horse continues to maintain correct impulsion, correct bend in the arc, pure rhythm and all this in relaxation. So listen to your horse. He will tell you when the tightening of the circle must be terminated. He will either lose impulsion and rhythm or "fall in on the shoulder" or skid out with his croup to evade further bending of his joints and musculature. Some horses may also hollow their backs, come above the bit and push, rather than lift with the hind legs. Should any of these messages reach you, proceed to enlarge your circle through the spiral line, for the horse is telling you that he can do no more.

Practicing this exercise will develop the physical suppleness of your horse. In time, the *volte* will no longer be the goal, but one of the circles that you can perform, without strain and in proper balance.

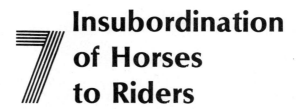

Insubordination of Horses to Riders

The Nervous Thoroughbred

The Thoroughbred is basically a very fine horse. Having been bred to excel at speed, he developed into a potentially fine sports horse, for it is running that nature meant horses to do. Thus, how could a fine runner be anything but a terrific horse? Yet, for dressage purposes, the Thoroughbred has often proved to be a difficult prospect. Even those that are physically without weaknesses, damage or injury, fail to excel in dressage because of their temperament.

Thoroughbreds are sensitive by nature. Added to this is their early and often ruthless training schedule. The young horse, often facing tasks more taxing than he is mature enough to bear, will soon develop a fear, mistrust and apprehension of the rider who induces his pain and agony. To relax such a horse, one with a past full of negative experiences, is indeed a challenge.

I thoroughly disagree with a common practice that calls for the relaxation of a horse at the trot. Most riders warm up their horse at a trot. To add a more unfortunate feature, they do it on a dropped rein, which for some reason is believed to induce relaxation in horses. The result is a madly rushing horse, falling on its forehand, trying to find its balance, remaining stiff both longitundinally and laterally. Basically this so-called "relaxation-limbering-warming up" effort becomes an exercise in stiffening, rushing and an ever diminishing chance to come into harmony with the horse. Much can be built at the trot and much time should be spent at the trot, to be sure. But all that must come in due course, after the horse has been relaxed.

Relaxation can be achieved at the walk. It is the slowest pace, allowing the horse to adjust to the foreign weight of the rider. Being the

163

slowest pace, it allows the rider to sit in harmonious balance and apply a minimum of aids, and that is done quietly. It is the only pace lacking a period of suspension, allowing the horse to have always a firm support of his weight on the ground.

At first the rider should walk his horse around the work area in both directions on a long rein; thereby allowing the horse to move any way he desires, to stretch all his muscles and to realize that he is trusted by the rider who does not encumber, limit or adjust his movements in any way. After having walked the horse freely around, contact should be sought gradually and gently. As always, contacting the horse should begin with the lower legs, continue with the assumption of the driving seat and terminate by the gathering of the reins into proper contact after all other contact areas have found their position and feeling.

The horse on contact is also one in control. He can now be asked to follow more exactly the rail of the arena or be ridden on large circles. He is now bent both longitudinally and somewhat laterally. Slowly he has a chance to accept the rider's control, then commands, without tension. If tensions arise, periodically the horse should be allowed to stretch out, as the aids are again relaxed and relinquished. One must always terminate demands (however simple they may be) and go back to an earlier, more simple stage of encounter when tension arises. Chances are, however, that the horse will react favorably to this patient, quiet and comfortable beginning.

When the horse is quietly on the aids, bending longitudinally and laterally on arcs and circles, suppling work may be added. One cannot emphasize enough the importance of work at the walk. Surely the most difficult pace to develop and improve, it is also the one during which important muscle developments as well as suppling of joints may take place. If the horse is advanced enough he should now be asked to do his two-track movements; all those he knows and some new ones can now be taught.

By now the reader will realize that prior to trotting or cantering I recommend a lengthy, patient session at the walk. During this session the horse will totally relax mind and then muscles, will supple his joints and will offer sustained attention to light aids. This kind of work readies horses, especially the mistrusting and therefore nervous ones, for the faster paces of trot and canter. Once the trot is assumed with this relaxed horse, it will be a trot ridden on the aids, therefore balanced. The trot will also show a certain degree of elasticity, depending on level of development. Certainly it will be slower (balanced) and therefore more engaged. The horse will bend easily in corners, for he has been bent during his walk work. Obviously the rider will be relaxed on a comfortably trotting horse, will be able to keep his balance better and chances for a harmonious pace will be many times improved. All this is due to the proper beginnings at the sustained period of work at the walk. Now, when properly relaxed and prepared, the horse will give that trot that indeed limbers him and warms him up properly for whatever other task is in store for him.

Opening The Mouth, Grinding Of The Teeth

Here is a young horse that resents the bit. Many do, and if the situation does not improve soon, this horse might develop a problem that will hinder him in dressage achievements throughout his entire career. There may be two major reasons for this horse's resentment of the bit. First, improper equipment might cause him discomfort. The rider must make sure to use the gentlest mouth-piece possible. Ideally, a rubber-covered, simple-jointed snaffle as thick as possible should be used.

Another major problem might be that the rider uses his hands improperly, thereby inflicting pain. Excessive pulling on the reins often causes the horse to evade pain by opening his mouth. That action on his part will get the bit off the sensitive gums and transfer the pressure to the less sensitive lips at the corners of his mouth. The opening of the mouth will often be accompanied by a stretching of the neck and an elevating of the head. Also, the horse may periodically shake his head or tilt it sideways, raising one corner of the mouth quite high. This kind of resistance at the mouth is a sure sign that the rider is inflicting pain with his hands.

It is obvious then that the rider must release the reins enough to eliminate all pressure on the horse's mouth. Initially he should even ride on a dropped rein to invite the horse's confidence in his hands. The weight of the bit itself should be the only thing for the horse to contend with. When he has accepted the weight of the bit the rider may periodically seek soft contact with it. At this stage the rein should still be regularly totally dropped and contacted only for short intervals.

It is typical of horses who develop anxiety towards the bit and consider it a threat of pain, to switch to teeth grinding when the mouth is forced closed with a tight dropped noseband. No force should ever be involved in correcting the problem and, consequently, a dropped noseband should never be used as an instrument of force. The dropped noseband should either be generously loosened or better yet, in this case, eliminated. The rider should use a cavesson noseband instead.

Without observing the situation, I must rely on being cued in by the questioner. He writes that the horse opened his mouth "when asked to come on the bit and be more collected." This phrase suggests to me that the rider asked for collection merely through the reins. In other words, he pulled, hoping that the horse will become shorter and will collect his strides. This cannot be done. To my mind it is questionable whether the horse should be collected at all at this stage of his training. But if so, he must certainly be asked to collect by the actions of the rider's legs and back and not at all by his hands! It is not my task now to comment on how to collect a horse. Let it suffice, however, to state that collection takes for granted a certain level of physical (gymnastic) and mental development of the horse. That development much depends on the horse's acceptance of the bit as an aid (area of communication) which is not true yet of this horse. Collection always develops from the hindquarters. It cannot occur as long as the horse shows resistance anywhere in his body.

Therefore, I must reiterate that the rider must yield the reins entirely to the horse until he can forget and forgive and become relaxed. At this time, I would not recommend any attempt to collect the horse and certainly not through the interference with the reins.

The horse will grind his teeth until he flexes, collects himself and accepts the bit. A horse that accepts the bit will never grind his teeth. Thus, what is here proposed as an "accepted bit" that terminates grinding, is not really an accepted bit! Rather, the rider must achieve relaxation when the horse finds the bit comfortable enough to carry and stops grinding his teeth. I presume that when the horse does relax, the rider's hands become gentle and the horse relaxes to these gentle hands.

I wish to avoid scrutinizing the terminology used in the question and rather suggest that whatever we call the event when the horse is not grinding his teeth, the rider must re-create that condition as often as he can!

If there is any reason for the rider desiring flexion in the horse's neck, at the poll, and at the jaw right now, he must go about it differently than he has been doing until now.

When contacting the horse's mouth, the rider should increase his driving aids. He must send the horse's hind legs towards the bit. If the horse responds to the rider's aids by rushing, he must perform gentle, repeated, and gradual half-halts. Therefore, the reins should be held short enough when this attempt is made to connect the rider's torso (weight) and back muscles directly to the horse's mouth. Thus, when the half-halts are performed, the horse will feel a coordinated aid that involves the rider's entire body: the legs forcefully attached to drive, the torso upright to weight the hindquarters and contact the reins, and the back muscles flexed along with the flexed abdomen that is pushed forward between the elbows. This is simultaneously driving the hindquarters while inviting the forehand to slow down. Done gently and with utmost coordination, these aids will let the horse shorten his body and flex his muscles correctly, while having no pain or disharmony to contend with, in a relaxed manner.

These aids must be dynamic, constantly and rhythmically yielding into periods of non-aid, or relaxation!

Let me summarize the essence of my advice: The rider should see to it that the horse has the most suitable gentle equipment in his mouth. He should either not use reins for the time being or use them from time to time, releasing them as soon as any irregularity develops in the horse's attitude at the mouth. If the rider desires to collect or flex the horse, he should do it gently, gradually, and only by the correct aiding methods (which exclude any pulling on the reins). The problem here described can, indeed *must,* be corrected. Help by a knowledgeable instructor seems essential to me for this particular problem.

The Horse Leaning On His Rider's Hands

Indeed, depending on the cause of the problem, its remedies may vary. First of all, the rider must identify (possibly with the help of an expert) the cause of the problem, for the horse's leaning on the rider's hands is merely a symptom.

Let me hypothesize that the horse is heavy on the hands because of insufficient and incorrect use of his hindquarters. If the horse is leaning on the rider's hands evenly, he is likely to push the composite weight (of himself and the rider) forward, rather than lifting it off the ground, thereby progressing in space through flotation during periods of suspension. If this is the cause of the problem, then slowing down the horse's forehand progression through a half-halt and urging the hindquarters to get closer to his forehand with stronger legs is, indeed, the correct remedial technique. In short, the rider should communicate to the horse that he must slow down the traveling of the weight of his front area, in order to allow the hindquarters to catch up with it, thus enabling the hindquarters to carry rather than push it. The result will be a shorter horse, bowed into a keener flexion, now capable of striding under a contracted mass of weight, which has its center of gravity further back.

If, however, the horse leans heavier onto one of the reins than the other, then in addition to the above suggested slowing down of the traveling of his mass, another remedy needs to be employed. The cause of being heavier on one of the reins is that the horse uses the opposite hind leg (from the heavy reign) incorrectly. This can be done in two different ways:

(1) When the horse steps shorter with one hind leg, though tracking up towards the direction of the corresponding foreleg, he must lean on the rein opposite the hind leg which is tardy. To improve the situation the rider should rhythmically yield the heavy rein at the very time when the insufficiently striding opposite leg is strongly aided by the rider's leg on that side. In the meantime the lighter rein is held firmly, offered in a strong support (direct rein) to become the point of reference against which the heavier rein is oscillated.

(2) The other possibility may be that the horse is not tracking towards the corresponding foreleg on the side opposite from the heavier rein. He is, as a matter of fact, tracking outside the path of

the corresponding forehand, thus moving with a slight "rump-out," leaning heavily on the opposite shoulder (falling on the shoulder) making the rein heavy there too. If this is the cause of the problem then the rider must oscillate the heavy rein identically to the above suggested way, but instead of driving the troubled hind leg forward, should push it sideways into place on the track.

Beyond these specific devices to correct the use of the horse's hind legs, there are certain exercises that are highly valuable. Let us not forget that a horse that moves somehow incorrectly with one or both of his hind legs has a physical reason for doing so. Basically, the reasons for such shortcomings are: (a) weak joints, (b) weak muscles, (c) stiff joints and (d) stiff muscles. *Therefore, exercises that strengthen joints, develop muscles or supple both the joints and muscles are in order.*

In the specific case we are discussing I would recommend the frequent use of the following gymnastic exercises:

If the horse is heavy on both reins evenly, rein back to encourage coordination, the shortening of the body and the carrying of more weight on the hindquarters. Make frequent transitions between trot and canter, so as to ride twice as many trot steps as there are canter bounds (i.e. twenty trot and ten canter). You may reduce the number of each gradually as the horse learns to shift his center of gravity backwards, which is manifested in the lightening of the rein contact.

If the horse is heavier on one rein only, there can be two causes, as mentioned above. If it is the cause described under (1), I recommend frequent canter departures from the walk on that lead where the rein is contacted heavier by the horse, extended trot, turning onto the diagonal before the movement from that side where the rein is lighter and serpentines at the trot.

Cause described under (2) requires shoulder-in and circles to the side where the rein is lighter, half-pass to the side where the rein is heavier, rump-in to the side where the rein is heavier, canter departures from the walk on the lead on which the rein is lighter.

I have offered the above gymnastic exercise suggestions at the risk of sounding like a textbook. Let me caution the riders with these problems that such exercises are offered because of their particular value in strengthening or suppling those joints or muscles that need improvement. Furthermore, it is imperative to realize that good riding continually "mirrors" each exercise. That means that when a rider does something on one hand, he must, within reasonable time, repeat the same exercise on the other hand. The suggested exercises should assume, for the time being, a predominant role, but they are not to be an exclusive diet. In short, the rider should do these exercises until improvement occurs, but for every two of them he should do one "mirror image" exercise. As soon as the problem noticeably improves, exercises should be done in pairs, "mirror images," to keep the improvement stabilized.

The
8 Rider's Seat
and Aids

The Development Of The
Rider Through Lunging Exercises

Dressage horses cannot be created by "dressaging" them only. The diversification of work awakens the horse's mind. Movement over open country and acquaintance with varied terrain is indispensable for the development of forward zest, from which impulsion can grow. Climbing, sliding, moving up and down hills, jumping natural obstacles, stretching over ditches, wading through water, all of these are natural tasks for the horse before he is trained in the controlled environment of his gymnasium, the dressage arena. The means toward the desired dressage ends, the ability to perform a Grand Prix test well, are not all found in the small indoor arena.

Analogously, riders who take only "dressage lessons," ride only with long stirrup leathers, sit all the movements, and remain with their horses in small, fenced-in areas, will never become adequate—let alone outstanding—dressage riders. A dressage rider is primarily an athlete who must breathe correctly and be strong, yet supple, in muscle. This person must also be wonderfully balanced and coordinated and should, at the same time, be flexible and able to stretch. One should remain relaxed and absorb huge movement without becoming

171

as limp as a dish-rag, and have muscle tone and strength, but without tightness, stiffness, or tension.

The dressage rider has to be, first of all, a horse-person who is acquainted with a diversity of equestrian activities, as only by these means can the nature of the horse be discovered. A dressage rider cannot be "made" by riding dressage only. Knowing the feeling of forward zest can be best learned by riding cross-country. The concept of the impulsion, the bold and powerful paces of an alert horse negotiating a natural environment, cannot be experienced in a fenced-in ring. To feel rhythm and to judge distance, one must negotiate cavaletti and jumps. To know the horse's attention to aids, one must experience trotting approaches to fences with exact aiding for canter before the jumps. And on goes the catalogue of experiences which are indispensable to riders before they deserve the title of Dressage Rider.

Dr. Reiner Klimke and other well known riders of international dressage eminence rode cross-country and over fences before specializing in dressage and producing the outstanding results for which they are known. Dr. Klimke competed in international combined events and was, in 1960, a member of the German Olympic squad. Other dressage riders have had experiences much the same. None that I know of have become international dressage riders without first having been well-trained over open country as well as jumps.

Riders should begin their training on the lunge line, while the horse is under the control of the trainer. Even after becoming an outstanding rider, one should be lunged time and time again for the needed athletic adjustments and equitation.

Preliminaries To Lunge Work

Many things should be done in the saddle during a lungeing lesson. First, the rider should be "sculpted" by words or by being actuallly placed in the correct position. Legs must be in contact with the horse's sides, with contact cultivated through the inner calf. Toes should not be braced outward. Ankles should be relaxed and mobile, knees turned inward (heels close to the horse), thighs stretched downward, buttocks wide open, seatbones spread, spinal column and lower back straight and stretched upward. Shoulder blades must be flat against the back muscles and almost touching, thereby lifting the rib cage upward so the lungs can breath and the heart cavity is open. The neck should be straight, with the head up, eyes looking forward. Arms hang relaxed at the sides or with lower arms resting on either thigh. This is the so-called **Basic Position** which is assumed on command when the rider is allowed to discontinue exercise and show the ability to return to correct riding balance and position. This is seen in Fig. 8-1, at the walk. However, the basic position is to be assumed at the trot and canter, as well as during the lunge lesson.

A few guidelines before beginning:

1. Do all exercises slowly and in a continuous motion, not jerkily or abruptly.

2. Start down and move up; feet first, then legs and on up to shoulders and hands.

3. Exercise first in walk, then trot, and finally canter. Almost all exercises can be done in all three paces.

4. Start from, and return to the *Basic Position*. In lungeing, this means to sit without stirrups, yet with knees bent enough to contact the saddle and pull the seat into the saddle for adhesiveness.

5. Intersperse exercises with brief rest periods for the benefit of both horse and rider.

Fig. 8-1. The BASIC SEAT is assumed on the lunge between exercises when the rider rests and returns to correct riding balance and position.

In Fig. 8-2, the rider has been asked to sit as correctly as he can. He does fairly well, though there are two notable exceptions which need adjustment. The lower back is slightly too round (this may be necessary for driving, but not at the halt), which raises the crotch too high and denies stretching and downward pressure on the thighs. The rider's legs are too far forward, showing no stretching. The toes are ahead of the knees, which are too high. All of these factors contribute to a

Fig. 8-2. An example of a rounded lower back and lifted crotch, leading to a limp, ineffective leg position.

"limp," ineffective leg position. These faults are a natural conse-quence of the rounded lower back and lifted crotch.

In Fig. 8-3, one can see the rider from the front, "squaring off" as best he can. While the shoulders and arms look square and balanced (neither is raised nor pushed ahead of the other), one can see that the left knee and heel are stretched lower than the right. The right side needs stretching downward to match the left, but before that is done, one should ask the rider to stretch both sides much further down and place both legs further back and down from the hip.

Illustrated in Fig. 8-4 is a driving seat with the shortcomings of a stiff ankle that turns the toes out and pushes too much with the heels,

rather than with the calves. The rider has also lowered her head in an attempt to visually monitor the horse's progress. However, the use of the lower back, the tilt of the torso, and the use of pressure through the buttocks and thighs are well illustrated here as commanding driving aids.

Exercises On The Lunge

An exercise that relaxes and limbers the ankle joints and stretches the calf muscles can be done early in the lunge session by rotating the ankles (moving both toes to describe circles). Start inward, upward, outward, downward, moving both toes, and ending with toes sharply lifted,

Fig. 8-3. The rider's left knee and heel are stretched lower than the right. The right needs stretching downward to match the left. This should be done by having the rider stretch on BOTH sides.

Fig. 8-4. In this example of the "driving seat," the rider's ankles are too stiff, resulting in too much pushing with the heels rather than the calves.

Fig. 8-5. An excellent exercise for relaxing the lower back, deepening the seat, and producing an awareness of unilateral aids. The rider swings her legs in alternate directions, on either side of the horse.

heels depressed, and feet more or less parallel with the horse's sides. Always keep the calves in contact with the horse's rib cage.

The rider in Fig. 8-5 is swinging her legs loosely and freely, in alternate directions, on either side of the horse. This produces awareness of the mechanics of unilateral aids (such as in canter departs), opens and widens the seatbones, rotates the hips and deepens (by widening) the seat. This exercise limbers and relaxes the lower back, making it an antidote for hollow back. It also helps to correct a collapsed hip position, square off the hips and suggests the feeling of refining the leg contact so that the leg is there for aiding, but without gripping.

The very important exercises that develop proper leg position and strong leg aids are shown in Figs. 8-6 & 7. The proper positioning of the lower back, pelvic bones, hips, thighs and knees is paramount to good riding. The exercise which consists of holding the ankles with straight arms, making sure the spine is straight and the rib cage lifted, will put the knee in the properly deep position, which in turn determines the correct placing of all other elements in the seat and legs. Often one must start with one foot at a time before stretching allows both to stay, with torso tall. One should be able to manually pull the boots up, then keep them there without holding them, thereby freeing the hands for additional exercising. While legs are in that stretched position, the rider should go through many combinations of exercises such as tilting the torso forward and back, rotating the shoulders sideways, and both stretching and rotating of the arms. When stretched enough, slowly lower legs on the horse's sides until the heel becomes the deepest point, toes well up and just behind the knees.

As is seen in Figure 8-7, the rider finds his balance

Fig. 8-6. By holding the ankles, the rider can put the knees in their proper deep position and proceed with various exercises that will strengthen a correct seat and leg position.

Fig. 8-7. Riding with kees lifted upward and legs spread away from the saddle is a good exercise for gaining balance. (The knees are too high in the photo.)

Fig. 8-8. An example of a "maximum vertical stretch." The rider's arms should be lifted more vertically and the legs should be stretched more downward.

Fig. 8-9. Arm rotations can be combined with other exercises to increase the limbering effect. This is also a good way to concentrate on individual problems.

Fig. 8-10. Stretching the back and side muscles by reaching across the horse's neck and down—the seat must remain deep in the saddle for this exercise to be effective.

Fig. 8-11. This is a variation on Fig. 8-10, reaching downward on the side of the shoulder. These exercises stretch all of the muscles in the torso area.

Fig. 8-12. Contributing to the driving ability of the rider's seat, the push from the legs is coordinated with a push from the shoulders downward through the lower back.

Fig. 8-13. The rider learns the effectiveness of the seat through exaggerated positioning of the torso.

Lunging Sequence (Figs. 8-1 thru 8-19):
Demonstrated and Photographed by Paul Drake & Susan Derr Drake

Fig. 8-14 & 15. Exercises done with arms on a horizontal plane help to flatten the shoulder blades, consequently widening the rib cage and lifting it upward.

Fig. 8-16 & 17. Using both arms in torso and stretching rotations is beneficial in relaxing and strengthening the lower back.

by contacting the horse only through firmly placed seatbones by lifting both knees (while pulling firmly with hands on the pommel) to the height of the hands. One must not touch the saddle or the horse with the legs. The straight and stretched torso remains anchored, seatbones "drilling holes" in the saddle. Riding this way (knees are too high in this picture) is important for gaining balance. This way, one feels that the earth's gravitational pull can keep one on the horse without any need to grip. This exercise also centers the seat in the middle of the saddle and harmonizes the rider's center of gravity with that of the horse in motion. It is an indispensable exercise for the strengthening of the abdominal muscles, without which there is no half-halting.

While the rider in Figure 8-8 has been asked to stretch and reach as high as he can (evenly, with short, upward thrusts), he has also been warned to keep his legs stretched down as deeply as he can. This is a "maximum vertical stretch." The spine should be straight, and the arms lifted into a more vertical position than is shown here. The legs should also be stretched more.

In Fig. 8-9 the rider is rotating the arms in opposite directions — a limbering exercise which can be done either in the manner of swimming the Australian crawl, or in the opposite direction, depending on the posture needs of the rider. The exercise should be done with straight arms (no bend in the elbows) and without altering the deep stretching of the legs. The arm rotation exercise can be combined with others to supply whatever corrections are needed; for example, while swinging or rotating arms, one could tilt forward and back, or add a sideways rotation of the body to increase the limbering effects.

Stretching of the back and side muscles can be accomplished by reaching either across the horse's neck and down (Fig. 8-10) or just reaching down on the side or the shoulder (Fig. 8-11). These exercises are very important (as is the one in Fig. 8-8) in the stretching of the muscles in the torso. During these stretchings, the seat must remain fully placed in the saddle.

Figures 8-12 and 8-13 show an exercise which contributes to the ability to drive with the seat. The push from the legs is coordinated with a push from the shoulders down through the lower back into the saddle in such a way as to urge the horse forward and apply aiding to the back muscles properly. First, exaggerate the aid by tilting well behind the vertical with legs kept scrupulously stretched back and down at the knees. The same, combined with an exaggerated rotating back of the outside shoulder while pushing the inside shoulder forward, should produce a canter departure (through the seat). After that, "squaring" the shoulders by suddenly pushing the outside shoulder forward and pulling the inside one back (making the shoulders part of an imaginary spoke of a wheel which is represented

Fig. 8-18. The rotating of the torso which induces shifting of the seatbones and hips is demonstrated here. The rider's legs are still too far forward, and lack downward stretching.

Fig. 8-19. Same as Fig. 8-18 shown from the front.

by the circle on which the horse moves) brings the horse back to trot. The rider should learn through the exaggerated position of the torso, the effectiveness of the seat (Fig. 8-13). Leaning back "accelerates," while leaning forward (to the vertical, never in front of it) "breaks" or collects the horse. Awareness of the rider's shoulders and hips remaining parallel with those of the horse should be developed through appropriate exercises.

The exercises shown in Figures 8-14 and 8-15 are done with the arms moving on a horizontal plane. Flattening of the shoulder blades can best be done with such exercises, widening the rib cage and lifting it upward can also be accomplished. This rider is following her hand with her eyes as it moves back and forth on a horizontal plane. The arm should be pushed as far back as possible. Using both arms in stretching and torso rotations (Figs. 8-16 & 17) is most beneficial in relaxing, yet stretching and strengthening the all-important lower back area. This should be done only with the buttocks remaining firmly in the saddle.

As illustrated in Figures 8-18 & 19, the turning (rotating) of the torso induces shifting of the seatbones and hips. While this can be useful in aiding (canter, etc.) it can also be a sign of a collapsed hip and crooked seat. In that case, one corrects by rotating temporarily more toward the opposite side. If the right hip is collapsed, one should pull the left shoulder backwards and push the right one ahead. In these pictures, however, the legs are still too far forward, lacking stretching adhesiveness, and the toes are hanging with the musculature limp. These are things that should be avoided when doing thse exercises.

Conclusion

Exercises that are performed on the lunge should be one of two basic kinds — stretching or rotating. In both cases, balance continues to be developed. The instructor should know the appropriate exercises to correct faults as they emerge. For instance, if a rider has a hollow, arched back with the hip bones tilted forward, one should not suggest the exercise of folding the arms behind the back and bending backwards. That would accentuate an already grave fault. Yet, in another case, such as a slumped-backed rider, this exercise might well be appropriate.

Again, the rider's position should be adjusted for them to feel when the angles are correct. The "sculpting" of the rider at the halt is very important, for one understands only what one has a chance to feel. Memorizing correct feeling is synonymous with learning to ride. A rider who is never made to feel that which is correct, cannot be expected to perform correctly.

Lungeing riders takes a certain knowledge. Such work should not consist of the rider sitting in an approximation of the Grand Prix rider's seat. Often one sees people being lunged, and being perpetually adjusted to the "ideal posture." This does not achieve the desired goals of lungeing. During a lungeing session, the rider's all-around athletic ability should be developed. Balance, coordination, strength, suppleness, stretching of muscles, and rotating of joints should be encouraged. When a sensible lungeing program is incorporated with jumping, cavaletti work, and cross-country riding, the result will be the development of a rider who is physically capable of aspiring to meet the myriad of demanding requirements for becoming a skilled dressage rider.

The Reasonableness Of
The Correct Seat

Without a correctly sitting rider the horse cannot move without pain or discomfort. The absence of these signals the beginning of cooperation between horse and rider. Based on such cooperation we can gain the horse's trust in us and attention to our desires. Only a correctly seated rider can apply the aids effectively. By the combination of being a pleasant weight and communicating properly, we may achieve the desired athletic development in our horse.

As in most athletic endeavors, the rider must develop the seemingly contradictory qualities of relaxation and strength. Relaxation allows horse and rider to harmonize, not only by virtue of absence of discomfort or pain, but by finding pleasure in moving through space in cooperative unity. With appropriate strength in the necessary areas of the rider's musculature, he can communicate through his aids to direct the horse's athletic development. That development is based on the ability to ride the horse in gymnastically helpful patterns and in an athletically appropriate frame or bodily situation. In the process, both horse and rider learn balance, their muscles are suppled, and their joints elasticized.

The balance of the rider in the saddle is the first step. So long as the rider fears falling off, or even just losing balance by slipping, relaxation cannot be expected. When losing balance we instinctively tighten many sets of muscles (wrong ones) in the hope that sheer strength and gripping will secure us in the saddle. Lungeing by an expert, providing the rider with many hours in the saddle without having to concentrate on controlling the horse, gives a sense of safety to the rider and allows instruction to improve balance. At first the rider should help his balance by holding the front of the saddle or a neck strap (certainly not the reins). He then relaxes the manually induced safety and balance aid for increasingly longer periods, and thus will grow gradually independent of the necessity to hold. Soon, initial balance will be established. But further refinement is necessary, so when the rider has stopped slipping in the saddle at the basic gaits, he can begin exercises that involve moving various parts of his body independently.

An independent rider emerges through the long process of these exercises, both *suppling* and *stretching,* done at the three basic gaits. Since they enhance independent control of specific parts of the rider's body, they are indispensable in enabling the rider to assume control over his horse and begin rudimentary but meaningful application of the aids. The exercises should involve every part of the body, literally from the toes (uncurl them for heaven's sake!) to the eyelids (close them often).

An equestrian becomes a rider as soon as he has a *balanced* and *independent seat.* Now he should be allowed to take control of his horse. Prematurely allowing control of the horse by the novice rider accounts for terrible habits of seat and aids that may never be completely corrected, only mellowed. Also, the psychological effects of being victimized by the horse who soon discovers that the unbalanced, tense and ineffective rider is easy prey for frolicking and so uncomfortable a burden that he should be gotten rid of, can remain detrimental to the rider forever.

So now let me call your attention to some particulars concerning the rider's seat and aids. These are the ones most often lacking in many riders' performances. Unfortunately, to adjust and make proper a rider's seat is not possible in print, but takes personal instruction.

The rider's head should never be tipped or inclined sideways, with the chin to one side. The neck should be back as if leaning against a head support in a car: the neck has vertebrae that must remain part of a straight (and upright) spinal column. The neck muscles should be relaxed, so that the rider is able to look sideways without affecting his functions elsewhere. Obviously, we ought to look around in both flat-work and jumping. A good exercise is to turn the head from side to side slowly until the chin is placed over the collar bone but remains high.

The shoulder blades should be straightened and tightened to make them lie flat in the musculature (not visible butterfly wings) and have only an inch or so between them. This lifts the rib cage (chest out), insuring good breathing and a straight spine. The rider must concentrate on correct body posture *constantly*, including when dismounted, even while driving a car. Shoulder blades flat into the back! The upper arms must *hang* in a relaxed fashion; imagine that the elbows are weighted with lead. The great mistake is to stretch the arms forward, thereby rounding the shoulders and rendering the chest concave.

Do not ever arch (hollow) the lower back and so stiffen it. That horrible position annuls the functions of the lower back, which, in my opinion, is *where riding is!* Riders who slant the pelvis forward, placing hips ahead of the seat bones, press the crotch down, and slant the lower abdomen over the pommel have never felt what riding is. They "limb ride" and eliminate the faintest possibility of feel, never know where the horse's quarters are, cannot sense the condition of the back muscles (which they pound stiff by that position), and only accelerate with legs and brake with hands. With a hollow back the rider's body cannot be used as the *"transformer"* (which I have written about previously) of the energy fed from the haunches, absorbed through the seat and returned to the horse's mouth forward in an appropriately altered fashion.

The rider's thighs should remain flat on the sides of the saddle and should be relaxed (unless in jump position or rising), but stretched from his hip, so that the knees stay low and back. To create this very important deep knee and long stretched contact situation the best exercise is to rise to the trot without stirrups! (Until blue in the face? Yes, sometimes.) It will also vastly improve the rider's balance (even eliminate falling off!).

The stretching of the calf muscles (ankle extensors) and ability to contract those around the shin bone (ankle flexors), producing the heels down, toes up position is crucial for stable, quiet, strong, and appropriate pushing (driving) and bending aids. Without properly formed (and used) calves there is simply no effective riding! A common fault is that riders wanting "dressage" attempt to ride "that style" by lengthening their stirrup irons by four notches. *Wrong! The rider must earn* the long stirrups *gradually* as he stretches his muscles and sinews: his legs "get longer" from the hip to the heel and *necessitate* the lengthening stirrups *one hole at a time* as this development takes place! So, start with *very short* stirrups, rise or stand in your knees until they are worked down and back while the heels are *forced* to sink down as the stirrup irons insist on keeping your toes high. Then in sitting trot and canter keep trying in short stirrups, always taking care that the knees remain pressed down and back: *bend your knees!* The feeling is similar to going down on your knees in church. It takes concentration and *perpetual readjustment* of the slipping knees and lower legs: down and back with them all!

The upper arms should *hang* (not be extended forward), and the elbows should feel weighted. Do not flare the elbows away from the rib cage. Start by hanging the arms straight down, then bend at the elbows, and put your two fists close together in front of your abdomen. Adjust the reins so that you can hold them in that relaxed position. There should be both relaxation in the arm muscles and tranquility (steadiness) at the shoulder and elbow joints. Without these qualities there can be no independent hands; the rider's hands will jolt, jar, dance and jiggle around.

The wrists should be straight; that is, the top of the rider's hand should be on the same plane (straight continuum) as his forearm. If you assume that correct position, the large joints of your fingers should touch when you press your fists together. The wrists bent out so that they can touch on the inside is stiff and incorrect, as is overbent wrists that make the knuckles touch.

All fingers should be closed all the time; a full fist should be made, with all the fingertips lined up in one row in the middle of the palm. Open fingers do not demonstrate light hands! They are dreadfully wrong (even dangerous), for such a rider will constantly lose some of the rein and will have to repeatedly readjust. The contact will be upset, altered, restless. Because riders do not learn initially to ride with closed fingers and a closed fist, at higher levels they keep losing the contact with the snaffle and remain only on the curb bit, thereby overbending and tensing their advanced horses. The thumbs should point down into the sharp angle formed by the large joint of the bent forefinger. The pressure on the reins should be there, the friction for holding a steady contact produced by that thumb pressure holding the reins tightly against the forefinger.

Well, these suggestions should take a while to carry out, and I wish you fast progress in acquiring these skills.

While instructing, a "straightening of the wrists" is often called for and the same request is frequently repeated at the end of judges' score sheets. The rider's wrists should not be stiff, a fault which is often caused by incorrect angling. It should not be "hinging" either; that is, it must not be allowed to rotate in and out. This is an action of the wrist frequently, if mistakenly, employed for a softening action in the hand.

The wrists should be simply quiet and relaxed, which is the natural consequence of the "straight wrist" position. The rider should never deviate from this. A riding whip may be used to help straighten the wrist. Holding the wrist correctly, the lower arm and the top of the rider's hand will form *one continuous and flat plane*. The whip will continuously touch the arm, wrist and hand. The whip touches only at the elbow and the knuckles which are pointing out. This is a common and grave fault! An equally grave fault is the "thumb down" stiffness. The line should remain straight below the wrist in the hand, as well as above the wrist in the arm.

The rider's legs represent the most important elements of a harmoniously coordinated aiding system. They are the primary sources of impulsion and bending. Horses are most often *not* on the aids (nor consequently on the bit either) because of ineffective legs of the rider. Ineffectiveness of the driving and bending aids is most commonly due to incorrect positioning and use of the leg.

A common, incorrect leg position develops when the thigh and knee are held too tightly (gripping) on the saddle. The rider's lower leg is pushed away from the horse, preventing contact by standing in the stirrup irons. The ankles are locked stiffly (not rotating with the motion of the horse or while aiding) and the toes are turned out. While there is a false "heel down" position, the leg is rendered useless. When working in such a position, the aid comes suddenly, from a distance. It is ill-timed and becomes a kicking action upsetting the seat of the rider. This kind of leg can neither produce pushing aids (the only powerful yet relaxed aids) nor can it supply rhythm based on supple contact.

At the expense of bringing both the knee and the toe out, the "closed on the horse" look can be produced by contact with the horse's rounding sides. Consequently, the ankles are locked stiffly. The turned out knees pinch the seatbones tightly together, as opposed to the correct wide distribution of the seatbones on either side of the saddle. The aids produced by these legs are often rhythmical but banging, giving the impression that the horse is being rhythmically beaten up by a pair of rubber truncheons. Highly visible and rude aids like these can dull the horse and sour him to the aids. Also, there is not modulation to such aids; for they come at the horse at the same rate all the time. They over-aid for the most part, but never modulate in power.

When the stirrup irons are positioned under the ball of the foot (good for jumpers but not for dressage riders) and the rider is applying undue pressure downward onto the irons the position is considered wrong. The ankle is again locked, preventing free circulation of the joint, forcing the foot and toes into immobility. Aiding is affected by an upward scratching on the horse's side. Both heel and knee are pushed upward by the rider "pedaling down" on the stirrups, like a bicycle. Meaningless aids develop.

A great deal of strength is exerted by the rider (many calories burned) but a dull horse that cannot interpret the annoyance of a heel pushing into his sides is the result. Such "heel rubbing" aids never suggest to the horse to go forward or bend. Lightness of the rider's seatbones and tension in the lower back accompany this incorrect leg position. The toe behind or flush with the knee of the rider is good, as is the "near parallel to the horse's sides" foot position. These are the reasons why this rather ineffective position is commonly but mistakenly accepted as OK.

Another example of *incorrect* position of the leg develops when the rider wrongly reacts to the request of "put your leg back." Yes, put it back, but stretch it back from the hip. The leg should always be stretched down and back from the hip so the knee and thigh are pushed down and back! Often the rider is pulling the stirrup leather back behind the vertical, pulling only the lower leg back. This produces a raised heel, no calf power, high gripping knee position and locked ankles struggling to hold the stirrup irons by turning out and pushing down. No aids, other than anemic kicking are forthcoming. Usually the rider's torso is also slanted stiffly forward to counter-balance the "I have a feeling of falling forward" sensation.

Photography by D. Edmund-Jones, England

*An instructor must step up to a rider to "sculpt" him into a correct position.
One can only learn that which one feels or has experienced. Therefore, here
the author moves the ankle for Andrew Rymill, Esq. while in England, offering the experience of feeling the rotation rather than just hearing many words,
that may be available for misinterpretation.*

The last example of *incorrect* position occurs when the rider pushes forward and down on the stirrups in the "stepping on the brakes" position. This eliminates all chances of aiding in contact with the horse. Such a leg position also pushes the buttocks of the rider onto the cantle of the saddle and the rider sits stiffly and totally out of harmony. Instead of *one* vertical weight vector acting down on the horse's back, there develop several restless, ever-changing weight vectors. The rider tries to stand up on the stirrup irons to steady himself and a vicious circle develops.

Correct leg position can be seen in photographs, films, and best of all actual riding of the great internationally competing masters of dressage. The greatest thrills to me are offered by the leg aids used by Dr. Reinert Klimke and Mrs. Karin Schlueter of Olympic renown. There are others to watch of course, and it is from this distinguished group that our models should be chosen.

The Use Of Aids
That Prevent Pulling

The reins in the rider's hands are tools and as all tools can be put to good or bad use. Pulling on the reins, even in transitions, is misuse of the reins. In fact, with some but not much exaggeration, one could think of dressage as aiming at the elimination of pulling hands or painful contact in general. Thus, strong stress through the reins, whether constant or occasional, is counter to the goals of dressage.

If riders pull because they are misguided, not understanding enough gymnastic theory to know why it is harmful to the horse's development, some good reading, clinic instruction, or conversation could set them on a new, more appropriate training track. However, in this chapter, I would like to deal with the rider, most commonly met in my work, who wishes to do well, understands that he must not pull, but feels he has to in order to be effective.

Many riders pull because they do not sit properly and therefore cannot apply their aids correctly. Their riding remains, therefore, often uneffective or only partially effective, and in their frustration they return to attitudes contrary to the spirit of dressage. They use the legs by kicking the horse to accelerate and use the arms to pull in order to brake. To them these thoughts are addressed, and I hope will be of help. For these riders mean well, are eager to learn how to do it right, and are theoretically not misguided.

Let us not forget that only that which is felt by the rider can be learned. Words never teach, they can only guide one to situations producing the proper feelings, results, and harmonies that will carry the message. Thus, my words on this page are worthless until the reader tries the suggestions they contain next time (and forever) in the saddle! I shall try to be as descriptive as possible in order to facilitate your actually *doing* what I suggest.

Riding is a sport, depending as it does on skills of coordination and *proper* use of muscles and the skeleton. Without further elaboration, let it suffice to say that a sack of potatoes, a bag of mush, a bowl of Jello® , or a flapping hat cannot effect the horse, even if placed on top of a saddle. Muscle tone, skeletal coordination, and strength in some areas are all necessary, as they are in any other sport this side of chess (strengthens the ear lobes?).

During riding instruction, one may often hear the teacher's oft-repeated suggestion and request for relaxation. However, indiscriminate or inappropriate relaxation is very harmful! Certain areas should be relaxed but others should not be! One must carefully define each area to give the rider an effective seat that can either drive or restrain without the pulling of the reins.

In general, the proper and therefore effective seat demands that the rider *be silent* (tight, muscled, in tone, not moving) *from the waist up and active* (relaxed, loose, light, pushing, tapping) *from the waist down.* Unfortunately, riders often have misunderstood the requests for relaxation and collapse with their torsos but grip with their legs. Often the rider with a loose top looks like someone in the process of kneading dough, including the detail of attentively looking down and sweating. Since that kind of hyperactive, but mushy torso can in no way stay in the saddle but bumps, pumps, and slushes on top of it, only the strong grip of the lower legs keeps the rider on the horse. In fact, the situation should be reversed!

The rider's torso should not only be properly stretched, straight, and perpendicular, but also in a constant state of isometric contraction. The rider should feel in the torso muscle tone induced by his own inner toning and flexing. Without that, the "silence" of the torso cannot occur, for the horse is very definitely moving, and the torso must accompany the horse's movement. All that depends on flexion and tone in the muscles. Let me suggest what actually to do when sitting in the saddle. This must necessarily fall short of personally "sculpting" the rider, but it is all words can offer:

1. *Sit* on the saddle *without pressing down on the crotch* (in order to get the three-point seat which, incidentally, has nothing to do with pressure on the crotch). In other words, *do not tilt the pelvis forward,* but keep it directly above the seatbones.

2. *Do not hollow your back* (that is *not* stretching up) or in any other way curve and therefore paralyze your spine. In other words, *sit on your buttocks* (that is their function) rather than pushing them out behind yourself. Keep your spine straight, which includes *pointing the tailbone (bottom of the spine) into (not away from!) the saddle.*

3. *Tighten your shoulder blades and flatten them into your back* so as to have no more than an inch between them; that is "stretching up," because only in that way can you *elevate the rib cage and stretch the abdomen!* That will also, very importantly, *stabilize your shoulders.*

4. The abdomen should *not* be relaxed and scoop, shove, wiggle, or otherwise remind you of an oriental dancer. Instead, *the abdomen must remain tight* to hold you up, stretched, and *to enable you to perform the half-halt.* A steady abdomen allows the lower back to follow the movement. The lower back should be relaxed so that the lower spine and lower back muscles can perform the half-halt properly. The abdomen is necessary for strengthening the seat (more adhesiveness and depth) so essential to half-halting. Occasionally lean behind the vertical to give yourself the correct feeling of how tight the abdomen ought to be, how it should work the torso back and forth (necessary in half-halting), and how adhesiveness in the saddle *really* feels!

5. *Keep your arms immobilized* rather than "feeding" the reins in walk and canter. The feeding of reins in order to follow the horse's head movements does not help the horse's contact and balance, but rather severely disturbs it. In addition, the horse will be whiplashed by the generously feeding hands that less generously jerk back on the jaw as well. Besides, both the feeding and jerking that follows are usually out of synchronization and disharmonious. *Arms rocking like that "unseat" the rider.* That is, the rider's aids do not go through to the horse but "short out" by being emptied through the arms onto the horse's neck (just like wiggling the abdomen does) instead of moving the aids down into the saddle properly. The horse, instead of feeling one rider, is disturbed by what seems to be many.

6. *Perfectly steady hands are a must in correct riding, and that includes straight and steady wrists and fingers closed into a full fist.* The lightest contact is not obtained by hinging the wrists nor with daintily opened fingers. In such hands there is frequent change, restlessness, inconsistency, and loss of contact.

The essence of these suggestions for adjustment of your position is simply this: *there is no aiding unless it is through a totally harmonized, continuous system.* There should be a firm feeling of "one riderness" (rather than loose mush) in order to create the lightest possible contact everywhere. Regardless of how many thousands of miles an underground pipeline supplying water is or how long an electric transmission wire, if these systems are broken at one tiny point, the whole system will fail. Analogously, in riding, if your seat, hands, legs, anything at all "shorts out" by wiggling independently from the rest of your body, your aids will fail to go through to the horse! That is why you then must use the unfortunate emergency measure of pulling (pain) to restrain.

I *know* that all horses can be ridden with the lightest of contact, without any restraint through the reins. It only takes proper equitation to be effective through lightness, ease, grace, and elegance, totally without force.

The Half-Halt

The *half-halt* is almost synonymous to dressage riding, for classical riding is without the force of hands. The half-halt, let us never forget, is a rebalancing aid that is "handless" when properly done. Pulling, jerking, or sawing with the hands is *not* a half-halt but its antithesis!

The half-halt is dependent on the rider's steadiness from the seat upward, in the torso. For it is based on anchorage (friction at the seat). The driving aids, so intimately part of a proper half-halt, cannot propel the haunches forward without a firm anchorage at the seat. The half-halt is "double everything," both restraining and driving.

All goals are achieved by proper means. Try to do some of the following, to get feelings, as means toward the ideal end.

Check the *steadiness of the torso* by tightening your muscles, so that when someone steps up to you on the ground and pulls on your arms (jerks even), you should not get loose anywhere: fingers, wrist, elbows, shoulders, abdomen, and so on. In fact, feel firmer down in the saddle as a consequence of the pull. Now make sure you pull on yourself, *not on the horse's mouth*. For these ideas about *your* being steady must be carried out with the tenderest rein contact on the horse's mouth.

Check the firmness of the abdomen by pushing the hip bones *upward* (not tilting forward!) toward your firmly lowered forearms, thereby elevating the crotch and lightening contact with the inner thigh muscles. When you deepen your seat (a must for the half-halt), you cannot do it by wishing for it. You must create adhesiveness with your buttock muscles, and that you can do only by pressing the hip bones upward and tightening the abdomen.

To get the feeling of deepening the seat, try to lift your inside knee for a few strides during canter and experience how that *does* put you down into the saddle properly. Or perform some "sit-ups" while trotting, leaning way back behind the vertical and slowly returning to the vertical position.

Do not fear losing "style," for just before the Olympic selection trials, you will be able to sit up just fine; these are *means* towards ends, not the way one competes in international contests. But by only imitating the posture of international riders, that is using the *ends* as *means*, you will never develop your seat and aids.

Only when the seat is deep and properly anchored will you begin to feel that you do not need to ride your horse with effort, for you have given your horse a chance "to ride himself through you." When you are mushy, hanging, wiggling, and loose in the saddle, the horse cannot use you gymnastically. It is analogous to a human gymnast using other items to create the gymnastic development and display. Without the floor mat, the parallel bars, or the rings, gymnasts can neither develop nor display their prowess.

The legs are the most important part of the aiding system. They both propel (provide the necessary energy) and bend the horse. There are no legs without an anchored seat, and there are no legs without their independence of balancing functions. Legs should *never* grip the horse's sides in order to hang on. Balancing by gripping with the legs is only necessary for those who do not sit anchored; rigid legs always go with an out-of-balance torso position (either loose or frozen).

Most riders' legs are positioned so as to rub backwards and upwards onto the horse's sides, toes out and down (locking in the stirrups), heels pulled up and pressing backwards. The opposite is necessary:

relaxed legs, deep heel position, and pushing action on the horse's sides downward and forward. Easily said, but how do we do it?

Put your stirrups out toward the tip of your toes; that gives you a longer foot, enabling your heels to drop. Only with dropped heels can you give supple strength to your calf, with which you must aid (rather than with the heels). A short foot, with stirrups at the ball of foot (good for jumpers but not dressage) or locked further in to the heel, cannot rotate properly to give pushing aids.

To use the calves and not the heels, the ankles have to be relaxed and rotating. When your legs are back where they belong (toe behind the knee), then you can slowly turn the toes inward, followed by lowering of the heels, which pushes the toes slightly outward, followed by turning the toes inward again. The feeling in walk and canter is slow, rhythmic pushing forward and down on the horse's sides. In trot, the rhythm is much faster, and on a green horse some bouncing of the calf off his barrel is all right, but later one wants a smooth undulation of the calves without their leaving the horse's barrel completely.

To build the skill and the feeling, you should aid the horse "with your toes" by bouncing (or circling) the toes inward toward the horse's body. You will *never* touch the horse with your toes, and you should not; but by bouncing the toes inward, you succeed in suppling your ankles and actually aiding with the calves! Ignoring calf aids, the only pushing aids possible, and insisting on aiding with the heels is the ruin of many riders.

Once the legs are capable of aiding, propel the horse by repetitious and rhythmic aids. For by repetition in good timing, the value of the aid increases the horse's motion rather than misguiding him to hurry with stiff steps. Just as one can break a glass by repeating the same note in proper intervals, so can one accummulate huge driving power effortlessly by repeating the message with the correct timing. By riding with stiff, strong, gripping, and kicking aids, you will only make the horse sour, stiff, or annoyed.

A good seat is an effective seat. Good aids are the consequence of it. Only through constant adjustment can one acquire such a seat and aids. Of course, one must constantly work toward a correct seat and aids. When riding, I feel myself perpetually readjusting, and in fact, often my aids are part of the readjustment process. Heels don't stay down because one pushes them down. They stay there because one keeps them there by readjustment during every stride. That readjustment is the circling with the toes, rotating the calf from the shin bone forward toward the back (thick) part.

When it all comes together, one has the fantastic sensation of having the horse ride himself through one's own effortless body, which is merely lent to him as are the rings to the gymnast.

The half-halt is the result of the synchronized use of all aids in an exaggerated form. Simply stated, it is "doubling everything!" When performing a half-halt, the rider should increase appropriately his leg, torso/back and rein aids.

The rider will increase his driving aids (legs) to facilitate improved impulsion (more engagement of the hindquarters). Against this, he will use retarding back and rein aids. As a result, a shorter but taller-moving horse, moving with more athletic resolve, will be made ready to change something in his position.

Half-halts should be performed prior to any major changes requested in the horse's position. As in good riding there is perpetual gymnasticizing, purposeful exercising of joints and muscles, half-halts should be performed with great frequency. To exaggerate their importance, one could state that riding is synonymous with the perpetual variation and interaction of half-halting, driving and relaxation.

Half-halts are performed in order to make changes easier for the horse and to allow him to change his position without reduction in his athletic involvement. Without a half-halt, the horse cannot make transitions (changes in longitudinal position), nor can he bend (changing lateral position), without compromising the major requirements of his athletic performance: relaxation, suppleness, balance, elasticity and maintenance of rhythm.

Prerequisites to half-halting:

The rider should be able to ride with an independent and balanced seat. Also, he should have developed effective use of his musculature. Because the half-halt's success depends on well-synchronized and appropriately strong (or mild) aiding, the rider must be faultlessly "on time" with it, as gentle (yet effective) as possible and perfectly capable of coordinating it with the movement the horse is then performing.

The horse should be well on the aids, that is, bending longitudinally, using his back supply to communicate impulsion from the hindquarters to the absorbing forehand. He should have a formed mouth that will respond elastically (without resistance) to both yielding or restraining reins. He should be, above all, eager to engage his hind-quarters when aided forward, without reluctance or sluggishness.

Maturation of both horse and rider must have reached a level at which both are athletically muscled enough and elasticized enough (in the joints) to expect of each other smooth, harmonious coordination.

Half-halts in any motion serve the purpose of suppling. Usually a horse will have a stiff side and a hollow side. As he moves, he will lean on the rider's hand on his stiff side, not accepting the bit on the hollow side. The rider should perform half-halts on the rein that is heavily contacted by his horse. The rider will gently present the bit and then relax its contact on that heavy side. The activity should be rhythmically performed to the beat of the hind leg on the stiff side. The most important feature of the half-halt is the fact that it is "half," and therefore terminates each time in yielding. As an example, the left leg drives while the left rein contacts, and alternates with both left leg and left rein relaxing.

Half-halts in transitions are indispensable for a supple arrival from one pace to another. The sign of such suppleness is that the horse does not need to change either his rhythm or his length when going from pace to pace. When going from a potentially faster pace (canter or trot) to a potentially slower one (walk or halt), repeated half-halts will make for a "soft landing," as the horse moving with considerable impulsion will settle lightly down to a slower pace without "falling" into it. The first stride of each pace has to be as pure and impulsive as the later one. Only by increased engagement of the joints (bending) prior to a new pace, can the horse gather his quarters under the weight to support it correctly. The half-halt repeatedly yielding will ensure an elastic entry into the new pace, with ample forward zest that is not inhibited by a paralyzing, steady pull.

When the transition occurs from a potentially slower to a potentially faster pace, the half-halt serves as a preparatory warning device. It also enhances improved engagement of the hindquarters. Thus, the prepared horse will be making a few more exuberant (engaged) steps and be more capable of lifting up into and propelling a trot or canter, rather than pushing forward and falling into the same.

Half-halts in lateral work should be employed to prepare each bending. Actually, every corner should be preceded by performances of half-halts. Without this, a horse usually will not bend, but rather fall through each corner. On lateral half-halts, diagonal aids are used.

Thus, a half-halt before a corner should be performed with the inside leg and the outside rein.

Depending on the horse's natural suppleness and elasticity, on his level of development and his responsiveness to the aids, half-halts may be repeated more or less often. An advanced horse that is moving well into the full bridle will respond to half-halts performed without the hands. This is to say that the horse will respond to the leg and seat aids only (the seat having a mild suggestion on the reins).

Thoughts On The Seat

Following is a symbol that can visually aid one's understanding that the harmonious seat results from balance (no slipping), relaxation, and appropriate flexion. The often-heard urging to "sit completely relaxed" is not clever, for *only certain parts of the body should be relaxed while others must flex!* Even when the thighs do not grip the saddle, there is flexion in them in order to push the knees down and back.

The calves should always be stretched by pushing the heels down and elevating the toes. The abdomen should not be slack (or worse yet, wiggle), for it is needed both for the driving aids through the seat and for the half-halt (restraining aids).

Common faults include over-relaxation of the shoulders, manifested in a mushy, deboned look of the rider, whose shoulders move up and down as well as sideways, disturbing balance. Others, who sit incorrectly with arched backs, pressing down on the crotch, will wiggle the abdomen and never absorb feelings from the horse's haunches nor be able to put anything back into the saddle. All pressures for driving "bubble out" through the abdominal wiggle and are emptied over the horse's withers. Instead, through a steadied abdomen the forces of riding, both the drive and the half-halt, should be placed into the saddle in order to affect the horse!

Note on the illustration that, in my opinion, harmony through the seat is not only a by-product of balance, relaxation, and flexion, but is *synonymous with aids.* For I know from feeling that when I ride, I cannot separate the two! When I move in harmony with my horse at the sitting trot, for instance, I am aware of my aiding him effortlessly, unconsciously, automatically by just that feeling of togetherness, that sensation of not knowing where my horse ends and where I begin. So I am convinced that there is no harmony without aiding, nor correct and successful aiding without harmony. But my message is that harmony leads *inevitably* to correct aiding without special effort. Therefore, learning the balanced, relaxed, correctly flexed seat is the very essence of riding, for without it there can be no perfect harmony that allows effortless aiding through unison.

A *balanced seat* is the so-called vertical seat, which incidentally appears "leaning behind the vertical" to some alarmed observers. The term "vertical" implies a vertical spinal position: the neck of the rider as well as his tailbone are both part of the spine and the neck should be directly above the tailbone. In order to produce a weight vector perpendicular to the ground, the line from the shoulder blades to the tailbone should be vertical, and *not* the line from the shoulders to the crotch!

As mentioned, when a rider works with an arched back (hollow and stiff with buttocks out behind the movement), the abdomen will undulate forward to act as a shock absorber (following the motion?). In such a case the rider's weight and driving force fall into the crotch, thus escaping through the horse's withers. Instead, the rider's lower back should be straight, and with the flexion of the abdomen (that holds the rider upright) the spine should slightly undulate in the opposite direction than it would with a hollow back. The sense of direction in the seat will come from feeling that the pressure of the shoulders down and back arrives in the saddle at the back of the seat, pressing the seatbones *forward toward the withers* (in every turn the inside one at least has to be pressed there).

A novice rider, or one who had an incorrect seat and has just been adjusted, should feel sore in the abdomen, thighs and calves.

The Collapsed Hip

Watching and judging competitors for a day, I often see some with a collapsed hip and naturally remark on it, for it affects the rider's score and is a severe enough fault to warrant the strongest urgings for correction. Sometimes, after the classes end, these riders come around to ask me what the collapsed hip really is and what am I talking about... So let's talk about it!

To identify a collapsed hip, you observe the rider from the front (or from the back). Let us suppose that the right hip is collapsed. Then this is what you will see:

1. The right stirrup looks (or is) shorter, the right ankle very stiff with the toe turned out and down more than the left.
2. The right knee higher and more forward than the left.
3. The right seatbone permanently pushed up to the center of the saddle while the rider "hangs away" from the horse to the left.
4. The whole seat falling away from the horse to the left; the rider's spine not straight upright above the horse's spine, but out to the left.
5. To compensate for falling away to the left, the rider, finally, drops the right shoulder down (bends torso to right) and looks stretched on the left (with high shoulder position) and hollow (collapsed) to the right.

Needless to say, the rider, just described, sits very crookedly. And since riding is based on harmony, such a seat will permanently impair progress. It therefore needs urgent and permanent correction.

Collapsed seats result from some stiffness in the rider. Stiffness may be initially isolated in a certain area but will inevitably spread to other parts of the rider's body. The collapsed hip syndrome is usually caused by *ankle stiffness*! If a rider cannot absorb the motion of the stirrups by properly resting the toes on them (rather than pressing down or walking on them), the ankles will stiffen. Stiff ankles are usually set or locked in a toes out position. By posting unevenly, by sitting into the hollow side of the horse, by misadjusted length (uneven) of stirrups, or by some native tension on one side, riders with stiff ankles will always turn one ankle out more sharply or press down with one toe more forcefully. This slight change in that tiny ankle area will push one entire side of the rider out of balance in the saddle and produce a collapsed hip!

Sit on a chair at home, put both feet on the floor, then push your right toe down, pull the heel up, and press, and you will feel your right seatbone move to the center of the seat and your hip collapse in the chair, producing the whole syndrome.

To correct it, eliminate the cause of the problem, do not just chip away at the symptoms. Thus, mobilize and supple the ankles (follow the stirrups with them; I wrote on it in past), press the toes up and heels down as you do it.

The collapsed side of the seatbone must be pushed forward. Take all leg contact away from the saddle and ride in walk (later some trot) with legs lifted away from saddle contact (knees higher for balance); feel how the seatbones can be pushed forward into place and how the lower back must work in order to keep them there!

In all turns, arcs, circles, etc., where the horse is expected to bend, you must ride with the inside seatbone pushed *forward towards the withers*. Many riders seem not to know about that, yet it is urgently necessary in order to drive properly. A rider who thinks that "the inside seatbone is heavier on circles" because one pulls it *back* (!) to the center of the saddle and leans over it (motorcycle syndrome!) is wrong! We feel heavier on the inside seatbone because in every bending situation the outside knee and thigh must be pushed *back and down*, steadying the lower leg on the outside in order to bend. Heels must be down!

Try the above leg position and feel that you are *automatically* heavier on the inside seatbone (the outside having climbed up in the buttocks) without leaning! Then push the inside seatbone *forward*, not sideways!

Use of Aids In Collection

The horse should be brought into collection without the use of hands. I urge riders to try it, for it is not only possible but the only correct method. You cannot learn anything in riding but what you feel — experience with awareness and develop a memory of it! So try it, do not let it remain just words.

Collection should be through a change of balance produced by *isometric contraction in the rider*. Just trot (or canter) and try this: Round your lower back by lifting the crotch off the saddle with the abdominal muscles. Press your shoulder blades together and tighten the muscles there without affecting the reins. Lift an imaginary ton of bricks with your lower arms without daring to actually elevate them or in any other way affect the horse's mouth. Lighten contact on the saddle until you feel none at the thighs, thereby making the seatbones float forward towards the withers. Then lighten the inside rein contact to a loose contact, as if you were sending down a little air-bubble to the inside corner of the mouth. Then relax (drop the ton of bricks), exhale (for heaven's sake!), follow with your back and tap with the inside leg. *Repeat! You will get collection*, and without pulling, tensing, or any artificiality.

Such transitions to collection can be easily understood by the horse through repetition and practice, and it feels pleasurable to them (as anything without force does). When the transition to collection is performed the horse should feel "uphill," as if you could raise him slightly with your spine . . . . just a feeling!

The Horse's Gymnastic Development

Riding logic in daily work and throughout the years grows like this:

WHAT WE WANT . . . . **MANIFESTS ITSELF IN:**

A) **Relaxation** . . . .
1) Longitudinal bending (on the bittedness).
2) Acceptance of driving aids (stepping under rather than speeding up, or lengthening rather than hurrying).

B) **Balance** . . . .
3) Lateral bending (with continuous spinal flexion and without speeding up or slowing down).
4) Transitions from gait to gait (without impurities or uneven footfalls).

C) **Rhythm** . . . .
5) Lengthening and shortening strides (the base of the horse) without losing flexion (relaxation and stretching of muscles while skeletal balance changes).

D) **Impulsion** . . . .
6) Controlled energy, manifested in slower but more suspended action; more fluent, continuous, and round action; supple use of joints owing to elastic musculature.

F) **Engagement** . . . .
7) Cadence: effortless flight (suspension); minimum energy produces maximum suspension, because the haunches carry maximum weight, liberating the forehand.

What we want must happen *in exactly the order in the chart.* If it is lost, steps must be retraced to an earlier stage.

The left-hand column is also the progression of suppleness. Gymnastic development is all about suppleness (not stiff horses running around with uneven steps and open jaws!). The terms on the left denote levels of suppleness, from the most primitive manifestation (relaxation) to the most sophisticated (engagement).

The right-hand list should help you understand what you feel when you have it or what you see in standardized competition tests. The tests we ride were written *with this purpose in mind*, that these stages of development be demonstrated for evaluation. Thus, when you see a movement that calls for canter left lead, turn onto the diagonal, trot at X, and canter right lead at H, you know the horse's *balance* is being tested!

Participating
in Courses,
Clinics,
Competitions,
and Judging Forums

What Is Expected Of A Rider Who
Participates In A Clinic?

Every instructor will have preferences as to the appearance, equipment and preparedness of students. I can speak about mine only, while hoping that they correspond to some of the expectations of fellow instructors.

Expectations vary somewhat, depending on the frequency of instruction for a particular pupil. I most often instruct people either once a month, or for the first time in an area where there has been either no dressage instruction or, let us say, a clinic once a year.

The horse should be in continuous training of some sort prior to a dressage clinic. He should be strong enough to take an hour of serious riding. Good muscle tone and good wind should result from both regular riding and correct feeding prior to a clinic. A horse conditioned this way will also have an acceptable attention span and certain ability to concentrate.

The rider should also be in athletically acceptable condition. Sick, injured or weak riders will have a low tolerance level, both physically and mentally, to cooperation in a serious, prolonged lesson.

Ideally, riders with an independent, correctly balanced seat will benefit most from a "one shot" clinic. I have learned that the seat of riders, as well as their use of aids, needs frequent and considerable attention. Few have been started correctly and therefore I accept that equitation becomes part of clinics. However, one should be able to "co-teach" the horse with the rider during clinics.

Also ideally, daily instruction (otherwise three times a week) may still be warranted for riders who need to acquire an independent, balanced seat with which aids can be supplied in a correct manner.

The horse's equipment should include a dressage saddle, well adjusted headgear and the proper bit for the level of the horse's development. Regulations concerning those are to be found in the Rule Books. However, I inevitably find many unnecessarily long leather pieces, particularly on the chin strap. These should be trimmed to such a size as to be tucked properly without hanging over. Riders also often come to lessons with stirrup leathers uneven. They had gotten accustomed to riding in such badly adjusted stirrup lengths and had reinforced a poorly developed seat with a collapsed hip. All of the tack, needless to say, should be clean!

The rider's equipment should approximate, as closely as possible, proper competition attire (Rule Book). Competition attire is correct attire in which riding can be most properly done and the rider most accurately observed. By all means, if you do not wear a properly tailored riding coat, do wear something that reveals the position of the torso and the use of the back muscles. Never come to instruction in bulky raincoats, ski sweaters or windbreakers. Wear proper riding boots for the sake of proper aids.

Carry at least one, but preferably two, riding whips. Both the rider and the horse have two equally important sides and one rides on both sides, the other is aided on both sides. Thus two whips might be a great asset in effectiveness. I prefer riders without spurs when riding horses developed under Third Level dressage. Sensitivity to mild leg aids is paramount in dressage riding and can best be developed on phlegmatic horses with the aid of whips. Spurs are warranted when collection and cadencing work commence. They are instruments of sensitivity, as is the double bridle.

At the beginning of a lesson the rider should walk up to the instructor and halt there. They exchange greetings and the instructor can learn the student's name. While the instructor inspects the equipment and adjusts it when necessary, the rider should offer a short and relevant report on the horse. This should include information on the horse's age, background, current work and training, particular problem areas and strengths in performance as well as weaknesses.

After the equipment, including stirrup leathers, has been inspected and properly adjusted when necessary and the rider's report has come to a conclusion, the lesson may properly begin. I prefer adjusting the rider's skeletal position while still at the halt. This is the time to sculpt the rider's position.

Then I ask the rider to leave for the rail or large circle and perform all three basic paces with the necessary transitions leading to them, very briefly, and then come back to a halt. This brief performance enables the instructor to diagnose the problems the rider may have with his seat and aids, and the horse with basic paces or fundamental development. The results of the observation can be discussed and then the lesson may begin in earnest!

Some Suggestions For
Riding A Dressage Test

As I make my rounds of travel conducting clinics, I am delighted to hear questions concerning showmanship and competition performance during our theory sessions. This is one more good sign that dressage riders are maturing in mass toward not only competition, but higher level test riding as well. Thus, comments on test riding are timely.

I chose the discussion of a Fourth Level test for several reasons. The most important of these is the ever increasing number of riders entering that rather sophisticated level of competition. Also, the Fourth Level test is one that serves as a bridge between training tests and "real"dressage riding as accepted internationally. Furthermore, riders preparing the Fourth Level test no longer need equitation suggestions, allowing me to concentrate on showmanship.

Let us begin with generalities. Once again I must make use of musical analogies. Playing the piano is not enough alone for a great performance. The skill of performing must be added or acquired before sucess is achieved. As the great concert pianist will not look at musical notes but play by heart, so will the great dressage rider ride his test from memory, without having it shouted to him by his mother-in-law at the side of the arena. Practice makes perfect, and the rider who has the test called, concentrating on finding the letters of the arena, will perform as poorly as would a pianist who is searching for the notes in a music book while playing. Only a well practiced test will show brilliance.

There is a myth about not riding tests frequently in practice. The reason given is that the horse will learn the ride and anticipate its movements. They must be kidding! Ride your test daily, then let your horse loose in the dressage ring and see if he will perform the test by memory. If riders miss test sequences even when they have a friend read the test for them, how could such vast intelligence be presumed of the horse as to suppose that he will learn it by heart! International riders often perform the Grand Prix test for a decade on the same horse. Yet, the horse never "messes up the test" by anticipation, let alone performing of his own volition movements that he has memorized.

Every dressage test is a logical composition unfolding a sequence of gymnastic exercises that allow the rider to show how well developed his horse is mentally and physically. As a composition, the test has fluency and beauty inherent by logic and balance. Dressage tests must be performed in their totality, not in bits and pieces or as patchwork. Once again let us be reminded. A concert pianist does not perform notes or measures, but rather a whole composition that is beautiful only in its entirety.

Nor are uneven musical performances delightful. Some parts played harshly, and others with poetic softness will show either a lack of understanding of the piece or a lack of skill in unfolding it correctly. Riding a dressage test often owes its greatest beauty to consistency. Once your horse and your temperament develop a bold and distinct style, carry it out persistently. Should there be a dainty, poetic or minor key revealing your greatest strengths, present your tests in that mood.

Practicing the parts of a dressage ride is as necessary to the rider as it is for a pianist to rehearse certain passages of his music. However, that activity should be relegated to practice sessions. It is painful to listen to only a few repeated bars of music, however brilliantly they may be played. Likewise, it is rather tedious for both horse and spectator to find that kind of repetition in unending dressage exercises. So once again, do ride the total test often. It will establish your mood and reveal your shortcomings. Then repeat the exercises that are weak.

Next, do not ride the test, ride your horse! You must know the test so well, have ridden it so often and polished it in such detail, that you should never really know which letter you ride by. You should know the composition of your ride, forgetting the letters that aided you to memorize it originally.

Often horses enter the arena tensely or above the bit. Sometimes they are lacking impulsion, attention or obedience. But what is worse is that often riders placidly accept these shortcomings and go through motions of the test without ever having attempted any correction of their horses. Although this is not always the case, it many times takes just seconds to re-establish your rapport, win his attention or relax and supple your horse. You should do it when at all possible. He is your instrument for the performance, and must be tuned ahd serviceable.

We have already discussed the transition to the halt from the canter, so I will not go into it again (see unit 1). Reining back while facing the judges would suggest that straightness is of the utmost importance here. Take time to prepare your horse for the backward strides while he is still at the halt. Adjust the position of the aids subtly before actually using them. Do not look down "into" your horse. On the center line, look unconcerned, as this attitude can pull together this demanding sequence of longitudinal transitions on the center line. Your attitude can be the greatest harmonizer and can give a last, but lasting impression of having effortlessly ridden an "automatic" horse. At the free walk, approach the judges still on the straight line and leave the arena on the long wall opposite the spectators' stand.

When should a dressage competition rider advance to the next higher level of showing?

Ideally, the rider should compete on a level where his horse can perform the gymnastics called for by the test effortlessly. This, then, presumes a proper athletic and mental development of the horse, who will consequently show the test in a seemingly effortless manner and with genuine relaxation. When such is the case, when a horse is really mature in the test, then under a knowledgeable judge he will receive a 60% or higher score result.

Riders should not enter their horses in tests where less than a 50% score can be reasonably expected. Should they receive, however, 60%

or higher scores from a reputable judge, they can interpret that as encouragement to go on the next higher level of tests in showing.

It is imperative to understand that in dressage one does not compete against others for a place (ribbon). In this art form, one competes against oneself only. Improvement should be understood only in terms of score percentile and not in terms of placement. It is, in other words, important to know the difference between a first place with a 42% score and an 11th place with a 62% score. The latter score signifies true achievement and the "right" to advance to the next level test. Despite winning, in the first case, the score indicates severe shortcomings in the horse's development which "forbids" one to advance for the time being.

The significance of the 60% score as one indicating fulfillment of the expected requirements for that stage of gymnastic development is underscored by the Danish System of awarding. According to that system of evaluation there are no place ribbons awarded to riders, but rosettes are given to all riders who scored 60% or more.

Often, ironically, riders score higher on more advanced tests than on lower ones ridden on the same day. The reason for this occurrence may be that the horse actually improved on the higher level test by having been warmed up in the earlier, lower level test ride. Or, more often, some horses can show their best gymnastic achievements on tests that allow them better to display that development.

Let me remind you that there are only four dressage tests that are ridden in international competitions. The lowest of these is the Prix de St. Georges, more difficult are the two Intermediate tests, and the most difficult test is the Grand Prix de Dressage. Yet all nations have lower level tests than these to allow riders to show, for educational purposes, during the lengthy preparation period for the real dressage tests. On these lower level training tests, Combined Event and Stadium Jumping horses are also shown. These training tests are basically, then, educational in value. Some of them are so undemanding that, indeed, an athletically well-advanced horse may not be able to show off his true achievements in them. However, this horse on a more advanced level may receive scores more truly indicative of his achievements.

Many riders will show their horses on two consecutive levels simultaneously. The lower level, presumably, is the more accomplished, more polished achievement. The higher level is the one on which the horse is "breaking ice." This is a good competition strategy. However, decisions concerning the advancement of the horse should be based on the highest percentile score received on a test. Thus, if a horse is shown on AHSA Second and Third Level tests and receives a 62% score on the Third Level test, but only a 58% on the Second Level test, he may still be advanced to the Fourth Level.

Serious dressage riders are well aware of the fact that their horses must be doing gymnastic exercises more advanced that those they show during competition test rides. It is presumed that a horse which shows well in the Third Level dressage exercises during competition is already being gymnasticized by exercises that will be part of the Fourth Level test. This is why, after receiving a 60% or higher score on a currently shown test, the rider should soon be able to show his horse on the next higher testing level.

In the USA our special circumstances of lacking a sufficient number of good coaches suggest that riders enter shows and ride tests even if they feel insecure about their having attained a show-worthy level of development. We must keep in mind that many riders must use competition opportunities as their only instructional opportunities. They must compete in order to be evaluated by an expert (the judge) and seek his comments for further improvement. Thus, it is forgivable to lower the standards of propriety in showing when doing so on an insufficiently prepared horse, for the purpose of instruction.

How does one go about composing a Kuer?

The general conditions of a Kuer should be noted and adhered to by riders setting about to compose one. These are listed on page 27 of the "Supplement to Rules on Dressage and Combined Training", which is reprinted below. Particular attention should be paid to paragraph (2), as it is most relevant for the proper composition of Kuer.

FREE STYLE KUER: Rider is to create and execute from memory an original ride showing off his horse to his best advantage. (Music optional).

1. Combination Class. Horse to be shown in prescribed dressage test Third Level or above and then to be shown in a short (5 minutes or less) Free Style Ride. The rider shall create a ride which highlights the horse's ability and which is not necessarily limited to the requirements of the prescribed dressage test. Highest combined percentage score for

both rides to win.

2. Free Style Ride. Horse to be shown in a Free Style Ride. Prize List to specify Dressage Level(s) Third Level or above. Rider shall create an artistic ride which includes movements appropriate to the Level prescribed by show management. Time allowed: six, seven, or eight minutes, to be specified in the Prize List.

3. Free Style Ride may be employed to break ties in dressage tests Third Level or above. This procedure must be specified in the Prize List.

4. Scoring: One score for artistic composition and design of ride (0-10). Failure to include all movements required as per prize list shall be penalized under the score for composition. Warning bell shall be rung one minute before end of the ride. Movements performed after the time limit will not be considered by the judge, and the ride will be penalized under the score for composition.

5. Except where specifically requested by show management in the Prize List, riders shall not be required to present in written form a copy of the Free Style Ride. Furthermore, since the total ride is to be judged, no errors of course can accrue.

In my opinion, the Kuer is the king of dressage competitions. Judging it, is a pleasure far surpassing that afforded by judging prescribed tests. The element of novelty, the manifest ingenuity in composition, the thrill of the unexpected, all contribute to that feeling of evaluating something that is now "world premiered." The Kuer lets the rider emerge not only as a performing artist, but as a composer-creator of art as well. Watching a brilliant Kuer may give one the same thrills audiences felt when Rachmaninoff played Rachmaninoff piano concertos in concert. Perhaps even more so for often a Kuer is seen for the first time, while Rachmaninoff's works may have preceded his performing them, or recordings or renderings by other artists.

Riders earn merit equally by the propriety and ingenuity of their composition on the one hand and the level of perfection of its performance on the other. The scores of these two elements weigh equally (scoring - paragraph 4).

The propriety of the Kuer demands that the rider display all the paces and movements appropriate to their level of development and entry, and that these movements fit comfortably into the time allowed for the performance.

The ingenuity of the Kuer, in general, depends on the rider's artistic creativity, sense of proportion and thorough knowledge of how to display the horse to his best advantage (half the score is on quality of performance). Specifically, I can give some hints as to my preferences for good compositions as follows:

The test should display fluency. Movements should easily flow from one another and offer a sense of riding (gymnastic) logic: progressing from simpler towards complex. Part of fluency is a vigorous beginning and crescendo ending. Remember that musical symphonies (and there is much in common with music) usually begin with lively attention-getters, and drive to an impressive conclusion, rather than fainting away.

When composing an impressive beginning, keep in mind that you have to top that by a magnificent ending (that is when the judge scores!). For instance, in a Grand Prix Kuer, entering with a passage would leave you little if any choice for an ending that tops that!

Building from simple to complex can be expressed by:

Patterning: larger patterns (i.e. circles) to smaller. Commonly used, familiar patterns (i.e. center line) to surprise ones (i.e. quarter lines, or serpentines limited to only one side of the arena as divided by the center line). One word of caution: while using new patterns can add to the interest and novelty of your test, avoid making transitions at rarely used or non-existent points (letters), for that may make the impression that you meant them somewhere else but could not manage to get them at the letter you wanted.

Transitions should also become more complex as the test progresses. To give you an idea, note that the "king of transitions" is made up of many, all difficult, and graces the Grand Prix test. It is movement 34 in the test, as follows: Down center line at collected canter to halt at L, to rein back four steps, to passage! Now that is what I mean by complex (many transitions) and sophisticated (as difficult as you can get). One should provide such transitional feats later in the Kuer, not at the beginning.

Paces should be shown from simple to complex. Obviously a working or medium mode of a pace is simpler than the extendedor collected manner. Obviously the walk is simpler than the canter (particularly when a figure like pirouette is involved!)

The symmetry of the patterns is of utmost importance. Not only because the symmetrical test is aesthetically more beautiful, but also because good riding logic demands it: the horse has two equally important sides that must be properly gymnasticized. However, even the symmetry of your design can progress from simpler to more complex. When the symmetry is simple then an exercise performed on one rein is immediately repeated on the other rein (i.e. figure-eight). When it is complex, an intricately sequenced pattern that includes several transitions may be repeated in its mirror image on the other rein. Note that this is time consuming: you cannot do it often in a short Kuer.

The balance of the Kuer depends on an equitable distribution of time to all three basic paces (walk, trot, canter). Yet I have two suggestions here:

Show more at your best pace and much less in your worst to cleverly influence the performance score. You can manage that without compromising balance by showing your worst pace in a novel pattern, at an unexpected place, or following a brilliant movement. Show your best pace as much as possible: give the judge a chance to feast his eyes! Besides, "shows" are all about showing that which is show-worthy, not our weaknesses. That is why, if you handle this cleverly, you can get a better performance score than on your standardized tests where your worst pace has to be shown all too much for comfort.

Show slow paces (walk or collected trot and canter) on short patterns (such as while changing hand on half-arena line or from K to F). Show bold paces on longer lines and for longer durations: that is gymnastically logical and also gives the impression of a bold, forward thinking performance.

In conclusion, remember that the Kuer is artistic when it is logical (rather than ambitiously confusing), is aesthetic (by means of symmetry and fluency) and artistic (novel and daring). When you compose one, even before riding it, scrutinize it as to its fluency, complexity, symmetry and balance. Ride it, to see how it feels as to performance quality, and have the courage to alter it when needed. Do not forget that it should reflect perfect riding logic and the best performance (unhindered by required, standardized test) of your horse!

Riding a Kuer to musical accompaniment is optional. However, keep in mind that even judges have a subconcious (so said Freud and Jung) and good music can pave your way to a better score: for one thing it helps the judge know what pace is occurring (no longer subconcious merely). Besides, are we not riding for the pleasure and beauty of it all? Music so increases both!

Music should be started at the moment you depart from your salute, not when entering, and should be stopped when you halt to salute at the end, not left on during the salute, which should be made in silence.

What Is The Correct Way To Salute The Judge During Competitions?

In spite of the phenomenal improvement in the quality of some competition rides, I continue to see the majority of riders salute poorly. Since I fequently remark on this on the test sheets, upon completion of the shows riders question me concerning the correct way to salute.

The illustrations are the result of the willingness to cooperate of two Californian professional riders, Elizabeth Friedlaender-Searle and Jeff Moore. To the joy of many spectators, they have ridden together some fine "Pas de Deux" and their saluting exemplifies the differences between a lady's and a gentleman's proper salute.

A proper salute is very important because it is not only the first major impression the judge receives of the rider but it also is the only real personal contact between competitor and judge. The actions of the salute crystalize into a formal tradition (protocol) that is based on adherence to elegance as well as making provision for not disturbing the horse or his balance during the halt.

The salutes at both the beginning and end of the test should be identically performed:

Correct Performance Of The Salute:

1. Settle the horse into a balanced (four-square) halt. Riding down the center line facing the judge, including the transition, establish eye contact with the judge. Do not appear anxious about the horse or preoccupied with your transition. Halting still as a monument, put all reins into left hand. Be careful not to shorten set of reins on one side since that will bend the horse's neck and head to that side during salute. The horse *must* remain straight (See Fig. 9-1).

2. **Lady** drops right arm straight down. Arm should be relaxed and fingers should be naturally, relaxedly folded rather than outstretched with tension. **Man** should reach for his hat and hold it somewhat in front of his right ear (See Fig. 9-2).

3. **Lady** tilts her head in relaxed, continuous motion. She does not drop her head down abruptly. She *will* have to lose eye contact with

Fig. 9-1

Fig. 9-2

Fig. 9-3

Fig. 9-4

Correct Ways of Saluting During Competition

Saluting Techniques (Figs. 9-1 thru 9-7b) demonstrated by:
J. Ashton Moore and Elizabeth Searle   *Photographed by Kerry Schroeder*

the judge. **Man** lifts his hat *without* losing eye contact with the judge (See Fig. 9-3).

4. **Lady** will sustain tilted head somewhat longer to correspond to the time it takes for the man to perform with the added activities concerning the lifting of the hat (See Fig. 9-4).

5. **Lady** must maintain her salute with tilted head without anxiety or tenseness. **Man** drops arm straight down, holding the hat in a manner as to show its top facing outside, with inside lining facing the horse's side. No tension should be visible in the arm. The hat should be close to the horse and not visible to the judge at this point (See Fig. 9-5).

6. **Lady** re-establishes eye contact with judge and separates reins into proper hands. **Man** replaces his hat firmly enough not to lose it during the ride, doing so with a minimum of fuss.

7. Depart from halt.

The Most Common Faults And Mistakes Encountered:

1. Too fast or hyperactive salutes upset the horse's balance and project an attitude of ignoring the judge rather than honoring him.

2. Where **Men** are concerned, lack of continuous eye contact with the judge while riding down center line and during salute. We greet someone by looking into his eyes and the same procedure is used here since the salute is essentially a silent greeting. Eye contact while riding on center line is essential to riding a straight track. We go in the direction we look; the horse follows our subconscious body attitudes. Therefore, you cannot ride on a straight track from "A" to "C" (the judge), unless you *look* towards that point.

3. **Ladies** should not tilt from the hip or waist to salute. Only the head salutes. Otherwise the seat contact will be lighter, upsetting the horse's balance and possibly making him step back. Theatrical, sweeping arm gestures are both unbecoming and humorous. (See comparison in Figs. 9-7a and 7b).

4. **Men** should not stretch saluting arm to the side since it may collapse their hip, frighten the horse or upset his balance. Showing the inside of the hat in the begging position is also theatrical and humorous. The hat's label is irrelevant to the judge.

5. **Men** should *never* lose eye contact with the judge during the entire proceedings. Do not tilt the head (see Fig. 9-6a and 6b).

Fig. 9-5

Correct
Salute

Fig. 9-6a

Fig. 9-6b

Incorrect
Salute

Correct
Salute

Ways of Saluting

Fig. 9-7a   **Incorrect**

Fig. 9-7b   **Correct**

Ways of Saluting

What Are Some Of The Ingredients
Of Good Judging?

I have had, for many years, the honor of being invited to judge dressage competitions. In recent years, I have been working with California apprentice judges on several occasions, preparing them for a judging career. My conducting judges' courses in England and Canada, has forced me to prepare an extensive program which in a nutshell may serve as an answer to the above question.

While spectators are invited to our yearly judges' forums and turn out in substantial numbers, those interested in dressage voice an increased need to know more about judging and what good judges are looking for. During past summers, to accommodate such needs, I worked some judging days into my long summer clinics. Not only those hoping to become future judges have been interested. Competitors, understandably, are interested in the standards of dressage judges. They want to know and ought to know on what principles their work will be evaluated.

A good judge is an expert and good judging is a by-product of thorough knowledge. Knowledge ought to increase. Theoretical and practical knowledge are both needed for expertise. As in all other fields of discipline, the experts, the evaluators, have been "doers," have had vast experience in the practical field. Beyond that, reading, conversation among experts, watching knowledgeably and with attention focused, and teaching are some of the ingredients that both prepare for judging and improve it with time. Probably active riding in competition and teaching are the two most valuable assets in good judging.

A judge is not a scoring machine. His expert opinions are sought not only on his score sheets. He is asked many questions before, during and after shows. His knowledge, expertise, must be so great as to stand up to these questions. His foremost duty should be to promote the classical standards of horsemanship. He must do that on his scoresheets both with scores and comments: reward all tendencies that are correct and punish the wayward, false and compromised efforts. If a judge is ill-acquainted with the classical principles of dressage, or worse, knows them but for various reasons is willing to compromise them, soon dressage in its pure form will disappear. Scoring should never accommodate situations. Thus, in areas where dressage is new, riders are novice or where combined eventers show on ill-prepared mounts, the same standards must prevail as elsewhere. Otherwise, the curious situation may occur that the rider gained his highest test score percentile when he was novice and as he became accomplished his percentile scores concurrently diminished. There is nothing wrong with winning a combined event dressage contest with an honest 32% score and advancing from there. There is something tragic in getting a 70% score with a horse above the bit in an "underdeveloped area". Scores are not numbers: they are an efficiently fast code-language for the communication of how closely the rider approximated the ideals judges are here to promote and uphold.

Judging consists of the interaction of three activities:

Knowledge of the rules of dressage competitions; of the goals of gymnastic development in the horse and their appropriate developmental stages.

Skills to observe accurately that which actually happens; to quickly decide on the hierarchy of importance of all that was observed; to make an instant value judgment and express it by a numerical score based on the hierarchy of importance.

Insight into the natural sequential development of the horse; into the conditions under which they are shown; empathy towards the rider and the horse as relevant in the pursuit of an ideal.

Not all individuals desirous of judging should be allowed to do so. Only the skills of judging can be acquired. Neither appropriately thorough knowledge of dressage nor insight can be developed easily to the level of expertise. Only those who are familiar with the classical principles of dressage and thoroughly trust them (for they know they work) can be expected to be dedicated to the correct standards uncompromisingly! Both theoretical and practical knowledge supply that factor of commitment that can uphold and promote the classical goals of dressage.

Scoring is a by-product of expertise. Therefore, constantly observe what is going on right now rather than referring to memory of what you know of the rider and horse from the past. More importantly, observe keenly in order not to judge by the memory of what went on in just the previous movement. One often has occasion to follow a score 3 with an 8 if prejudicial memory is not involved.

Translate what is perceived in terms of the hierarchy of its importance in the horse's development. The score must represent a knowledge of what is most important, less important, and least important in each movement. Knowing that the movements of each test were designed to demonstrate certain specific achievements by the horse, the judge must look for the proof that those standards have been attained. As movements flow with "connecting tissue", the essence of what is shown is often introduced through an "overture" which must not be overemphasized. For instance, the first movement of each test requires a straight entry at some pace, a halt and salute and a continuation; it involves two transitions among other things. Two bad judges looking at the same movement may score it anywhere from 1 to 10 depending on which unimportant feature they isolated for purposes of scoring. But if they are good judges and know the hierarchy of importance in that movement, their scores will be close or identical.

Make a quick decision on both the score and the succinct comment appropriate for guidance to the rider. In order to do that the judge has to computerize what has been observed, both as to its relative value to all the other rides observed in the class, and its relative value to the ideal of what should be shown. This ideal should be clearly in the judge's mind like a transparency over which the actual ride is superimposed. For each level test the "transparency" is a different ideal against which the horse performing is compared and contrasted.

The most important judging activity is the perception of the horse's activity and its comparison to the uncorrupted vision of the classical standards of requirements. Only when the perception is correct can the knowledge of the required classical principles be put to use to evaluate the activities observed.

To know the essence of each movement in a test is indispensable for correct evaluation. In a sequence of activities the judge must know, for instance, that the shoulder-in or rein-back or the halt is the most important, and weigh that feature more heavily in scoring than complementary features leading into or away from that action. Then he should observe that the required pace is pure and energetic, that is, natural and active; that the transitions are fluent, i.e. continuous, rhythmic yet clearly defined; that one pace terminates with as pure a stride as the new pace begins with.

In the observation of both the purity of paces and the definition of transitions, the following hierarchy of values should prevail:

Relaxation, a prerequisite to all other components of correct performance of a horse. Without mental and physical relaxation, only the horse's legs move; with relaxation, the horse renders himself into an athletically capable position and the entire horse becomes involved in motion and therefore develops athletically, improving his muscles, joints and coordination. A horse not relaxed is comparable to two moving-men lifting up a grand piano and carrying it across a room. The grand piano gets transported but is not involved in the movement. Similarly, a horse that only moves with his legs, due to tension, is not gymnastically involved. A relaxed horse is easy to recognize by its being longitudinally bent toward the bit. A horse not flexed in his length is neither relaxed nor stepping through his whole body. Therefore, from First Level on, a satisfactory grade can only be given on condition that the horse is longitudinally bent, thereby involved in motion in its entirety and developing as a consequence.

Balance may develop once the horse is relaxed. It is revealed most importantly through periods of transitions. Every movement in every test has a meaning, revealing one of these components to the judge for his evaluation of the degree of achievement in the area relative to the absolute standards of the ideal. When in balance, the horse must appear as a harmonious unit. His neck should not be artificially shortened or set higher than the stretching back muscles would suggest as correct or uninhibited. Thus, depending on the level of development in the horse, the harmonious look is different at various stages, through various tests. A balanced horse is not overdeveloped in one area at the expense of another. His movements reveal balance when the transitions are smooth, without loss or gain in rhythm, yet clearly defined: the last step of the preceding pace and the first step of the continuing pace as good, clear, pure and harmonious as expected to be when performed within a certain space and time. A balanced horse will also move in pure rhythm and pace when changing from straight to bent (such as from wall through corner) without either speeding up or slowing down.

Rhythm develops as a consequence of consolidated balance. It is best revealed by the added sophistication of lengthening and collecting the stride without losing the purity of the pace and the evenness of the rhythm. When the horse no longer rushes when asked to extend nor slows down when asked to collect, rhythm is a proven accomplishment.

Impulsion is energy controlled so as to increase the periods of time the horse is suspended and decrease the periods of touching down on the ground. In the walk, where there is no suspension period, the relative time the horse's limbs travel above the ground (roundness, elevation, reach) can reveal the degree of impulsion. Impulsion is certainly based on the horse's natural forward zest and enthusiasm, yet a fast, running horse that moves stiffly and close to the ground will be working through speed rather than impulsion. Impulsion presumes the kind of muscular and joint development which allows the horse to carry the rider slowly, yet with powerful vigor, by using his joints to promote an effortless locomotion that is smooth and suspension-oriented by its roundness and largeness. Needless to say, such impulsion may not be shown without relaxation, balance and rhythm. Unfortunately, as impulsion is often misunderstood, hurrying due to excessive driving by the rider is often accepted as its substitute. Judges should be very conscious of not promoting that mistake, for speed is the enemy of impulsion.

Engagement develops as the latest sophistication in the horse's gymnastic advancement. Therefore, it is cautiously and gradually introduced as a requirement in the tests, beginning with the brief and mild shoulder-in exercise in the Second Level test, thorough and sophisticated engagement is required throughout the entire test only on the FEI international levels. Engagement is revealed by the horse's ability to carry more weight over the haunches, thereby lightening the forehand and making all movements, both extended and collected ones, look equally effortless. As a result, all movements have an excessively cadenced look. That is, immaculate longitudinal and lateral flexion, perfect balance and rhythm, buoyant impulsion are all united to make the horse get off the ground by lifting rather than pushing actions of the haunches, which are well under the center of gravity. This enables the horse to perform with the lightness of a dancer and the litheness of a gymnast.

The natural hierarchy of the above-explained development should be appropriately weighed by the judge who evaluates the horse. Once the judge knows which of these stages is required in each test to be fulfilled and accomplished and knows through which movement each of the developmental stages are best revealed, correctly grading the movements will become automatically easy and decisive. The judge should punish much more the lack of lower development which is prerequisite to others than the missing of the higher developmental stages. For instance, if relaxation is missing, even a First Level horse is deemed unsufficiently accomplished. When it is missing from a Grand Prix horse punishment by low grades should be intensified. Conversely, as a

First Level horse is not required to show engagement the lack of it must go unpunished, and when the same is missing from a Fourth Level horse, let us say, punishment should be milder than if the Fourth Level horse is not in balance.

A Grand Prix horse moving without relaxation is so incorrect that it could not even be labeled circus (good circus riding is relaxed). Such a horse is merely showing a false super-structure that not only has failed to improve him, but actually made a caricature of his potentials and presents him as a puppet on a string.

Scoring philosophy should be based on the ideal, not the expected performance! Expectations are prejudicial, relativistic, indefinable. If competitors have to ask, "What does this judge like?," there is something wrong with the judge. Also, if in an area of beginning dressage interest or during a combined event the judge makes concessions to absolute standards by reasoning, "What can we expect of them? After all we are here to encourage...," judging will be biased and misleading. That kind of attitude of abandoning the ideal standards (or not knowing them!) creates the peculiar situation of the beginning rider scoring in the sixty percentile with a weak ride and as he progresses (and the judge's expectations and biases rise) progressively scoring in lower percentiles! Is he then regressing?

The ideal score is 10 and the judge should start with that in mind! If one of the basic requirements, such as relaxation or later rhythm or balance or impulsion, etc., is missing from the horse's development, the judge should drop down to a 4, "insufficient" being the highest possibility. From the 10 or 4 standards the judge may recede by additional points as additional faults of more-or-less severity occur in the movement, and by the time the movement is finished, arrive at the appropriate numerical description.

While a certain amount of "computerization" of what the judge has been seeing and how it was weighed by scores earlier is necessary during a competition, a very good judge, having weighed against the ideal standards of that level, will find few occasions to adjust his scores to do justice to the relative achievements among the contestants.

Keenness of observation cannot be overemphasized. Never forget that for the rider, those few minutes in the arena are the most important minutes, for which months or even years of preparation have been done, time and expense not spared. A judge cannot afford to be tired, bored or disinterested in any of the horse, any of the rides! Only when he sees everything can a correct meaningful score be given even by the most knowledgeable judge.

Terminology as well as appropriate commenting on score sheets is vastly important. Contestants, if they are mature sportspeople, will come to a show to be evaluated and guided rather than as a ribbon-gathering endeavor.

Comments should be concise and therefore not only succinctly phrased, but relevant to the most important issue on each movement. Nit-picking on details while ignoring major shortcomings is neither helpful guidance nor appropriately evaluative. One should never underestimate the intelligence, knowledge and sensitivity of the contestant, who in turn judges the judge designated to judge him!

Use standardized, classical teminology that refers appropriately to the gymnastic meaning of the movements performed. Say "balanced and rhythmic" rather than "nice". Nice means nothing and is an appropriate comment when the milk-man sends you a Christmas card. For lack of time and space and for their instructional values, negative comments are appropriate, particularly when the score is low and major improvement is desirable. However, they can be stated in a positive manner, for example, "A straight, rhythmic entry followed by inattentive halt," denoting the judge's eagerness to notice and reward the good parts of the movements and encourage more of them to happen. Do not waste time stating the obvious. Comments like "horse spun around, reared and backed instead of halting" sound defensive rather than instructional. The rider noticed those happenings and the low score substantiates the story.

Comment in full sentences rather than just words or phrases. Saying "not enough" is an unacceptable comment; what is not enough? Relaxation, rhythm, bending, engagement, what?

Once the appropriate scoring range is established by the judge, receding from the "excellent" 10 or "insufficient" 4, the judge should keep in mind an additional hierarchy of importance. One can add (and I hope you will) to the terms listed here ad infinitum. Basically, one should say what one observes. Never state your emotions about a movement, such as "I don't like it." Remember that both your score and comment should emphasize the more important (i.e. the paces) over the evaluation of the less important (size and shape of patterns). This is a scale that needs adjustment in emphasis as the tests ridden grow more sophisticated in advancement. At Grand Prix level, all aspects are important! Even exactitude! Remember to reward that which is good particularly if it is something leading the hierarchy, such as relaxation or the pace.

Remember that riders look for improvement as they compete against their own earlier scores and comments. If a rider could manage to improve from a comment "resistant" to "somewhat tense", he can rightly have a sense of achievement. That is why the appropriate strength or mildness of the commenting vocabulary is important and must never be neglected.

The cumulative scores at the end of tests, as well as the comments accompanying them, are vastly important. Often their importance is emphasized by coefficient scoring and good riders pay much attention to their cumulative, overall emphasis on the fundamental requirements concerning the horse on that level. The score of the rider is the only one he gets and in my mind there is great competition in improving that score relative to earlier ones earned! Those are also tiebreaking scores. So do not neglect consideration of them. Show managements should provide two or three minutes in addition to riding time in order not to rush the judge who wants to stay on schedule (as he should) and eliminate the meaning of these last scores and comments.

Commenting on the rider should be as positive as can be managed, yet corresponding to the numerical grade. One cannot say "excellent rider" and give a 5, for the grade for excellent is 10. One could, however, make statements such as "your well relaxed torso and light use of hands deserve the compliment of a more relaxed ankle."

Finally, the third hierarchy of judging values should be based on punishing more severely mistakes that are harder and take longer to correct than those that are easily correctible. Thus, a well-schooled horse that jumps a spot of sunlight in a dingy covered arena should not be severely punished if at all, for that is not a gymnastically unsound activity. On higher levels where absolute obedience is required such an event may be punishable, but not on lower levels. A horse moving with a "broken neck" or tongue over the bit, however, is in serious trouble, for those faults are hard to overcome, and if at all possible would take a long time.

Dressage is concerned with the horse as a gymnast. All that contributes to that ideal should be rewarded and those developments that hinder it should be punished. The goal of this gymnasticizing is to straighten your horse and ride it forward, so that he can carry you with maximum efficiency. That can only be achieved by a relaxed, balanced, rhythmic, impulsive and engaged horse that is allowed to develop gradually to improve his natural abilities and look naturally beautiful.

The ethics of judging require of us an unswerving adherence to the classical principles of gymnasticizing, requires us to chastise all falsehoods, shortcuts and gimmicks. We are not to promote by rewarding temporary success, but to uphold in its pure form the tradition that has been proven to produce happy horses. All other ethical standards are derivitive of this one and can logically be arrived at. Nothing substitutes for knowledge of these classical standards, of perceiving them and of knowing how to rate them in their relative values to the horse's natural development. All judges should be experts who coincidentally adjudicate.

10 Equipment and Facilities for Dressage

How Does One Choose A Proper Dressage Saddle?

If saddles were not extremely important for increasing the rider's effectiveness and the horse's comfort we would still be riding bareback. Horsemen recognized centuries ago, however, that saddles are necessary. The importance of riding in a suitable saddle cannot be emphasized enough. The best rider on the finest horse can lose much of his effectiveness as a master of the art for lack of a good saddle.

The fundamental purpose of a saddle is to allow effective communication of the rider's bodily attitudes to the horse, while ensuring the maximum comfort for the horse. A saddle is meant to facilitate unity and harmony between two vastly different body structures; that of the rider and that of the horse. Therefore, a good saddle's top line must approximate a negative mold of the rider's bottom line. Similarly, the saddle's bottom line should be a negative mold of the horse's top line or a portion of the back.

Needless to say, the ideal saddle is either custom-made, or customized (adjusted) to the shape of the rider (on its top line) and to the shape of his particular horse (on its bottom line). Saddle makers will look at your horse, measure him, and even make molds of his back.They will measure the rider carefully and inquire about the riding purposes for which the saddle is to be used. Based on this information, they will create the ideal saddle.

The bottom of the saddle, in general, should distribute the rider's weight on the horse's back over as large an area as possible. Therefore, a saddle that is constructed on the principle of an old fashioned rocking chair, pressing and pivoting on the horse's back at one limited point will be very uncomfortable for the horse. Rather, the opposite should be sought: a saddle that rests evenly on either side of the horse's spinal column over long, parallel contact areas. The saddle should at no time press against the bones of the horse, that is, the saddle's bottom stuffing (cushioning) should be ample so as to provide a deep tunnel that arches high above the horse's spinal column and withers.

The top of the saddle should be as short as possible for the accommodation of the rider's buttocks. The rider should not be slipping back and forth on the top of the saddle. In addition to having a short saddle, the rider should insist on a very "deep ditch" to sit in, with the deep point, or center of gravity of the saddle placed as far forward toward the withers as possible. This deep point should be well defined, rather than extended over a few inches of flat, "river bottom-like" area.

A person standing and spreading his legs will create the shape of an upside-down "Y". When sitting in a saddle, the rider's seatbones should be widespread and evenly placed on either side of the saddles's center line. Thus, it is good to have a narrow saddle which will allow the deep drop of the knees resulting from comfortabley resting thighs. The human bottom is shaped like an inverted "V", the legs coming to a direct meeting point. Therefore, logically only a narrow saddle will allow the seatbones to separate widely. If the horse is a wide one, in order to keep the saddle narrow on the top, it will have to be elevated higher above the horse's back by more stuffing and a higher frame. Conversely, on a very slender horse, the saddle can be lowered toward the horse's back without compromising its narrowness, yet allowing for closer communication contact.

So far, I have confined my comments to matters relating to the saddle's frame and shape as they best meet the requirements determined by the horse's back-shape and the rider's bottom shape. Beyond this, the rider should pay attention to the quality of the leather. A saddle serves us for a long time and constitutes a major investment. The better the quality of leather used, the longer and more comfortably the saddle will serve the rider. Thus, the expensive, fine leathers are in the long run the "cheap" purchases. There should be ample and soft padding and cushioning for both the horse's and the rider's comfort.

The side flaps should be of a length that will not interfere with the rider's boots; that is, the flaps should not catch or push down on them. There should be as little leather separating the rider's thighs and boots from the horse as possible. Some newer saddle types exist whose girths buckle under the horse's belly or fasten in a way similar to airplane seat-belts. This eliminates the excess bulk created between horse and rider by buckles and thick leather straps hidden under the saddle's side flaps. These flaps should be shaped to as to guard the knees and thighs, but not so as to eliminate direct contact with the horse at the boots.

The expense of custom-made equipment being as it is, it is wise to think about ready-made saddles as well. When buying a ready-made saddle, one should purchase a reputable brand, for example, Kieffer, Passier, or Stubben. The rider should ask the manufacturer or dealer to stuff about two more inches of foam rubber cushioning into the very back of the saddle before shipping. They accept that condition and this will ensure enough forward tilt in the saddle's position toward the withers. Also, such stuffing lengthens the area at the bottom of the saddle where it is in contact with the horse's back, Eventually, with use, all saddles sink in the back, and the extra padding will promote longer wear, with the saddle staying up in a correctly centered position.

In my opinion, most riders should first buy a dressage saddle, for the young horse's training will initially be on the flat, involving gymnastic exercises (synonymous with dressage). Moreover, the dressage saddle will most appropriately develop the rider's correct seat. Dressage competitors will naturally always need a dressage saddle, but jumpers too, even past their initial training stages, will be schooled continuously on the flat and the dressage saddle is still useful here. For jumping, of course, a specialized jumping saddle is indispensable. However, I am personally against buying an all purpose saddle. Their purported use is so diversified that they are actually not suitable for any specific endeavor. They are the average "catch-all" saddles and as such are more a statistical idea than a realistic piece of equipment.

As staying in close contact with the horse is essential to good riding, saddle pads should be as thin as possible and of course, shaped to fit the saddle. Overhanging saddle pads are ugly and inappropriate, and thick ones serve no real purpose. Let us not forget that a good saddle, well shaped and softly padded, can sit on a horse's back without anything underneath it. Pads are really only useful when the saddle is unsuitable, and therefore irritates, hurts or bruises the horse's back. Although pads preserve the saddle by preventing damage to the leather from horse sweat, during dressage competitions it is better to ride without any pad or saddle cloth at all. Remember, dressage represents elegance through simplicity. Should a saddle pad be used, however, the rider must be sure to pull it way up into the tunnel of the saddle so that it does not touch or press down on the horse's withers. That sustained pressure, however mild, will cause profound discomfort and pain; something like wearing tight shoes.

Prevent the Sliding of the Saddle

The position of the saddle on the horse's back should always be firm and on the right spot. There is always only one place where the saddle belongs on a particular horse. The saddle should never travel forward or backward while the rider works. If it does, there are reasons for it and they should be eliminated. Let us examine the possibilities.

1. The saddle placed incorrectly will slide to adjust itself to the correct location where it finally lodges itself. When placing the saddle one should start from the withers (neck) and slide the saddle back (on contact with horse) with a short, firm push until it "lands" just behind the withers. The horse's back (depending on its shape) "receives" the saddle because friction makes sliding it further back difficult. Pushing the saddle back from the withers with a short downward pressure defines the area by "feel" for sliding the saddle any further back "feels wrong" as the horse's back widens and a saddle too far back will not "mold into the horse" but sit above his ribs.

2. A correctly placed saddle should be tightly cinched up. One should adjust the girth three times to tighten: before mounting; after few walking steps on a long rein (from the saddle of course); after about six to eight minutes of further warming up. With a tight girth the saddle will not slide. The girth should be pulled as tight as possible! It does not hurt the horse (like a tight belt would hurt a human).

Only a very tight girth will provide a safe ride! A loose girth, in fact, hurts the horse as it allows the saddle to travel on his back and creates friction that rubs and blisters his back. We have similar human experiences with loose shoes and sandals that blister our feet. Often resistance and lack of relaxation in the horse are caused by such dangerous wobble on a saddle which is not tightly cinched.

3. The saddle should fit the horse. Often saddles are not created wide or flat enough to settle on the horse's back properly. The points of contact between the saddle and horse's back should be as large as possible. A saddle that touches on only one point on each side and curves upward from there will rock on the horse and besides causing him pain might move forward or back. Some horses have different structure of the back(hollow, perhaps) or the back's connection with the withers and shoulders. The horse's physiology might demand a readjustment or custom made saddle in order to fit properly. It should be fitted to prevent discomfort for the horse and provide safety to the rider.

4. A saddle might slide because the rider does not sit in it correctly. Some riders make the mistake of "riding the saddle" by shoving it with the hips and lower back. Or they might "scoop" the saddle with their abdomen, lifting in a gyrating motion rolling the contact from a pressure down the crotch and back towards a tucking under with the tailbone on each stride. None of the seat actions that are actively "riding the saddle" are correct!

5. Seldom will there be a situation in which the above causes for sliding saddles cannot be eliminated. But should that be the case, use leather strapping equipment that prevents the slipping such as a breastplate (to prevent sliding back) or a strap that is held in place by a loop going under the horse's tail to prevent forward sliding.

Don't be afraid to go to these extremes as preventing saddle slippage is most important.

Appropriate Stirrups

Offset stirrups are inappropriate for dressage! By their construction they mechanically prevent the correct position of the rider's leg, stiffen the ankle and prevent correct use of pushing aids. Ironically enough, often the most difficult area to relax while riding is the ankle. The offset stirrup, instead of contributing to relaxation, forces the rider to lock his ankle and thus instead of contributing to correct leg usage it makes habitual his paralysis at the ankle.

Stiffness anywhere in a rider will spread from one area and eventually affect most of the rider's body. That is why suppleness in the ankle is particularly important. Without this suppleness the rider's effectiveness decreases, and when actual stiffness sets in, the possibility of adequate and smooth aids is eliminated.

The primary purpose of the rider's leg aids is to create impulsion (forward locomotion, energy) and the secondary role of the legs is to create and maintain proper bending. In essence all riding depends on appropriate use of the legs because all dressage achievements are based on the control of the horse's hindquarters. Therefore the correct position and use of the rider's legs are of the greatest importance. Offset stirrups preclude a proper leg position, and hence, proper use!

Offset stirrups force the rider to press down into the irons with the ball of the foot in such a way as to create the greatest contact pressure at the area of the big toe, that is, the inside of the stirrup. This forces the toes to turn outward, the ankles to turn inward and lock into a rigid foot position. These unfortunate changes in the rider's foot position and this rigidity at the ankles then produce a leg contact that is at the seam of the boots rather than the inner sides of the calves. Once the rider contacts with the seam of the boot, he is forced to use the skeletal rather than muscular aids. Skeletal aids are not only meaningless to the horse but often disturbing by their uncomfortable pressure and their inability to produce rhythmic contact. Once the rider is gripping the horse in this manner, lateral (bending) aids become difficult. The rider solves the problem by pulling up her heels to aid the horse by "scratching" with the heel upward, pressing toes down and out.

Unfortunetely, the incorrect position and use of rider's legs is all too often seen. Many riders acquired this impotent, and also ugly, use of legs by having ridden in offset stirrups. Those who still use them, of course, have the documentation of their jeopardy right at their toes! By all means never use an offset stirrup!

Let me briefly describe how to create an effective leg position and contact with a correct, ordinary stirrup. Use a heavy stirrup iron for better feel as well as for the occasion when you lose it: a heavy stirrup will come to rest in a vertical hanging position faster and will not dance along the horse's side when lost; therefore you can reclaim it easier. Place your foot into the stirrup so as to touch with the outside rim of your boot the outside edge of the iron. A stirrup too wide for your foot will not look good, leaving too much visible iron after you have properly placed your foot to its outside extremity. When you place your foot into the stirrup, do not forget that it is a resting place for the toes and not an area of support. Do not press down into the stirrup, do not attempt to hold it by secretly curling your toes inside the boots — I, for one, have x-ray eyes and can detect when "the monkey grips with the toes" in the secrecy of the boots! Place the stirrup iron forward close to the toes rather than to the back on the ball of the foot. The more forward you contact the stirrup, the deeper your heel can be pushed down to create the all-important stretching of the calf muscles! Make sure the big toe, the inside of your boot, is not contacting the irons but rather only the outer side alone: this helps keep the toes turned inward and in a near parallel position to the horse's side. Without this position, the legs (calves) cannot curve inward along the horse's barrel for that soft, perpetual contact with his sides that is so necessary for driving in rhythm and controlling the haunches tracking and activity.

Initially, adjust your stirrups short enough to facilitate good stretching of the thigh and calf muscles. As you stretch these muscles and achieve a deep seat and longer legs, you will earn a longer stirrup leather and you may lower it notch by notch. But never drop the stirrup irons way down and fake a long-legged deep seat; that will force you to sit with slack muscles that cannot aid, toes down (ballerina?) fishing for the irons. Remember that two hundred years ago the stirrups were shortened precisely for the reason that de la Gueriniere recognized: that riding improves by perpetual contact with the horse's sides and by supple rhythmic aids that come from the muscles and not from the skeleton! The shorter stirrup enables you to keep the legs folded into and under the rounded rib-cage. It will stretch the leg muscles and eventually enable you to earn your long legs! Look at the old engravings of western riders who learned from the pre-de la Gueriniere Spaniards. Their legs are not in contact with the horse: they make contact impossible by having too long a stirrup leather adjustment, which makes their legs dangle on the horse's sides straight down. And you know the horse's sides are not vertical and straight down — they are curved!

The rider's legs act, move, accompany, harmonize or aid differently in the three different paces. Yet in all three paces their activities and their effectiveness are dependent upon a supple ankle, a well-stretched thigh to keep a deep knee position and a well-stretched calf to deep heel position. Without such leg position there is no relaxed rider with an independent seat and there can be no effortless yet powerful aids coming from the rider's stretched musculature!

When the foot is resting correctly in the stirrup irons that are not hanging lower than your current ability to stretch the leg to the horse's barrel, then learn to work with pushing aids, rather than banging! These pushing aids best develop when you can use a supple ankle joint to rotate the stirrup irons with your toe in a smooth continuum and circular fashion. Try it out first with great exaggeration while halting the horse; toes in, then up, then out, then down, then in...etc. You will feel that when the toes go in and up, your calf performs a pushing stroking aid forward on the horse's sides. The exaggerated circling with the stirrups is a teaching device. Eventually when you can handle the stirrup contact with suppleness this activity is minimized until it is imperceptible to the onlooker. Yet the ankles will continue to remain supple and in contact with the irons; and the pushing aids now on, now off, in rhythm with the horse's movement, will remain active without ever relinquishing contact with the horse's sides!

These activities very much depend on the correct stirrup equipment and the correct resting of the foot within it. The result will be perpetual contact and effortless but powerful pushing aids that are harmonious with the horse. A big change from the offset stirrup, paralyzed ankles, turned out toes, gripping with seam of the boots, skeletal banging or gripping — and the resultant stiff and agonized horse that cannot understand what is going on and why it's so painfull!

Why Are Snaffle Bits
With Copper Mouthpieces Not Popular?

As you can see in the FEI Rule Book, in the Notes on Dressage (by the AHSA) and all other rule books, only certain mouthpieces are proper for the horse. One with copper wires on it is certainly inacceptable because of its cruelty. It is used to restrain horses through the mouth, an activity we don't promote in dressage.

Proper bits, those allowed in dressage riding, are perhaps not made of copper because the price of that metal is high and the cost of such bits would be prohibitive. In the "good old days" when I, for one, rode in carriages in Europe (during my childhood), the elegantly fitted carriage horses were bitted up with copper. Other metal parts of the harness and equipment were also of copper or brass. You can still find brass harness ornaments in gift shops throughout the Western world; they are now used as wall decorations. But in those days elegance demanded, if not pure gold, at least the color of gold to be used in harnessing horses. Even then poor people could not afford such elegant tack and used aluminum or steel or even iron bits and fittings.

Now that copper and brass have become much sought-after industrial metals their price has soared. Who would buy them? But consider that stirrup irons and spurs are also metal and to make things look nice on a riding horse, copper bits would look out of place when coordinated with stainless steel stirrup irons and spurs! In short, the matter is one of "supply follows demand". For the above mentioned reasons there is no demand for copper bits!

I know of no serious evidence that horses like the taste of copper. Horses develop a moist mouth as a result of correctly gentle and pleasant rein contact. When the horse is correctly invited to bend toward the bit, he changes the position of his neck and head carriage by flexion. This physical position, when coupled with mental relaxation, and pleasure, will produce saliva by virtue of activating the digestive salivating glands at the base of the horse's tongue. All wetness in the horse's mouth when ridden and driven is produced by the activity of this digestive salivating gland. Thus, horses will have a wet mouth when correctly contacted by the bit: any bit, not just copper or brass! Thus, I hope, you will see and ride yourself, horses with wet mouths!

As there is no regulation against metals, why don't you try custom made brass bit, stirrups and spurs: no kidding, you might inspire a new style!

Side Reins, Draw Reins, Running Martingales
Their Purposes, Benefits or Disadvantages
In Dressage Training

Draw reins and running martingales have no place in dressage. They are tools used by those who fail to gain desired results because they do not know or are unwilling to use the methods of dressage. These tools affect the front of the horse, his neck and shoulders and head, without doing anything beneficial to the hindquarters. In fact, they both in-hibit the correct use and therefore the correct development of the hindquarters. The horse's front should behave in a certain desirable way as a result of correct engagement of the hindquarters. But by manipulating the neck into a false flexion, the rider merely works on the symptom and not on the cause.

Side reins, however, are useful at times in dressage and therefore have a legitimate place in dressage discussion. One may use side reins both when the horse is being worked from the ground (lunging and long-reining) or when working under the rider.

When the horse is worked from the ground, being lunged or driven on long-reins, he should always be equipped with side reins. Like all tools, side reins are beneficial only when properly applied, that is, properly adjusted. The horse should stand relaxed, with an extended neck and head when the side reins are adjusted and when the horse is in this correct position the side reins should just barely (gently) offer contact.

At the horse's head, the side reins may be attached to the ring of the cavesson or the rings of the snaffle, depending on which is used. On the horse's body, the other end (buckled) may be attached to the lower rings on the surcingle or to the girth of a saddle. When attached to a girth, they function best when placed just below the saddle's side flap, where the girth emerges visibly from the saddle.

Side reins should always be adjusted evenly; that is to be of equal length on both sides, regardless of the fact that the horse is moving on a circle while being lunged. To shorten the inside side rein while lung-ing encourages the horse to track away from the line of the circle with outside hind leg and remain straight in the body, bending only in the neck. As the side reins should always be generously adjusted, as described above, the equal length of the outside rein and that of the in-side will not encourage the horse to counterflex and look away from the circle. As the side reins were already generous at the halt, they should remain so for the walk and actually hang at the trot and canter during which the horse naturally shortens his neck.

The side reins gently inspire the horse's acceptance of a generous frame supporting his neck and position. It introduces the visual and weight acceptance of the reins that will be held by the rider. When at-tached to a snaffle, side reins will prepare the horse for the calm ac-ceptance of the bit.

Draw reins and running martingales encourage merely a false neck and head position that is neither correct in its flexion nor warranted by any desirable engagement of the hindquarters. They merely belabor the symptomatic areas to the detrimental neglect of the hindquarters.

The Appropriate Use of the Full Bridle

The double bridle is comprised of a curb bit and a snaffle. The width of both mouthpieces should fit the width of the horse's mouth exactly. Otherwise the equipment will lose its effectiveness and will cause problems by being uncomfortable for the horse. The thicker the mouthpieces are, the less their severity and therefore, for horses with sensitive mouths, thicker mouthpieces are recommended. The bit has an arched elevation in its structure to accommodate the horse's tongue, and in order to prevent painful pressure there, this curvature (the port) should be suitably large for the accommodation of the tongue. Yet a highly arched port is more severe than a lower one and therefore care should be taken to select a bit with sufficient, yet not oversized arch.

The severity of the effects of the bit are determined by the thinness of the curb bit and snaffle, the height of the port on the curb bit (as explained above), the proportions of the upper and lower parts of the cheek piece, the length of the cheek piece and the length of the curb chain. The longer the cheek piece, the more severe its effect will be. The longer the proportionate size of the lower part of the cheek piece is to the upper part, the more severe its effect will be. The tighter the curb chain is fitted the more severe its effect will be. Adjustment of all sizes of these pieces of equipment should be carefully planned according to the horse's needs, keeping in mind that the lightest possible effect on a particular horse is the most desirable!

The curb chain, fitted into the chin groove of the horse (under his jaw) should be adjusted so as to have a lesser effect (pain induction) than the bit in the mouth. The thinner and smaller the chain links are, the more severe their effects become. For sensitive horses a large linked chain flatly lying into the chin groove and adjusted with some looseness, is most appropriate. The curb chain must always lie flat against the horse's chin and its links should be carefully flattened; the

The Double Bridle

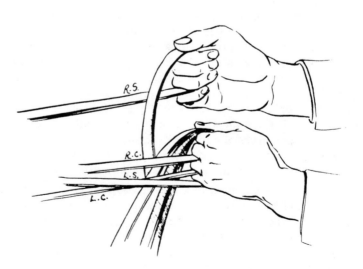

Fig. 10-1

last one so hooked onto the left hook that the point of that receiving hook points out and away from the horse's lips.

The full bridle, consisting of the above described pieces of equipment (curb bit with port, snaffle, cheek pieces with leverage and curb chain) is capable of very severe action on the horse's mouth. Therefore it is an instrument of refinement, not of powerful restraint. The full bridle has to be earned by both the horse and rider. The horse has to become physically and mentallly so developed that beyond relaxation and balance, he will show elasticity (in joints) and suppleness (in muscles) and therefore will be able to move with proper engagement of the hindquarters. The horse should be able to perform truly collected and extended paces in order to demonstrate his readiness for this instrument of sensitive refinement.

The rider should not only be a craftsman, but accomplished enough to have developed his own horse to the level of proper collection and extension. He should be able to work the horse with leg and seat aids, needing his hands merely as a sensitive termination point of his communications. His hands must be able to maintain a forward feel and be always free of restrictions. Hands should be those of a *giver,* not those of a *miser.* A rider's hands should reflect ever so mildly only the actions of his seat, rather than being seperate instruments.

About six months prior to putting the horse into the full bridle, the rider should begin to work with spurs. As the development of the horse must always proceed from his hindquarters toward his mouth, rather than the other way around, the horse's impulsion must be secured, strengthened and improved by the spurs prior to the curbing effect. Only when the horse's increased impulsion is developed to a higher level (in about six months) will he "beg for" the refinement at the termination point of the mouth.

If the full bridle causes the horse to overbend, open his mouth, move with a "broken neck" (bent at the third vertebra instead of the poll), lose impulsion or throw his head around, the use of the full bridle was surely premature. Even when the full bridle is offered at the right time and used with proper refinement, the horse should continue to work in the simple jointed snaffle periodically. The frequency of returning to the simple snaffle should be determined by the reactions of the horse when in the full bridle. As the full bridle should never serve as an instrument of restraint, as soon as the horse reacts to it as if it were restricting (loss of impulsion and engagement, stiffness, resistance) the rider must return to the use of the simple snaffle.

The horse must be gradually accustomed to the full bridle. Initially, every riding session should start in the snaffle and later, during the work, the full bridle can be put on the horse for a short period of time. Initially, more days in a week should be spent working in the snaffle than in the bridle. Gradually, the length of time the horse spends in the full bridle can be increased both as to its use during a lesson, and as to the number of days it is used during a week.

Beyond the double bridle's ability to reduce communications to its utmost sensitivity at the horse's mouth, it also supplies a steadying effect that cannot be acquired on the jointed snaffle bit. This bit can affect the horse's mouth more strongly on one side than the other (joint in the middle), which may be useful in a less advanced horse. But on a more advanced horse, an even effect over the bar is indispensable for the steady development of movements. By the time the horse has earned the double bridle, he is to be straight and not in need of uneven uses of the bit from side to side.

The four reins of the full bridle (two from the snaffle, two from the curb bit) may be held in two different ways. One either distributes them so as to hold two reins in each hand; the snaffle and curb bit reins each on appropriate sides. They are held in the same manner as the regular snaffle bit reins are held, except the curb bit reins are added on each side. Or, one can hold three reins in one hand and only one in the other (Fig. 10-1). In this latter case, the left snaffle and both curb bit reins are held by the rider in his left hand, while the remaining right snaffle rein is held alone in the right hand. This latter (three-in-one) distribution of reins is the more traditional, but currently less practiced mode of holding rein contact.

The advantage of the three-in-one position is that of increased steadiness of contact with the curb bit, which is severe. This makes the double bridle's use keener, for as said earlier, the dual purpose of this equipment is sensitive contact and a steadying effect. Both values increase when both bit reins are held in one hand. There is then no chance to "see-saw," even inadvertently, with the reins, nor to half-halt unilaterally.

Holding the four reins evenly distributed, two in one hand, two in the other, is an imitation of the simple snaffle contact position without any advantages to the art of riding other than easier adjustment for the rider, who is used to an even distribution of contact. It may add aesthetically to the image of symmetry. However, from a riding point of view (that is, the horse's developmental needs) this most commonly used position is inferior.

The rider should continue in the full bridle to contact his horse primarily on the snaffle bit and merely lightly connect with the reins of the curb. Initially only the snaffle should be contacted and the two reins connecting to the curb bit should hang loosely until the horse gets used to their weight, size, and presence. Since the rider should continue using the snaffle part of this equipment, it is well separated in the more beneficial three-in-one position. Yet the curb in one hand will provide increased sensitivity and steadying, even contact. (One hand is always coordinated with itself!) Guidance (turning) should certainly not be given with the curb bit. Guidance should be merely indicated through the snaffle which remains in separate hands.

The abuses of the full bridle are many and frequent. It is most often abused by use as a substitute of knowledge. An ignorant rider may use it to control his horse through pain, or to shortcut in training for a fancy, but wrongly, arched neck. As long as there are riders ignorant enough to ride the horse's neck and head, the areas visually perceptible to them, abuses of the double bridle will continue. A knowledgeable rider, however, will always remember that the rideable areas of the horse are not those visible to them; those being the hindquarters and the back. They will ride by feel rather than by gaze. They will know that the horse's neck and head position are merely symptomatic as to the activities of the all important hindquarters (locomotion) and back (communication). They will not use an instrument of sensitivity so insensitively as to inflict pain on the horse. The full bridle is not a break of locomotion.

In short, the full bridle is sophisticated only when horse and rider are both ready for its use. It has to be adjusted for the lightest possible effect and must be used sparingly and alternately with the simple jointed snaffle. It has to afford comfort to the horse rather than foster stiffness in him. It has to add, not detract from the horse's correct performance. The double bridle must balance with the horse's increased impulsion and elasticity and may never be used for restraint.

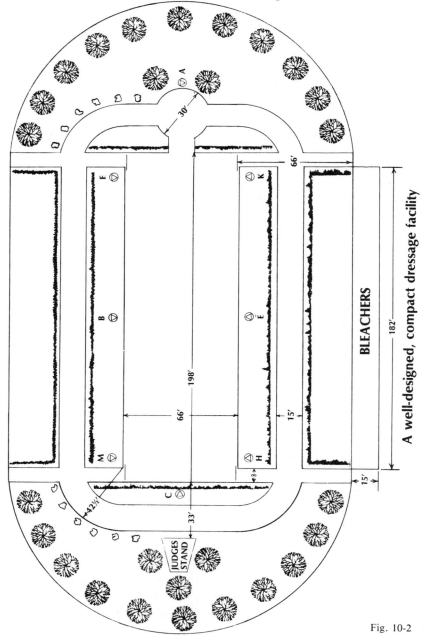

Fig. 10-2

The Physical Setup
of a Dressage Facility

When designing a dressage facility, one should really see the property and make suggestions on the premises. Much depends on the size of available land, its contour (drainage particularly), plans for future development, and so forth. One must also consider the number of horses that will be regularly trained there, the size of competitions expected, etc. More than one dressage arena may be needed for training purposes, or for holding large shows that require two arenas simultaneously in use, or for a second proper dressage arena for warm-up purposes.

I've decided to addresss myself to the minimum needs — one dressage arena, a good one — and leave it to my readers to elaborate on the plans or add to them when necessary.

Two things are essential to a good plan: it must be functionally correct and it must be aesthetically beautiful. A functionally correct set-up will pay attention to maximum utilization of available property as well as to its correct segmentation, and to making the actual riding arena (soil) as best suited as possible to horses' feet. Aesthetically speaking, the arenas in the West I worked or judged in have been rather unpleasing. We must never lose sight of the fact that we are riding for the pleasure of it. That may mean a variety of things to every individual, but surely for all, pleasure includes a beautiful environment. The more open country and large and beautiful gardens are disappearing, the more we yearn for their presence. In the West most areas are semi-desert, sub-tropical and generally arid, so vegetation is sparse and unattractive unless irrigated and tended landscaping is provided. The arenas I see are often rather ugly for their dusty, abandoned, desert look. I feel we owe it to ourselves as riders, to the art of dressage and to future generations to begin to create beautiful riding environments in addition to having them functionally correct.

Please refer to the "master plan" of my dressage facility, as I briefly explain what it consists of.

First of all, in the center you will see the properly sized dressage court. It should have proper footing and good drainage. It should be perfectly level and must be worked over to eliminate any "furrow" created near the rail as the horse is tracking there repeatedly. For the purpose of proper re-leveling and raking, and even for watering from a truck if necessary, note that the four corners of the arena can be opened. The railing should be removable so that tractors and equipment can move in and work the corners thoroughly.

The arena itself should be surrounded by a low fence slanted outward to avoid the horse's tracking on it by accident. While picket and light fencing painted white is rather beautiful, a solid board railing, also painted white (or crimson red?) may be more functional in keeping the sand of the arena inside (horse's stirring, wind, rain). The fencing around the arena should be permanently dug in except for the corner units that should open for equipment. The specifications for the height of the fence are in the FEI rule book and other literature. I can suggest the following profile:

The dressage letters should be high enough to be visible to both the rider and judges. Also they can be constructed so as to allow them to hold flower pots for additional decorative purpose. They should also be permanently dug in, after careful measurement of their position. Again, there is much literature about where to place them, and how far back they must be from the railing.

There should be a thirty foot diameter circle at letter "A". This circle can be used as a lunging ring as well as proper preparation for entering the ring during competition. Such a holding circle is missing from competition arenas and therefore riders are often forced to enter crooked, dodging letter "A" and making a poor impression on the judge. Needless to elaborate on the usefulness and indispensibility of a proper lunging circle, for that work is essential to the proper development of a dressage horse. The circle in this location is very important and useful. The letter "A" should be outside of it to avoid continuous dodging! This little circle should also be fenced around. It may have a taller fencing on the continous arc away from the dressage arena, but it should be kept as low as the fence around the dressage arena on the inner half-circle. This railing will keep the horse in lunge work properly tracking and will encourage even bending.

Around, outside the dressage arena and cutting through the lunging circle you will find the great canter ring. This is unfortunately missing from most facilities I have visited. Good work requires that one ride forward on straight and ample tracks. Horses need to be warmed up on larger tracks than a dressage arena offers. Horses need to be "cantered in" to develop the pace and the proper musculature and impulsion. Much can be done on the great canter ring, even collected work. Yet in a small facility, such as designed on the diagram, one can still fit in this large track. The canter ring has additional uses too. You may observe that the rider can go around on it to visit the judge's booth, making the horse get used to it (as riders like to do in order to avoid shying during the test). It can also be used for equipment to run on (tractors, rakes,etc.). This same canter ring also absorbs some of the otherwise useless area that is necessary to keep both the judge and the spectators at the proper distance from the rider.

Note that one proper judge's booth at "C" should be a permanent structure. All of it must be both functional and beautiful. Additional judge's booths can be set up according to the requirements of the shows and space for them is provided outside the great canter ring on the lawn. The main, permanent judge's booth will sit in the midst of an approximately semicircular landscaped area. There additional tables can be set up under trees for the secretariat, or the space can otherwise be utilized in addition to its aesthetic importance.

The bleachers should be properly removed (66 feet) from the nearest edge of the dressage arena. They can be carved into a hillside or be manufactured structures according to the terrain. They could be shaded by trees or a permanent roof. These details should be determined by the owners of the establishment, for there are many good ways.

Opposite the spectators' bleachers, one can landscape the area or make it a lawn for receptions, tabled, sun-umbrellas, etc., like a sidewalk cafe during shows. Concessionaires and toilet facilities, however, should be on the bleachers side.

The rest of the areas (around the perimeters of the illustration) and those between the dressage arena and canter ring, or those between canter ring and spectators, should be landscaped. One can give suggestions as to plantings; however, landscape architects should be consulted. Here in the West several low ground covers exist, some even blooming for many months. Climbing geraniums and jasmine could cover large territories. Ivy, low juniper and even a low but heavily blooming variety of red rose would make masses of greenery or a colorful sea of flowers. The area behind "A" and the lunging circle could be made a formal backdrop to the rider (like Schonbrunn, anyone?) with use of tall, slender Lebanese Cyprus or in other climates silver spruce, etc. Because the areas for landscaping are small, a formal Mediterranean gardening approach may make it more beautiful than a casual British park-like landscaping. While lawns need much watering and mowing in our area, they might be desirable elsewhere and would allow for more movement by spectators.

I am also presenting two designs for the permanent judge's booth. They can be infinitely altered to be suitable to climate (open or glassed in? heated or cooled?).

Judges' Booths

Southern California

Beautiful, simple,
inexpensive & so practical
it even slides (portable!)
on sledges